DATE DUE

SEP 5 1995	
DEC 21 1995	
ILL 2-26-96	
OCT 23 1996	
FEB 26 1997	
MAR 05 1998	

FOREVER

BARBIE

FOREVER

The

Unauthorized

Biography

of a

Real Doll

BARBIE

WILLIAM MORROW AND COMPANY, INC.
New York

M. G. LORD

AUTHOR'S NOTE

This book was prepared
in cooperation with Ella King Torrey,
who began researching Barbie
in 1979 as part of a Yale University
Scholar of the House project.

Copyright © 1994 by M. G. Lord

Library of Congress Cataloging-in-Publication Data
Lord, M. G.
Forever Barbie : the unauthorized biography of a real doll /
M. G. Lord. — 1st ed.
p. cm.
ISBN 0-688-12296-5
1. Barbie dolls. I. Title.
NK4894.3.B37L67 1994
688.7′221′0979493—dc20   94-18272
CIP
Printed in the United States of America

First Edition

1 2 3 4 5 6 7 8 9 10

BOOK DESIGN BY ALEXANDER KNOWLTON

For Ken

. . . er, Glenn

Horowitz

CONTENTS

Lily understood that beauty is only the raw material of conquest and that to convert it to success, other arts are required. She knew that to betray any sense of superiority was a subtler form of the stupidity her mother denounced, and it did not take her long to learn that a beauty needs more tact than the possessor of an average set of features.
—EDITH WHARTON, *The House of Mirth*

The daughter is for the mother at once her double and another person . . . she saddles her child with her own destiny: a way of proudly laying claim to her own femininity and also a way of revenging herself for it. The same process is to be found in pederasts, drug addicts, in all who at once take pride in belonging to a certain confraternity and feel humiliated by the association.
—SIMONE DE BEAUVOIR, *The Second Sex*

No nude, however abstract, should fail to arouse in the spectator some vestige of erotic feeling.
—KENNETH CLARK, *The Nude*

CHAPTER ONE

WHO IS BARBIE, ANYWAY?

The theme of the convention was "Wedding Dreams," and appropriately it was held in Niagara Falls, the honeymoon capital, a setting of fierce natural beauty pimpled with fast-food joints and tawdry motels. The delegates were not newlyweds who had come to cuddle aboard the *Maid of the Mist,* poignantly hopeful that their union, unlike half of all American marriages, would last. They were not children, who had come to goggle at the cataract over which dozens of cartoon characters had plunged in barrels and miraculously survived. Nor were they shoppers attracted by Niagara's other big draw—the Factory Outlet Mall—where such brand names as Danskin and Benetton, Reebok and Burberrys, Mikasa and Revere Ware could be purchased for as much as 70 percent off retail.

They were, however, consumers, many of whom had been taught a style of consumption by the very object they were convening to celebrate. They had fled the turquoise sky and the outdoor pagentry for the dim, cramped ballroom of the Radisson Hotel. There were hundreds of them: southern ladies in creaseless pant suits dragging befuddled Rotary Club–member husbands; women in T-shirts from Saskatoon and Pittsburgh; stylish young men from

BARBIE COLLECTORS' CONVENTION, 1992

SYLVIA PLACHY

Manhattan and West Hollywood. There were housewives and professional women; single people, married people, severely corpulent people, and bony, gangling people. A thirtysomething female from Tyler, Texas, volunteered that she had the same measurements as Twiggy, except that she was one inch wider in the hips. There were people from Austria and Guadeloupe and Scotland. Considering the purpose of the gathering, there were surprisingly few blond people.

These were delegates to the 1992 Barbie-doll collectors' convention, a celebration of the ultimate American girl-thing, an entity too perfect to be made of flesh but rather forged out of mole-free, blemish-resistant, non-biodegradable plastic. Narrow of waist, slender of hip, and generous of bosom, she was the ideal of postwar feminine beauty when Mattel, Inc., introduced her in 1959—one year before the founding of Overeaters Anonymous, two years before Weight Watchers, and many years before Carol Doda pioneered a new use for silicone. (Unless I am discussing the doll as a sculpture, I will use "she" to refer to Barbie; Barbie is made up of two distinct components: the doll-as-physical-object and the doll-as-invented-personality.) At other collector events, I have witnessed ambivalence toward the doll—T-shirts, for instance, emblazoned with: "I wanna be like Barbie. The bitch has everything." But this crowd took its polyvinyl heroine seriously.

Of course, people tend to take things seriously when money is involved, and Barbie-collecting, particularly for dealers, has become a big business. The earliest version of the doll, a so-called Number One, distinguished by a tiny hole in each foot, has fetched as much as $4,000. The "Side-part American Girl," which features a variation on a pageboy haircut, has brought in $3,000. And because children tend to have a destructive effect on tiny accessories, the compact from Barbie's "Roman Holiday" ensemble, an object no bigger than a baby's thumbnail, has gone for $800. While Barbie-collecting has not replaced baseball as the national pastime, it has, in the fourteen years since the first Barbie convention in Queens, New York, moved from the margins to the mainstream. Over twenty thousand readers buy *Barbie Bazaar,* a glossy bimonthly magazine with full-color, seductively styled photos of old Barbie paraphernalia. And twenty thousand is not an insignificant number of disciples. Christianity, after all, started out with only eleven.

In the shadowy salesroom, amid vinyl cases and cardboard dreamhouses, thousands of Barbies and Barbie's friends were strewn atop one another—naked—suggesting some disturbing hybrid of Woodstock and a Calvin Klein Obsession ad. Others stood bravely—clothed—held up by wire stands. Some were in their original cartons; "NRFB" is collector code for "never removed from box." Still others were limbless, headless, or missing a hand. "Good for parts," a dealer explained. Buyers, wary of deceitful dealers, ran weathered fingers over each small, hard torso, probing for scratches, tooth marks, or, worst of all, for an undeclared spruce-up. Even a skillful application of fresh paint can devalue a doll, as does hair that has been rerooted.

Emotions ran high as deals were cut. A stocky woman in jeans haggled furiously over Barbie's 1963 roadster; I later saw her in the lobby, cradling the car as if it were her firstborn child. Others schmoozed with reliable, well-known dealers—Los Angeles–based Joe Blitman, author of *Vive La Francie,* an homage to Francie, Barbie's small-breasted cousin who was born in 1966 and lasted until 1975; and Sarah Sink Eames, from Boones Mill, Virginia, author of *Barbie Fashion,* a photographic record of the doll's wardrobe. I learned the value of established dealers when I bought "Queen of the Prom," the 1961 Barbie board game, from a shifty-eyed woman who was not a convention regular. "The set's kind of beat-up," she told me, "but all the pieces are authentic." Right, lady. Barbie's allowance, I discovered when I played the game, was five dollars. The smallest denomination in the set she sold me was $100. (The bills were from another game.)

Selling was not the only action at the convention. There was a fashion show in which collectors arranged their not-especially-Barbie-esque bodies into life-size versions of their favorite Barbie outfits. There was a competition of dioramas illustrating the theme "Wedding Dreams"; one, which did not strike me as lighthearted, featured a male doll (not Ken) recoiling in fear and horror from Barbie and, implicitly, Woman, on his wedding night. (His face had been whitened and his eyes widened into circles.) Employees of Mattel were treated like rock stars. Early on the second night of the convention, veteran costume designer Carol Spencer, who has been dressing Barbie since 1963, settled down in the hotel lobby to autograph boxes of "Benefit Ball Barbie," one of her creations in Mattel's Classique Collection, a series promoting its in-house designers. At eleven, she was still signing.

Intense feelings about Barbie do not run exclusively toward love. For every mother who embraces Barbie as a traditional toy and eagerly introduces her daughter to the doll, there is another mother who tries to banish Barbie from the house. For every fluffly blond cheerleader who leaps breast-forward into an exaggerated gender role, there is a recovering bulimic who refuses to wear dresses and blames Barbie for her ordeal. For every collector to whom the amassing of Barbie objects is a language more exquisite than words, there is a fiction writer or poet or visual artist for whom Barbie is muse and metaphor—and whose message concerns class inequities or the dark evanescence of childhood sexuality.

Barbie may be the most potent icon of American popular culture in the late twentieth century. She was a subject of the late pop artist Andy Warhol, and when I read Arthur C. Danto's review of Warhol's 1989 retrospective at the Museum of Modern Art, I thought of her. Danto wrote that pop art's goal was elevating the commonplace; but what, he wondered, would happen when the commonplace ceased to be commonplace? How would future generations interpret Warhol's paintings—generations for which Brillo boxes, Campbell soup labels, and famous faces from the 1960s and '70s would not be instantly identifiable?

Danto's meditations got me thinking about the impermanence of living icons. What, for instance, is Valentino to us today? A shadow jerking across a black-and-white screen, campy at best, no more an image of smoldering sex appeal than, say, Lassie. What is Dietrich? To the millions who read her daughter's vindictive, best-selling biography, she is an amphetamine-ridden drunk with disgusting gynecological problems, so leery of hospitals that she let a wound in her thigh fester until her leg was threatened with amputation. What is Marilyn? A caricature, a corpse, the subject of tedious documentaries linking her to RFK and JFK. And what is Elvis? To anyone over forty, he's probably still the sexy crooner from Tupelo; but younger people recall him as a bloated junkie encrusted with more rhinestones than Liberace.

Barbie has an advantage over all of them. She can never bloat. She has no children to betray her. Nor can she rot, wrinkle, overdose, or go out of style. Mattel has hundreds of people—designers, marketers, market researchers—whose full-time job it is continually to reinvent her. In 1993, fresh versions of the doll did a billion dollars' worth of business. Based on its unit sales, Mattel calculates that every second, somewhere in the world, two Barbies are sold.

Given the emergence of the doll as a symbol in literature and art—not to mention as a merchandising phenomenon—it's time to take a closer look at how Barbie developed and what her ascendancy might signify, even though it's impossible to calculate the doll's influence in any sort of clinical study. By the time children play with Barbie, they have too many other factors in their environment to be able to link a specific behavior trait with a particular toy. But because Barbie has both shaped and responded to the marketplace, it's possible to study her as a reflection of American popular cultural values and notions about femininity. Her houses and friends and clothes provide a window onto the often contradictory demands that the culture has placed upon women.

Barbie was knocked off from the *"Bild* Lilli" doll, a lascivious plaything for adult men that was based on a postwar comic character in the *Bild Zeitung,* a downscale German newspaper similar to America's *National Enquirer.* The doll, sold principally in tobacco shops, was marketed as a sort of three-dimensional pinup. In her cartoon incarnation, Lilli was not merely a doxie, she was a *German* doxie—an ice-blond, pixie-nosed speci-men of an Aryan ideal—who may have known hardship during the war, but as long as there were men with checkbooks, was not going to suffer again.

Significantly, the Barbie doll was invented by a woman, Mattel cofounder Ruth Handler, who later established and ran "Nearly Me," a firm that designed and marketed mastectomy prostheses. (As she herself has put it, "My life has been spent going from breasts to breasts.") After Ruth and her husband Elliot, with whom she founded Mattel, left the company in 1975, women have continued to be the key decision makers on the Barbie line; the company's current COO, a fortyish ex–cosmetics marketer given to wearing Chanel suits, has been so involved with the doll that the *Los Angeles Times* dubbed her "Barbie's Doting Sister." In many ways, this makes Barbie a toy designed by women for women to teach women what—for better or worse—is expected of them by society.

Through the efforts of an overzealous publicist, Mattel engineer Jack Ryan, a former husband of Zsa Zsa Gabor, received credit for Barbie in his obituary. Actually, he merely held patents on the waist and knee joints in a later version of the doll; he had little to do with the original. If anyone should share recognition for inventing Barbie it is Charlotte Johnson, Barbie's first dress designer, whom Handler plucked from a teaching job and installed in Tokyo for a year to supervise the production of the doll's original twenty-two outfits.

Handler tries to downplay Barbie's resemblance to Lilli, but I think she should flaunt it. Physically the two are virtually identical; in terms of ethos, they couldn't be more dissimilar. In creating Barbie, Handler credits herself with having fleshed out a two-dimensional paper doll. This does not, however, do justice to her genius. She took Lilli, whom Ryan described as a "hooker or an actress between performances," and recast her as the wholesome all-American girl. Handler knew her market; if any one character trait distinguishes the American middle class, both today and in 1959, it is an obsession with respectability. This is not to say the middle class is indifferent to sex, but that it defines itself in contrast to the classes below it by its display of public propriety. Pornography targeted to the middle class, for example, must have a veneer of artistic or literary pretense—hence *Playboy*, the picture book men can also buy "for the articles."

Barbie and Lilli symbolize the link between the Old World and the New. America is a nation colonized by riffraff; the *Mayflower* was filled with petty criminals and the down-and-out. When Moll Flanders, to cite an emblematic floozy, took off for our shores, she was running from the law. Consequently, what could be more American than being an unimpeachable citizen with a sordid, embarrassing forebear in Europe?

TO FIRST-GENERATION BARBIE OWNERS, OF WHICH I WAS one, Barbie was a revelation. She didn't teach us to nurture, like our clinging, dependent Betsy Wetsys and Chatty Cathys. She taught us independence. Barbie was her own woman. She could invent herself with a costume change: sing a solo in the spotlight one minute, pilot a starship the next. She was Grace Slick and Sally Ride, Marie Osmond and Marie Curie. She was all that we could be and—if you calculate what at human scale would translate to a thirty-nine-inch bust—more than we could be. And certainly more than we were . . . at six and seven and eight when she appeared and sank her jungle-red talons into our inner lives.

Or into my inner life, anyway. After I begged my mother for a Barbie, she reluctantly gave me a Midge—Barbie's ugly sidekick, who was named for an insect and had blemishes painted on her face. When I complained, she compounded the error by simultaneously giving me a Barbie and a Ken. I still remember Midge's anguish—her sense of isolation—at having to tag along after a couple. In my subsequent doll play, Ken rejected Barbie and forged a tight platonic bond with Midge. He did not, however, reject Barbie's clothes—and the more girlish the better.

To study Barbie, one sometimes has to hold seemingly contradictory ideas in one's head at the same time—which, as F. Scott Fitzgerald has said, is "the test of a first-rate intelligence." The doll functions like a Rorschach test; people project wildly dissimilar and often opposing fantasies on it. Barbie may be a universally recognized image, but what she represents in a child's inner life can be as personal as a fingerprint. It was once fashionable to tar Barbie as a materialistic dumbbell, and for some older feminists it still is; columnists Anna Quindlen and Ellen Goodman seem to be competing to chalk up the greatest number of attacks. Those of us young enough to have played with Barbie, however, realize the case is far from open and shut. In part, this is because imaginative little girls rarely play with products the way manufacturers expect them to. But it also has to do with the products themselves: at worst, Barbie projected an anomalous message; at best, she was a sort of feminist pioneer. And her meaning, like her face, has not been static over time.

Before the divorce epidemic that swept America in the late sixties, Barbie's universe and that of the suburban nuclear family were light years apart. There were no parents or husbands or offspring in Barbie's world; she didn't define herself through relationships of responsibility to men or to her family. Nor was Barbie a numb, frustrated *Hausfrau* out of *The Feminine Mystique.* In the doll's early years, Handler turned down a vacuum company's offer to make a Barbie-sized vacuum because Barbie didn't do what Charlotte Johnson termed "rough housework." When Thorstein Veblen formulated his *Theory of the Leisure Class,* women were expected to perform vicarious leisure and vicarious consumption to show that their husbands were prosperous. But Barbie had no husband. Based on the career outfits in her first wardrobe, she earned her keep modeling and designing clothes. Her leisure and consumption were a testimony to herself.

True, she had a boyfriend, but he was a lackluster fellow, a mere accessory. Mattel, in fact, never wanted to produce Ken; male figure dolls had traditionally been losers in the marketplace. But consumers so pushed for a boyfriend doll that Mattel finally released Ken in 1961. The reason for their demand was obvious. Barbie taught girls what was expected of women, and a woman in the fifties would have been a failure without a male consort, even a drip with seriously abridged genitalia who wasn't very important in her life.

Feminism notwithstanding, the same appears true today, though many of my young friends who own Barbies have embraced a weirdly polygamous approach to marriage, in which an average of eight female dolls share a single overextended Ken. Some mothers facetiously speculate that they are acting out the so-called "man shortage," still referred to by dinner-party hostesses despite its having been discredited by Susan Faludi in *Backlash*. My theory, however, is that smart little girls were made uneasy by the late-eighties version of Ken. Unlike the bright-eyed, innocent Ken with whom I grew up, the later model bears a troubling resemblance to William Kennedy Smith: His brow is low, his neck thick, and his eyes too close together.

With its 1993 "Earring Magic Ken," Mattel perhaps overdid his retreat from heterosexual virility. True, the doll has a smarter-looking face, but between his earring, lavender vest, and what newspapers euphemized as a "ring pendant" ("cock ring" wouldn't, presumably, play to a family audience), he would have fit right in on Christopher Street. Watching my jaw drop at the sight of the doll at Toy Fair, Mattel publicist Donna Gibbs assured me that an earring in one's left ear was innocuous. "Of course," I said feebly, "the same ear in which Joey Buttafuoco wears his."

Barbie, too, has changed her look more than once through the years, though her body has remained essentially unaltered. From an art history standpoint—and Barbie, significantly, has been copyrighted as a work of art—her most radical change came in 1971, and was a direct reflection of the sexual revolution. Until then, Barbie's eyes had been cast down and to one side—the averted, submissive gaze that characterized female nudes, particularly those of a pornographic nature, from the Renaissance until the nineteenth century. What had been so shocking about Manet's *Olympia* (1865) was that the model was both naked and unabashedly staring at the viewer. By 1971, however, when America had begun to accept the idea that a woman could be both sexual and unashamed, Barbie, in her "Malibu" incarnation, was allowed to have that body and look straight ahead.

The Barbie doll had its first overhaul and face change in 1967, when it acquired eyelashes and a rotating waist. Although the new "Twist 'N Turn" Barbie was not that different from the rigid old one—its gaze was still sidelong—the way it was promoted was not. Girls who traded in their old, beloved Barbies were given a discount on the new model. Twist 'N Turn introduced car designer Harley Earl's idea of "dynamic obsolescence" to doll bodies. Where once only doll fashions had changed, now the doll itself changed; each year until the eighties, the doll's body would be engineered to perform some new trick—clutch a telephone, hit a tennis ball, even tilt its head back and smooch. Taste was not a big factor in devising the new dolls; in 1975, Mattel came out with "Growing Up Skipper," a preteen doll that, when you shoved its arm backward, sprouted breasts.

Fans of conspiracy theories will be disappointed to learn that Barbie's proportions were not the result of some misogynistic plot. They were dictated by the mechanics of clothing construction. The doll is one-sixth the size of a person, but the fabrics she wears are scaled for people. Barbie's middle, her first designer explained, had to be disproportionately narrow to look proportional in clothes. The inner seam on the waistband of a skirt involves four layers of cloth—and four thicknesses of human-scale fabric on a one-sixth-human-scale doll would cause the doll's waist to appear dramatically larger than her hips.

It is one thing for a sexually initiated adult to snicker over the doll's anatomically inaccurate body, quite another to recall how she looked to us when we were children: terrifying yet beguiling; as charged and puzzling as sexuality itself. In the late fifties and early sixties, there was no talk of condoms in the schools, *National Geographic* was a kid's idea of a racy magazine, and the nearest thing to a sexually explicit music video was Annette Funicello bouncing around with the Mouseketeers. Barbie, with her shocking torpedo orbs, and Ken with his mysterious genital bulge, were the extent of our exposure to the secrets of adulthood. Sex is less shrouded now than it was thirty years ago, but today's young Barbie owners are still using the doll to unravel the mystery of gender differences.

Of course, these days, kids have a great deal more to puzzle out. One used to wake up in the morning confident of certain things—among them that there were two genders, masculine and feminine, and that "masculine" was attached to males, "feminine" to females. But on the frontiers of medicine and philosophy, this certainty has been questioned. Geneticists recognize the existence of at least five genders; prenatal hormonal irregularities can, for instance, cause fetuses that are chromosomally female to develop as anatomical males and fetuses that are chromosomally male to develop as anatomical females. Then there are feminist theorists such as Judith Butler who argue that there is no gender at all. *"Gender is a kind of imitation for which there is no original,"* Butler has written. It is something performed, artificial, a "phantasmic ideal of heterosexual identity." All gendering, consequently, is drag, "a kind of impersonation and approximation."

No one disputes that from a young age boys and girls behave differently, but the jury is still out on why. Is such behavior rooted in biology or social conditioning? I think it's possible to look at femininity as a performance—

or "womanliness as a masquerade," to borrow from Joan Rivière, a female Freudian who labeled the phenomenon in 1929—without chucking the possibility of biological differences.

Indeed, some of Barbie's most ardent imitators are probably not what Carole King had in mind when she wrote "Natural Woman." Many drag queens proudly cite Barbie's influence; as a child, singer Ru-Paul not only collected Barbies but cut off their breasts. Barbie has, in fact, a drag queen's body: broad shoulders and narrow hips, which are quintessentially male, and exaggerated breasts, which aren't. Then there are biological women whose emulation of Barbie has relied heavily on artifice: the Barbi Twins, identical *Playboy* covergirls who maintain their wasp waists through a diet of Beech-Nut strained veal; and Cindy Jackson, the London-based cosmetic surgery maven who has had more than twenty operations to make her resemble the doll.

When Ella King Torrey, a friend of mine and consultant on this book, began researching Barbie at Yale University in 1979, her work was considered cutting-edge and controversial. But these days everybody's deconstructing the doll. Barbie has been the subject of papers presented at the Modern Language Association's 1992 convention and the Ninth Berkshire Conference on the History of Women; rarely does a pop culture conference pass without some mention of the postmodern female fetish figure. Gilles Brougère, a French sociologist, has conducted an exhaustive study of French women and children to determine how different age groups perceive the doll. When scholars deal with Barbie, however, they often take a single aspect of the doll and construct an argument around it. I have resisted that approach. What fascinates me is the whole, ragged, contradictory story—its intrigues, its inconsistencies, and the personalities of its players.

I've tried to pin down exactly what happened in Barbie's first years. Mattel's focus on the future, which may be the secret of its success, has been at the expense of its past. The company has no archive. This may help con-

DEAN BROWN, "OLYMPIA," 1981

ceal its embarrassments, but it has also buried its achievements—such as
subsidizing Shindana Toys in response to the 1965 Watts riots. The African-
American–run, South Central Los Angeles–based company produced ethnically correct playthings long before they were fashionable.

Although Barbie's sales have never substantially flagged, Mattel has been
a financial roller coaster. It nearly went broke in 1974, when the imaginative accounting practices of Ruth Handler and some of her top executives
led to indictments against them for falsifying SEC information, and again in
1984, when the company shifted its focus from toys to electronic games that
nobody wanted to buy. The second time, Michael Milken galloped to the res-
cue. "I believed in Barbie," Milken told Barbara Walters in 1993. "I called
up the head of Mattel and I told him that I personally would be willing to

invest two hundred million dollars in his company. There's more Barbie dolls in this country than there are people."

The Barbie story is filled with loose ends and loose screws, but unfortunately very few loose lips. In a world as small as the toy industry, people are discreet about former colleagues because they may have to work with them again. As for welcoming outsiders, the company has much in common with the Kremlin at the height of the Cold War. To a degree, secrecy is vital in the toy business: if a rival learns in August of a clever new toy, he or she can steal the idea and have a knock-off in the stores by Christmas.

Nor am I what Mattel had in mind as its Boswell. Inspired perhaps by Quindlen and Goodman, or, more likely, by fear and a deadline, I had owned up in my weekly *Newsday* column to having cross-dressed Ken because of antipathy toward his girlfriend. This was years before I gave serious thought to Barbie's iconic import, but it was not sufficiently far in the past to have escaped the attention of Mattel publicist Donna Gibbs, who, when I first called her, did not treat me warmly. Miraculously, after a few months, Donna and her colleagues became gracious, charming, and remarkably accommodating. I was baffled, but took it as a sign to keep—like the entity I was studying—on my toes. Still, it was hard not to be seduced by the company, especially by its elves—the designers and sculptors, the "rooters and groomers," as the hair people are called—who really did seem to have a great time playing with their eleven-and-a-half-inch pals.

Toys have always said a lot about the culture that produced them, and especially about how that culture viewed its children. The ancient Greeks, for instance, left behind few playthings. Their custom of exposing weak babies on mountainsides to die does not suggest a concern for the very young. Ghoulish though it may sound, until the eighteenth century, childhood didn't count for much because few people survived it. Children were even dressed like little adults. Although in 1959, much fuss was made over Mattel's "adult" doll, the fact was that until 1820 all dolls were adults. Baby dolls came into existence in the early decades of the nineteenth century along with, significantly, special clothing for children.

Published in 1762, Rousseau's *Émile,* a treatise on education, began to focus attention on the concerns of youngsters, but the cult of childhood didn't take root until Queen Victoria ascended the throne in 1837. "Childhood was invented in the eighteenth century in response to dehumanizing trends of the industrial revolution," psychoanalyst Louise J. Kaplan has observed. "By the nineteenth century, when artists began to see themselves as alienated beings trapped in a dehumanizing social world, the child became the savior of mankind, the symbol of free imagination and natural goodness."

The child was also a consumer of toys, the making of which, by the late nineteenth century, had become an industry. Until World War I, Germany dominated the marketplace; but when German troops began shooting at U.S. soldiers, Americans lost their taste for enemy playthings. This burst of patriotism gave the U.S. toy industry its first rapid growth spurt; its second came after World War II, with the revolution in plastics.

Just as children were "discovered" in the eighteenth century, they were again "discovered" in post–World War II America—this time by marketers. The evolution of the child-as-consumer was indispensable to Barbie's success. Mattel not only pioneered advertising on television, but through that medium it pitched Barbie directly to kids.

It is with an eye toward using objects to understand ourselves that I beg Barbie's knee-jerk defenders and knee-jerk revilers to cease temporarily their defending and reviling. Barbie is too complicated for either an encomium or an indictment. But we will not refrain from looking under rocks.

For women under forty, the implications of such an investigation are obvious. Barbie is a direct reflection of the cultural impulses that formed us. Barbie is our reality. And unsettling though the concept may be, I don't think it's hyperbolic to say: Barbie is us.

CHAPTER TWO

A TOY IS BORN

It is hard to imagine Mattel Toys headquartered anywhere but in southern California. A short drive from Disneyland, minutes from the beach, it is in a place where people come to make their fortunes, or so the mythology goes, where beautiful women are "discovered" in drugstores, and a man can turn a mouse into an empire. Barbie could not have been conceived in Pawtucket, Rhode Island, where Hasbro is located, or Cincinnati, Ohio, where Kenner makes its home. Barbie needed the sun to incubate her or, at the very least, to lighten her hair. This is not to say that Hawthorne, where Mattel had its offices until 1991, is anything but a dump—a gritty industrial district that cries out for trees. But it is a dump with a glamour-queen precedent: In 1926, Marilyn Monroe was born there.

Of course it's inaccurate to say Barbie was "born" anywhere. The dolls were originally cast in Japan, making, I suppose, Barbie's birthplace Tokyo. But Barbie's "parents," Ruth and Elliot Handler, are very much southern Californians—of the fortune-making variety—who fled their native Denver, Colorado, in 1937.

California was a different place back then: neither stippled with television

RUTH HANDLER PHOTOGRAPHED WITH PORTRAIT

BY ELLIOT HANDLER SYLVIA PLACHY

antennas nor linked with concrete cloverleaf. The McDonald brothers wouldn't raise their Golden Arches for another fifteen years. Thanks to the Depression, the Golden State had lost some of its glister. Okies and Arkies poured in from the ravaged Dust Bowl; and for many, the land of sunshine and promise was just as gray and bleak as the place they had left.

Not so for the Handlers. Just twenty-one when they uprooted, they were optimists; and because they believed in the future they were willing to take risks. The youngest of ten children, Ruth was a stenographer at Paramount Pictures; Elliot, the second of four brothers, was a light-fixture designer and art student; and their first gamble was to chuck their jobs and start their own business, peddling the Plexiglas furniture that Elliot had been building part-time in their garage. The wager paid off: In the first years of World War II, they expanded into a former Chinese laundry and hired about a hundred workers. They made jewelry, candleholders, even a clear-plastic Art Deco airplane with a clock in it.

Wartime shortages derailed that venture, but the Handlers remained on track. In 1945, they started "Mattel Creations" with their onetime foreman, Harold Matson, whose name was fused with Elliot's to form Mattel. Matson, however, did not love gambling with his life savings; he sold out in 1946, making him the sort of asterisk to toy history that short-term Beatle Pete Best was to the history of popular music.

Elliot not only believed in the future, he believed in futuristic materials—Plexiglas, Lucite, plastic. He set up Mattel to manufacture plastic picture frames, which, because of wartime rationing, ironically ended up being made of wood. When the war ended, however, it was the Ukedoodle, a plastic ukelele, that secured Mattel's niche in the toy world. A popular jack-in-the-box followed, and by 1955, the company was worth $500,000.

Although Barbie wouldn't be introduced for another four years, Mattel, in 1955, paved the way for the sort of advertising that would make her possible. It was a big year for child culture: Disneyland had opened in July and

Walt Disney, who seemed to have a golden touch with the under-twelve set, was preparing to launch a TV series, *The Mickey Mouse Club*. No toy company had ever sponsored a series before, and ABC, Disney's network, wanted to give Mattel the chance. There was just one catch: ABC demanded a year-long contract that would cost Mattel its entire net worth.

Ralph Carson, cofounder of Carson/Roberts, Mattel's advertising agency, thought the Handlers would be hesitant. He brought Vincent Francis, ABC's airtime salesman, to Elliot's office to make the pitch. What he failed to consider, however, was the Handlers' willingness to gamble.

The presentation "took fifteen or twenty minutes," Ruth recalls, and she and Elliot were "ready to jump out of our skins with excitement." But before they said yes, they consulted their comptroller, Yasuo Yoshida.

"Yas," Ruth recalls having said, "what would happen if we didn't bring much out of this? Would we go broke? And Yas's answer was: 'Not broke—but badly bent.' "

"Okay," Elliot remembers telling him, "we'll try the bent."

In Mattel's commercial, a little boy stalked an elephant with a toy called the Burp Gun; when the child fired, the film of the animal ran backward, causing it to appear to retreat. Kids loved the ad, and by Christmas the gun had sold out.

The Handlers' move, however, did more than create record sales for a single product in a single year. Before advertisers could pitch directly to kids, selling toys had been a mom-and-pop business with a seasonal focus on Christmas. But once kids could actually see toys on television, selling them became not only big business but one that took place year-round.

Ironically, in December 1955, *Time* magazine ran a photo of Louis Marx, founder of Louis Marx & Company, Inc., on its cover. He was king of the old-time toy industry—an industry that Mattel and Carson/Roberts were well on their way to making obsolete. Marx sneered at advertising. Although his company had had sales of $50 million in 1955, it spent a meager $312 on publicity. Mattel, by contrast, which had sales of $6 million, spent $500,000; it also pioneered marketing techniques that would send Marx and his ilk the way of the dinosaurs.

IN 1993, RUTH AND ELLIOT SHARED SOME REMINISCENCES with me in their Century City penthouse. With its gray marble floor, white pile carpet, grand piano, and vast semicircular wet bar, the dwelling is a far cry from the furnished one-room apartment they shared when they were married in 1938. Their daughter, Barbara, after whom the doll was named, was born in 1941; their son Ken, who also gave his name to a doll, in 1944, during Elliot's year-long hitch in the U.S. Army.

Together since they were sixteen, they have weathered things that might have daunted a lesser couple: Ruth's radical mastectomy in 1970; her indictment in 1978 by a federal grand jury for mail fraud, conspiracy, and making false statements to the Securities and Exchange Commission; and, after having pleaded no contest to the charges, her conviction, leading to a forty-one-month suspended sentence, a $57,000 suspended fine and 2,500 hours of community service, which she has completed. In 1975, they survived expulsion from the company they built. Theirs is the sort of romance that seems to happen only in the movies—or used to happen, before the fashion for verisimilitude precluded not only "happily ever after" but "ever after."

They have not grown to resemble each other, as many couples do. Ruth is compact and gregarious. She marches into a room with a combination of authority and bounce, rather like Napoleon in pump-up, air-sole Nikes. And indeed, on the two occasions I met her, once at home and once at Beverly Hills' Hillcrest Country Club, she was wearing sneakers and a stylish warm-up suit. Her hair is short and steely. She can be irresistibly charming; she's cultivated the ability to listen as if you were the most fascinating conversationalist in the world. But if your talk takes a turn she doesn't like, she can wither you with a glance.

"When she walks, the earth shakes," said her son Ken, a philanthropist, entrepreneur, and father of three who lives in New York's West Village. "She's a little woman, seventy-six years old, and the earth shakes."

Elliot is tall, lanky, and laconic. He lets his wife do most of the talking, occasionally interrupting with a sardonic aside. He dresses as casually as Ruth, wearing short-sleeve polo shirts on the two occasions I met him. Very little, I suspect, gets by him: he strikes me as a keen observer.

Elliot's paintings hang on nearly every wall of the apartment. One composition depicts an orchid on a mirrored table; in the foreground, blue and white jewels spill opulently from a case. Another shows voluptuous red and green apples in front of a cityscape. Yet another has as its principal element a giant pigeon. Often, these forms are displayed against a flat cerulean sky with clouds—a sky that recalls Magritte's and that, as the objects are painted many times larger than life and in intense Day-Glo colors, heightens their surreality.

There was a time, a little less than ten years ago, when the room was a museum, housing the Handlers' multimillion-dollar collection of Impressionist and Post-Impressionist paintings. A wintry Norwegian landscape by Claude Monet contrasted with brighter, sunnier spots by Camille Pissarro, Fernand Léger, and André Derain. Pierre-Auguste Renoir's *Baigneuse* and Picasso's *Baigneuse au Bord de la Mer* shared wallspace with Amedeo Modigliani's *Tête de Jeune Fille.* But considering whose success made the collection possible, perhaps the most intriguing canvas was Moïse Kisling's *La Jeune Femme Blonde:* a standing female nude, slightly stouter than Barbie, with her hair pulled back in a Barbie-esque ponytail.

In 1985, however, at the height of the art market, the Handlers put their paintings on the block at Sotheby's in New York. "One day I said, 'This place is no good for an art collection'—too much glass, too much window, too much daylight," Elliot explained with a smile. "We had to keep the drapes closed. So I said, 'Aw, to hell with it, I'm painting now.' "

If one were to believe in astrology, as many Californians do, one would suspect something strange and powerful was going on in the heavens over Hawthorne in 1955. Not only had Mattel caused an earthquake in the toy business, but the company hired Jack Ryan, a wildly eccentric, Yale-educated electrical engineer whose sexual indiscretions, extravagant parties, and sometimes autocratic management style would shake the company from within.

For Elliot Handler, hiring Jack was a great triumph. Elliot had initially met him when he pitched Mattel an idea for a toy transistor radio. Children's toys were not, however, Ryan's forte; a member of the Raytheon team designing the Sparrow and Hawk missiles, he made playthings for the Pentagon. But Elliot sensed that Jack had what Elliot needed: Jack knew about torques and transistors; he understood electricity and the behavior of molecules; he had the space-age savvy to make Elliot's high-tech fantasies real. Elliot courted Ryan for several years, sweetening his offer until Ryan had a remarkable contract: one that permitted him a royalty on every patent his design group originated; one that swiftly transformed him into a multi-millionaire.

Ryan "had a funny little body, very compact, and a kind of bird puffy chest—like he had just puffed himself up," recalled novelist Gwen Davis, who had met him through his fourth wife, Zsa Zsa Gabor. His hair appeared "painted on, like Reagan's, and he had a very peculiar tan that looked as if it might have been makeup." At his parties, he wore clothing that was very non–Brooks Brothers—khaki jackets with golden epaulets, imaginary uniforms, fantasy costumes for his fantasy life.

The setting for this strange life was the castle he built in Bel Air, on the site of the five-acre, eighteen-bathroom, seven-kitchen estate that had belonged to silent-screen star Warner Baxter. In Jack's mind, "residence" was a synonym for "theme park." He gave dinner parties in a tree house with a glittering crystal chandelier and occasionally forced his guests to down victuals without utensils in a tapestry-ridden, vaguely medieval curiosity that he called the Tom Jones Room. "He ruined a perfectly good English Tudor house by putting turrets on the end of it," chided Norma Greene, the retired liaison between Ryan's design group and Mattel's patent department.

But the castle was not all lighthearted fun and games. It also had a dungeon—Zsa Zsa described it as a "torture chamber"—painted an ominous black and adorned with black fox fur. Over the years the castle housed, often simultaneously, his first wife Barbara, his two daughters, his brother Jim, multiple mistresses, one or two fellow engineers, and a group Zsa Zsa called "Ryan's Boys," twelve UCLA students who did work around the place in exchange for room and board.

Zsa Zsa never moved in with Jack; but even with her own house as a refuge, she could only endure seven months of marriage. "Jack's sex life would have made the average *Penthouse* reader blanch with shock," she observed in her autobiography, *One Lifetime Is Not Enough.*

Meanwhile, in Hamburg, Germany, around the world from Mattel, 1955 was a key year for another designer who had a major influence on Barbie. Reinhard Beuthien, a cartoonist, had created the comic character Lilli for the *Bild Zeitung;* on August 12 of that year, Lilli acquired a third dimension. The Bavaria-based firm of Greiner & Hauser GmbH issued her as an eleven-and-a-half-inch, platinum-ponytailed, Nefertiti-eyed, fleshtone-plastic doll.

Lilli's cartoon antics fit right in with the *Bild Zeitung*'s sordid, sensational stories. A golddigger, exhibitionist, and floozy, she had the body of a Vargas Girl, the brains of Pia Zadora, and the morals of Xaviera Hollander. Beuthien's jokes usually hinged on Lilli taking money from men and involved situations in which she wore very few clothes. Male wealth was of

„Wieso hast du Bedenken, einen Mann mit sehr viel Geld zu heiraten — wenn du ihn heiratest, hat er doch sowieso bald weniger!"

LILLI COMIC STRIP:

"HOW DO YOU MEAN TO MARRY A MAN WITH A LOT OF MONEY—AS SOON AS YOU MARRY HIM IT WILL BE GONE!"

far greater interest to Lilli than male looks; she flung herself repeatedly at balding, jowly fat cats.

In one typical cartoon, Lilli appears in a female friend's apartment concealing her naked body with a newspaper. The caption: "We had a fight and he took back all the presents he gave me." In another, a policeman warns that her two-piece bathing suit is illegal on the boardwalk. "Oh," she replies, "and in your opinion which part should I take off?" In yet another, she shouts her phone number to a female friend on the street, hoping the rich-looking man nearby will overhear.

Her debut cartoon, which ran on July 24, 1952, set the tone for the others. It shows her with a gypsy fortune-teller begging, "Can't you give me the name and address of this tall, handsome, rich man?"

Even people inured to the peculiarities of Barbie's body might cringe at the sight of the doll based on Lilli. Unlike Barbie, Lilli doesn't have an arched foot with itty-bitty toes. She doesn't even have a foot. The end of her leg is cast in the shape of a stiletto-heeled pump and painted a glossy black. Never mind that her leg is a fetishistic caricature; never mind that she is hobbled, easily pushed into a horizontal position; that she might want to play tennis sometime or walk on the beach. Poor Lilli can never take the monstrous slipper off.

Sculpted by doll designer Max Weissbrodt, Lilli was never intended for children: She was a pornographic caricature, a gag gift for men, or even more curious, for men to give to their girlfriends in lieu of, say, flowers. *"Die höchsten Herrn haben Lilli gern"*— "Gentlemen prefer Lilli," says a brochure promoting her wardrobe, over a picture of the doll in a short skirt that has blown up above her waist. It adds: "Whether more or less naked, Lilli is always discreet." (*"Ob mehr oder minder nackt Lilli bewahrt immer Tackt."*)

Like Barbie, Lilli has an outfit for every occasion, but they aren't the sort of occasions in which nice girls find themselves. In a dress with a low-cut back, Lilli can be "the star of every bar"; in a tarty lace one, she can rendezvous for a five o'clock tea—either in a café or (wink) in private. Lilli isn't just a symbol of sex, she is a symbol of illicit sex.

"You should take Lilli with you everywhere," the brochure advises men. As a "mascot for your car," Lilli promises a "swift ride" (*"beschwingte Fahrt"*). The nature of this "swift ride" is suggested by Lilli's photo. In a tight sweater and microscopic shorts, she sits on a swing, her outstretched legs slightly splayed—a pornographic recasting of Fragonard's erotic *The Swing.* The brochure mentions that "children swoon" over Lilli; but the very notion of "swooning"—the way one "swoons" over a rock star—has a weird carnal innuendo, implicitly sexualizing kids.

Just what did German men do with the doll? "I saw it once in a guy's car where he had it up on the dashboard," said Cy Schneider, the former Carson/Roberts copywriter who wrote Barbie's first TV commercials. "I saw a couple of guys joking about it in a

No. 1113A

Neuheit!
Novelty!
Nouveauté!

"WHOEVER GIVES WITH LOVE—THINKS OF LILLI." BILD LILLI PROMOTIONAL IMAGE

... sicher
gefällt
Lilli
Dir
mit
einem
schönen
Tier

"LILLI WILL PLEASE YOU WITH A BEAUTIFUL ANIMAL." BILD LILLI PROMOTIONAL IMAGE

bar. They were lifting up her skirts and pulling down her pants and stuff."

Lilli is more, however, than a male wet dream; she is a Teutonic fantasy. And her Germanness is a critical part of her identity. Lilli reminds me of Maria Braun in *The Marriage of Maria Braun*, Rainer Werner Fassbinder's allegorical 1979 film about the relationship between the two parts of then-divided Germany. Not only does Hanna Schygulla, the relentlessly Aryan actress who portrays Maria, closely resemble Lilli; for much of the movie she wears the same hairstyle—a flaxen ponytail with poodle bangs. One gets the sense that Lilli, like Maria, has endured great privation during the war, and that even if it means using men, she will not starve again. Although Fassbinder is not around to clear up the mystery, one has to believe he was familiar with the Lilli cartoon character—so similar to Lilli's are Maria's clothes, makeup, and behavior.

In Fassbinder's movie, the parallel between Maria and the Federal Republic is clearly defined: Maria kills a black American G.I.; her German husband takes the fall, and she remains loyal to him while he is in jail—a situation analogous to the prisonlike condition of East Germany before 1989. Her loyalty, however, does not preclude exchanging sexual favors for cigarettes, silk stockings, and ultimately, corporate perks. Lilli first appeared in 1952, when the so-called German economic miracle was under way, though far from fully realized. And while Lilli doesn't bear the metaphorical burden of a marriage to the East, it's hard not to view her pursuit of wealth as similar to that of West Germany. She is the vanquished Aryan, golddigging her way back to prosperity.

Ruth Handler first encountered the Lilli doll when she was shopping in Switzerland on a family vacation. "We were walking down the street in Lucerne and there was a doll—an adult doll with a woman's body—sitting on a rope swing," Ruth told me, though she has in other interviews placed this epiphany in Zurich and Vienna. Her daughter Barbara, in her mid-teens and well past the age for dolls, wanted Lilli as "a decorative item" for her room. Ruth bought three—two for Barbara, one for herself.

. . . zu allen

Gelegenheiten

sollte

Lilli

Sie

begleiten

!

"I didn't then know who Lilli was or even that its name was Lilli," Ruth said. "I only saw an adult-shape body that I had been trying to describe for years, and our guys said couldn't be done."

"Our guys" were the male designers at Mattel. Since Barbara was a child, Ruth had tried to get them to develop a doll with a woman's body. She got the idea watching Barbara play with paper dolls who were "never the play-

"YOU SHOULD INVITE LILLI AT EVERY OPPORTUNITY!"

BILD LILLI PROMOTIONAL IMAGE_

. . . ob mehr oder minder nackt

Lilli bewahrt immer Takt

mate or baby type," but rather "the teenage, high-school, college, or adult-career type."

"Through their play," Ruth said, Barbara and her friends "were imagining their lives as adults. They were using the dolls to reflect the adult world around them. They would sit and carry on conversations, making the dolls real people. I used to watch that over and over and think: If only we could take this play pattern and three-dimensionalize it, we would have something very special."

Special was not how the male designers saw it. It was costly. In America, they told Ruth, it would be impossible to make what she wanted —a woman doll with painted nails and "real nice clothing" that had "zippers and darts and hemlines"— for an affordable price.

"Frankly," Ruth recalled, "I thought they were all horrified by the thought of wanting to make a doll with breasts."

But just because the dolls couldn't be made in America didn't mean they couldn't be made. In July 1957, Jack Ryan took off for Tokyo to find a manufacturer for some electronic gadgets he had designed. "Just as I was leaving," he said, "Ruth stuck this doll into my attaché case and said: 'See if you can get this copied.' " The doll, of course, was Lilli.

Jack was accompanied on the trip by Frank Nakamura, a recent graduate of Los Angeles' Art Center School whom Mattel had hired as a product designer in April. A United States citizen, Nakamura was also fluent in Japanese; during the war, he taught the language in a school run by the U.S. Military Intelligence Service at the University of Michigan in Ann Arbor. When the war ended, he was sent to Japan to debrief Japanese soldiers on their battle experiences and report their stories to General MacArthur.

Frank "knew his way around Japan very well," Jack said. "And in Japan, it's more important to know your way around and to be able to make connections than it is here. Here you walk into any office and you're doing business right away on face value. It's not so in Japan."

The trip did not begin auspiciously. Ryan, Frank recalled, became edgy when the plane took off. He had an odd phobia for an aerospace engineer: He was afraid to fly. Nor did things go smoothly on the ground. Frank contacted numerous manufacturers, none of whom was equipped to make vinyl dolls. After three weeks, Ryan returned to California.

Part of the problem was Lilli herself; she didn't exactly capture the hearts of the Japanese. "The Lilli doll looked kind of mean—sharp eyebrow and eyeshadow and so forth," Nakamura said. "And Japanese people didn't like it at all." But Frank pressed on, and by the time Elliot joined him in early August, Kokusai Boeki Kaisha (KBK), a Tokyo-based novelty maker, was ready to cut a deal.

KBK was not one big widget factory; it was a distributor for widgets that had been made by contractors and subcon-

Ihr guter Stern auf allen Straßen

No. 100

Schaukel
Swing
Columpio
Escarpolette

Lilli

LOOSELY TRANSLATED: LILLI IS "YOUR LUCKY STAR ON THE ROAD."

BILD LILLI PROMOTIONAL IMAGE

tractors all over Japan, from Hokkaido in the extreme north to Fukuoka in the extreme south. "The network was like a spiderweb," Nakamura said, "stretching two to three hundred miles in each direction."

KBK persuaded a dollmaker named Yamasaki to knock off Lilli, but that was only the beginning of the challenge. Lilli's body was as hard as her look, made of rigid plastic that had been "injection-molded"—squeezed into its mold like toothpaste from a tube. Mattel, however, wanted to make Barbie out of soft vinyl, and vinyl, when injection-molded, didn't always ooze into the tiny crevices of a mold. To ensure that Barbie had fingers and toes, her arms and legs would have to be "rotation-molded"—turned slowly in their molds while the vinyl hardened.

Yamasaki had never rotation-molded anything in his life. So in November, Mattel sent Seymour Adler, a Brooklyn-born engineer with a background in tool design, to teach him how. Adler arrived with the latest plastic-industry journals detailing the new process. Only one obstacle remained: Adler himself had never rotation-molded before either.

Back in California, Ryan was doing his best to make the doll look less like "a German streetwalker." He had befriended Bud Westmore, the makeup czar at Universal Pictures, who gave Lilli a makeover. The first thing Westmore eliminated was what he called her "bee-stung lips," the Maria Braunesque pout into which her tough little mouth had been formed. Next were her heavy eyelashes and what Ryan termed the "weird widow's peak" on her forehead. A sculptor was brought in to refashion Lilli's face, but, Adler told me, nobody at Mattel liked the results, so the head was cast, with slight modifications, from Lilli's.

Ryan also modified the joints that attached the arms and legs to the torso. Then he sent cast alloy masters of the freshly sculpted body parts for the Japanese to electroplate and make into molds. Before a mold could be used to produce the doll, Ryan had to approve six sample castings from it. Sometimes the castings had startling embellishments.

"Each time I would get a half dozen back, they would have nipples on the breasts," Ryan explained. "So I took my little fine Swiss file, which the Swiss use for working on watches, and very daintily filed the nipples off and returned them."

After several rounds of emery-boarding, KBK got the message. "The Japanese are very obedient," Ryan said. "They'll always do what you tell them."

KBK NOT ONLY MADE BARBIE, IT ALSO MADE HER CLOTHES. It didn't, however, design them. For Barbie's first wardrobe, the Handlers turned to Charlotte Johnson, a fortyish veteran of Seventh Avenue who had been working in the garment industry since she was seventeen. They found her at Los Angeles' Chouinard Institute, where she was teaching an evening course in fashion design. Many say Charlotte created Barbie in her own image. "The shocker was that the doll looked like her," Ken Handler said of his first meeting with the designer in the early sixties. "It had the same-shaped head and was wearing the same hair."

As often as the adjective "short" has been used to describe Jack Ryan, who stood about five feet seven, the terms "tall," "statuesque," and "imposing" have been applied by colleagues to Charlotte, who stands about five feet ten in heels. Her reputation for tenacity evolved during the year she spent in Tokyo, in Frank Lloyd Wright's aptly named Imperial Hotel, making Barbie's wardrobe. Six days a week, Charlotte met with a Japanese designer and two seamstresses, developing designs that minimized the sewing process. "She was very, very fussy about the fit of the costume," Nakamura said.

She was also fussy about the fabric, which translated into a headache for him. He had to convince textile merchants to make small batches of cloth to her specifications, and small batches were rarely profitable. After much haggling, he obtained the black-and-white striped fabric for Barbie's first bathing suit. With still more haggling, he got minuscule snaps, buttons less than an eighth of an inch in diameter, and yards of miniature zippers from zipper manufacturer Yoshida Kojko (YKK).

Charlotte was similarly fussy about foundation garments, which sent Nakamura scrambling for pastel-colored tricot. A doll like Barbie couldn't wear couture clothing over bare plastic, after all. Among Barbie's first garments were two strapless brassieres, one half-slip, one floral petticoat, and—God knows why—a girdle.

Unmarried and what people used to call a "career girl," Charlotte never suffered for male attention. "She was very resourceful," recalled Adler. "Before she would have dinner at the Imperial Hotel, she would survey the three dining rooms, and if she saw an eligible male eating by himself, she would eat in that dining room." Eventually, Nakamura said, "She found a boyfriend at the hotel. A Westerner—a gentleman from Germany or something."

Nevertheless, doing business was tough for a woman in Japan. Often Japanese men expressed their scorn by excluding women from work-related socializing. But textile consultant Lawanna Adams, who worked with Charlotte in the Orient, remembers the exclusion as a blessing. After a typical business dinner, the men "would go out to get bombed"; she and Charlotte, however, would be dropped off at the hotel, free to get a good night's sleep.

WHILE CHARLOTTE BRAINSTORMED IN TOKYO, HOUSE-wives all over Japan made her ideas real. Eyes straining, needles flying, they handstitched gold buttons onto Barbie's red "Sweater Girl" cardigan and attached flower appliqués to her "Picnic Set" sunhat. They added chestnut fur to her "Golden Splendor" jacket and tacked bows onto her "Cotton Casual" sundress. They trimmed her "Barbie-Q" outfit with white lace. Then, after their handiwork had been vetted for flaws, they gave the garments to other housewives who stitched them into cardboard display packages.

Called "homework people" because they toiled at home, they went blind so that Barbie could wear taffeta. They pricked their fingers so that she could have a ski holiday. They hunched over and wrecked their backs so that she wouldn't have to sleep in the nude. They were the original slaves of Barbie.

"I think Japan was the perfect place [to make the doll] because of the patience of the workers," said Joe Cannizzaro, the Mattel efficiency expert who went to Japan in the sixties. "And their desire to do it right. I never saw any dresses—even white wedding dresses—get soiled, though they were in the homes and on the tatami floors, because everything was so spotless, so well taken care of. They were delivered by bike and by pickup truck. They were handled four, five, six times. And they never got dirty. It's amazing, really. I don't think there's any other country where you could do that."

In factories, too, men sweated so that Barbie might dress. Machines pinged and clattered to make her clothes. One cut the fabric for her dresses and another sewed up their seams. Unlike homeworkers, who were paid by the pieces they produced, factory workers received a fixed wage. They lived in dormitories and were fed by factory owners. In August, however, everybody quit. "It was rice harvesting time," Cannizzaro explained.

By 1958, dolls had begun to emerge from doll molds in Tokyo. Filaments of gold or brown Saran were machine-stitched along their vinyl hairlines and pulled taut over their otherwise naked skulls. Ponytails were affixed. Eyes were painted with a masklike template that became clogged about every twentieth doll. Their glance was sidelong, formed by eerie white irises under ominous black lids. The dolls looked as if they had a history; as if they, in their Lilli incarnation, had seen the smoldering ruins of postwar Germany and knew the horrors that preceded them. The dolls did not look either innocent or American. It was Mattel's job to make them appear to be both.

AS STRATEGY SESSIONS BEGAN IN HAWTHORNE, THE
Handlers made a brilliant tactical move. They commissioned a toy study
from Ernest Dichter, Ph.D., director of the Institute for Motivational
Research in Croton-on-Hudson, New York. The study cost a staggering
$12,000 and took six months to complete, but when it was finished the
charge seemed low. Dichter had masterminded a cunning campaign to ped-
dle Barbie.

Dichter was already a legend when the Handlers approached him. Quoted
on nearly every page of Vance Packard's *The Hidden Persuaders,* a best-
seller in 1957, Dichter was hailed as a marketing Einstein—an evil
Einstein, but an Einstein nonetheless. He pioneered what he called "motivational research," advertising's newest, hippest, and, in Packard's view,
scariest trend—the manipulation of deep-seated psychological cravings to
sell merchandise.

Dichter's appeal to the Handlers was obvious. They had achieved their
success through space-age materials and futuristic methodology. Dichter's
approach, filled with Freudian symbols and clinical jargon, had a scientific
veneer. It promised control over an otherwise chaotic marketplace. It seemed
as daring in 1958 as advertising on television had been three years earlier.

Dichter also had much in common with Ruth. He was a Jewish immigrant,
just as her father had been. Born in Vienna, Herr Doktor Dichter studied
psychology at the University of Vienna and trained as a lay analyst. When
World War II broke out, he fled to Paris; then in 1937, the same year that
Ruth moved from Denver to Los Angeles, he tried to emigrate to New York.
But because he and his wife had neither $10,000 nor proof of a stateside
job, they were turned away.

Enraged, he lashed out at Llewelyn Thompson, the American vice consul
in Paris, who had stopped them. "All you care about is having people come
to the U.S. who have rich relatives," he said. If he were permitted to emigrate, he would revolutionize commerce by applying the principles of psy-

chology to the selling of products. Captivated, Thompson listened to Dichter's pitch. Then he intervened in Washington to have the Dichters admitted.

Dichter seduced corporate America in equally record time. He sent off unsolicited letters to six big firms, explaining why he thought they were in trouble and how his insights could help. Four responded, and the work he did for three—Ivory Soap, *Esquire* magazine, and the Chrysler Corporation—put him on the map.

Dichter didn't just compare brands for Ivory, he examined the role of cleanliness in American life. He didn't euphemize for *Esquire,* he confirmed what its editors "didn't dare" say—that "naked girls" sold the magazine. Sex also came up in his research for Chrysler. Men viewed sedans like wives; they were "comfortable and safe." Convertibles were like mistresses; they were "youthful," beckoning to "the dreamer" within. Thus to lure men into showrooms, car dealers should use convertibles as "bait."

Dichter packaged himself as cleverly as he advised clients to package their products. He worked out of a twenty-six-room castle on a Westchester mountaintop, the East Coast equivalent of Jack Ryan's fortress in Bel Air. There, he watched children play with toys from behind a one-way mirror. He performed "depth interviews" on a "psycho-panel" of several hundred neighborhood families. "He never asked a direct question," explained his wife, Hedy, because a confused interviewee was more honest.

For a man whom the Dale Carnegie Institute had retained as a consultant, Dichter was surprisingly adept at making enemies, among them Betty Friedan, who filled a whole chapter of *The Feminine Mystique* with his sins. So great was her outrage that she rarely referred to him by name, calling him simply "the manipulator."

Dichter's research, she found, documented her thesis: that being a housewife made most women miserable. But Dichter saw nothing wrong with their misery; rather, he sought to exploit it—by filling their anguished, barren lives with products. She paraphrases him: "Properly manipulated ('if you are not afraid of that word,' he said), American housewives can be given the sense of identity, purpose, creativity, the self-realization, even the sexual joy they lack—by the buying of things."

Unmoved by utopian sentimentality, Dichter strove to improve not the world but his clients' sales. If suffering made people reach for their checkbooks, why alleviate it?

By 1958, Dichter was so besieged with work that he relegated much of it to his staff. The Mattel project, however, he kept for himself. Toys were new to him, something no motivational researcher had ever investigated before. They were a pretext to expound a whole philosophy of play. Its purpose, he felt, was to relieve tension, to maintain children's "psycho-economic equilibrium" in the face of growing knowledge, growing bodies, and growing pressure from the adult world.

He investigated four types of toys—dolls, guns, holsters, and rockets—and based his findings on interviews with 23 fathers, 45 mothers, and 357 children plucked from a variety of social classes. The children included 191 girls and 166 boys. Dichter's gun-related observations are fraught with Freudian overtones—big guns are like big penises—or in the case of three-to four-year-olds, "The big long gun satisfies his need for power." But in an era characterized by exaggerated gender roles, he courageously advocated androgynous play: "Adults frown upon doll play on the part of little boys as 'sissy' behavior. In actuality, this type of play is emotionally as important for little boys as for little girls."

It is in his Barbie-doll inquiry, however, that his brilliance as a tactician comes forward. To read the Barbie study is to understand why he took Madison Avenue by storm. He asks blunt questions, gets blunt answers, then hatches a devilish scheme to make the bad news work to his client's advantage.

In his initial bid to Mattel, Dichter recommended probing Barbie's dark side to determine whether it should be played up or down. Is Barbie "a nice kid, friendly and loved by everyone, or is she vain and selfish, maybe even cheap? Does she have good taste or is she a little too flashy?" Could the doll be used to play out a child's rebellion against her parents, and if so, "should the wardrobe be sophisticated, even wicked?" He also suggested studying "the gift psychology of the adult." Is Barbie a conversation piece, a present "that will 'buy' the affection of the recipient?" Even more blunt, is Barbie a homewrecker? "Are men afraid of their wives' taunts should they bring home a 'sexy' doll?"

Dichter's answers told Mattel what it had perhaps suspected already. Barbie probably would "buy" the affection of a child; kids loved her. Mothers, by contrast, *hated* her. The report quotes a housewife and mother of three:

I know little girls want dolls with high heels but I object to that sexy costume. (POINTING TO SHEER PINK NEGLIGEE) I wouldn't walk around the house like that. I don't like that influence on my little girl. If only they would let children remain young a little longer . . . It's hard enough to raise a lady these days without undue moral pressures.
SAID THE MOTHER OF AN EIGHT-YEAR-OLD:
(MRS. B. SEEMED VERY MUCH EMBARASSED WHEN SHE LOOKED AT THE DOLL, ACTUALLY BLUSHING) One thing . . . my daughter would be fascinated. She loves dolls with figures. I don't think I would buy this for that reason. It has too much of a figure. (SHE STARED AT THE DOLL FOR A LONG TIME.) . . . I'm sure she would like to have one, but I wouldn't buy it. All these kids talk about is how the teachers jiggle. I think that would be all she would observe . . . . Maybe the bride doll is O.K., but not the one with the sweater.
ADDED THE FIRST MOTHER:
I'd call them "daddy dolls"—they are so sexy. They could be a cute decoration for a man's bar.

Eight- to thirteen-year-olds, however, were instantly hooked, though some had reservations. "The face looks snobbish," said one. "I think they call these Barbie because they are so sharp," said another. And a third used Barbie to reveal her ambivalence about the role of feminine artifice in snaring a mate: "I would like her better if there was a little less eye makeup . . . if she was a little less glamorous. But how else could she attract boy dolls?" The one girl who wanted no part of the doll, "who held her in her hand at some distance," was dismissed as a hopeless tomboy. All that interested her, the report says dismissively, were "sport clothes."

Although some girls said the doll's neck was "too long, and her figure and legs too thin," Barbie's body nevertheless gave her an edge over her rivals. Ginny, a potbellied, pug-nosed, flat-chested, eight-inch fashion doll that had been made in hard plastic by Vogue Dolls, Inc., since 1950, was as good as dead; her owners were eager to dump her and her "cheesily-made" clothes for Barbie. But Miss Revlon, a doll made in two sizes by Ideal Toy & Novelty Corporation, would be harder to defeat. She had incipient breasts, feet poised for high heels, and a less threatening body. "I like Revlon dolls the best," one girl explained. "They are . . . fatter."

Dichter also made marketing suggestions, which Mattel followed to the letter. He urged the company to package each outfit with a catalog of available clothing and with coupons to obtain other outfits at a reduced price. (In 1967, the doll itself became a coupon; girls traded in their original Barbies for a price break on the revamped Twist 'N Turn model.)

A lesser manipulator might have been daunted by the mothers' unvarnished loathing of the doll, but not Dichter. He swiftly located their Achilles' heel and formulated a plan to exploit it. One woman, who had found Barbie way too racy, changed her mind when she heard her eight-year-old daughter comment, "She's so well groomed, Mommy." Out of this came Dichter's strategy: Convince Mom that Barbie will make a "poised little lady" out of her raffish, unkempt, possibly boyish child. Underscore the outfits' detailing, and the way it might teach a roughneck to accessorize. Remind Mom what she believes deep down but dares not express: Better her daughter should appeal in a sleazy way to a man than be unable to attract one at all.

"The type of arguments which can be used successfully to overcome parental objection are in the area of the doll's function in awakening in the child a concern with proper appearance," the report says. And, as with all controversial toys, a well-coached child is the doll's best salesperson.

"The child exerts a certain amount of pressure, the effectiveness of which depends on his [or her] ability to argue sensibly with an adult," the report explains. "The toy advertiser can help the child by providing him [or her] with arguments which will satisfy mother."

Draft arguments to sway parents: Carson/Roberts had its marching orders; its campaign, in fact, was already under way. No stranger to hawking glamour—Hollywood makeup legend Max Factor was its other big client—it decided to introduce Barbie as a fashion model. Agency cofounder Jack Roberts, who made the sets for her first commercials, and copywriter Cy Schneider, who wrote them, strategically ignored the fact that Barbie was a thing; they imaged her as a living teenager and invented a life for her that was as glamorous and American as Lilli's had been tawdry and foreign. "The positioning from the very first commercial was that she was a person," said Schneider. "We never mentioned the fact that she was a doll."

Unhampered by current guidelines that force advertisers to show toys realistically, Schneider and Roberts animated Barbie. Head tilting, arms moving, she glided into outfit after outfit—from beach dates to high state occasions. Never mind that Ken wasn't even on the drawing board, the early spots showed Barbie's wedding dress, a celestial vision in white flocked tulle. Barbie didn't mince, as one might expect on her tiny feet. She floated. She was a teenage fashion model, and the world was her runway.

"Our findings suggest the desirability of advertising [that features] a variety of teen-age social activities," prescribed Dichter, and the ads fit his bill. In agency tests, girls gave them high marks, embracing Barbie as a real person, one they might even want to spruce up and emulate.

"We haven't superimposed a culture on the kids," Schneider explained. "The kids have dictated what their own culture should be. Every commercial was tested with children. And anything that didn't get through the barbed wire on the test never got on the air."

But Mattel was not yet out of the woods. "Advertising can make a good product better," Schneider said. "It can make a mediocre product slightly better. But the fastest way to kill a bad product is to advertise it. Because then more people find out that it's lousy. The kids tell each other. If they're disappointed, the product disappears."

MATTEL'S FIRST BIG PROMOTIONAL EFFORT, HOWEVER, was not to children but to toy buyers. If stores didn't stock the dolls, all the ads in the world wouldn't sell them. So in the dead of winter, 1959, Barbie made her debut at the American Toy Fair, the industry's annual trade show in New York City.

Toy Fair, old-timers say, has not changed much in thirty-five years; it has always had the trappings of Mardi Gras. For decades, people in costume— bunnies, pirates, spacemen—have passed out toy promos in front of the Toy Building at 200 Fifth Avenue. Inside, spies have combed showrooms, searching for ideas to knock off. And for seven long days, business lunches have merged into business dinners that have merged into hangover breakfasts.

It was into this chaos that Barbie strode, unseasonably bare in her black-and-white swimsuit. Voluptuous, half-naked, she curiously didn't make much of a splash. Perhaps this was because male buyers had human distractions; most toy companies hired breathtaking models to demonstrate their wares. But even when buyers glimpsed her, it was far from love at first sight. Condemning her sexiness, Sears buyer Lowthar Kieso, toy tastemaker for the catalogue empire that had been one of Mattel's biggest customers, rejected her—an odd bit of prudery at a trade show where, to make sales, models batted their eyelashes and stuck out their chests. Other buyers agreed to stock her: not, however, legions.

The Handlers returned to California. Was it possible that Ruth's daring, Elliot's vision, Charlotte's chicness, Nakamura's persistence, Adler's resourcefulness, Ryan's inventiveness, Dichter's insight, and Carson/Roberts's imagination had spawned a turkey?

Carson/Roberts began its commercial blitz in March, but still nothing happened. Spring came, then summer—meaningless seasons on the temperate West Coast. But it is doubtful that in Hawthorne the summer of '59 went unnoticed.

"When school was out, that doll just disappeared from the stock of the shops," said Charlotte. "Kids had to have the Barbie doll. . . . It just took off and went wild."

For boomers, it was one of those watershed moments, like Elvis's return from the army or the arrival of the Beatles in 1964. Barbie was a handheld piece of the one true Hollywood; scary and sleazy and spellbinding. Even her brunette version was golden. She was grown-up, contemptuous; yet *we* possessed her; she was forever susceptible to our rough little fingers. "Barbara"—the name means "foreigner," from the same root as "barbarian," and Barbie still had enough of Lilli in her to elude the dreariness of the homegrown. She was sunshine, Tomorrowland, the future made plastic. Not all that she promised was good, but we didn't know that at the time.

CHAPTER THREE

SEX AND THE SINGLE DOLL

ight months after Barbie's launch, Ruth was riding high. While most of her cogenerationists languished from the "problem that has no name," she was running a half-million-dollar business. "Ruth works a full day, driving away in a pink Thunderbird at 8:15 A.M. every day with her husband, leaving a gorgeous $75,000 home in Beverly Wood," the *Los Angeles Times* wrote in September 1959. "That's something not every woman would do. But Ruth wouldn't have it any other way. 'If I had to stay home I would be the most dreadful, mixed-up, unhappy woman in the world,' she cries."

The team at Carson/Roberts was also thriving, filled with a happiness so great it burst onto their lapels. If the agency didn't actually invent the smile-face button, it certainly popularized it. Long before such badges infected the lapels of the general public, Carson/Roberts used them for in-house promotions.

Mattel, however, was in turmoil, having begun a period of swift expansion that was not without growing pains. In 1960, the company went public, and by 1963 its common stock was listed on the New York Stock Exchange.

BARBIES SYLVIA PLACHY

Between 1959 and 1962, it had added 180,000 square feet to its Hawthorne headquarters and begun hiring people to fill it. Still, space was tight: in 1964, the company acquired a new plant east of Los Angeles in the City of Industry and built a three-story office building in Hawthorne, designed with reinforced foundations so that three more stories could be added later.

Asked to graph Mattel's expansion for a speech Ruth was preparing, Marvin Barab, who in 1960 established Mattel's first market research department, drew a line shooting up and off the chart. "If the growth Mattel has had . . . continues at the same rate," he told Ruth, "by 1980-something, the total volume of the company will exceed the Gross National Product." It was as if the Handlers had hitched their chariot to a puppy and now had to deal with a giant dog.

They did not always deal with grace. Seymour Adler, who had spear-headed rotation molding in Tokyo, found himself skewered back home. "I complained bitterly to Ruth that the data processing department was incompetent, which it was," Adler says. The incompetence caused a crisis after the 1963 Toy Show, when records lost during a change from one computer to another prevented Mattel from shipping goods for three months. Exasperated, Ruth said, "Seymour, you run the goddam department," Adler told me. And although he knew nothing about computers, he agreed.

Adler's new job may not have changed the balance of power in management, but it seemed that way to Jack Ryan, who was not one to keep his perceptions to himself. "Ruth became very unhappy because Jack was needling her about my having too much control in the company," Adler said. Tensions heightened, reaching a point where Ryan, who had caused the rift, curiously tried to heal it. He hoped to reconcile Ruth and Seymour through the equivalent of executive marriage counseling—a cutting-edge idea at the time. "People would get together and air all their problems," Adler explained. "It was very much like group therapy. But Ruth wouldn't attend the sessions. So they fired me."

Three years later Ruth had second thoughts. Mattel "had been having terrible problems," Adler said. "They had a walking doll that would not stay walking and they were getting returns at a rate of about eight percent. They wanted me back to solve problems like that—and to have the confidence that they would be solved."

As ever, what Ruth wanted, Ruth got; but Mattel had to buy the toy company Adler had founded during his absence.

Many employees say that during the Handler years, Mattel felt more like a family than a corporation. "Ruth and Elliot ate in the cafeteria every day and they walked through the factory and knew all the factory workers," said Beverly Cannady, who worked in promotion. "Those were the people who had the least turnover and who stayed until they retired. Ruth and Elliot knew the old ones, the original ones, and they'd stop and say, 'Hi Hattie, how's your granddaughter?' That kind of thing."

For some, however, Mattel was a dysfunctional family. Marvin Barab, who left market research to join Ryan's group, had terrible run-ins with his boss. Things reached a nadir when Ryan, during a party at his Bel Air house, ordered Barab, on penalty of dismissal, to dive into his pool and race him. This would have been annoying under any circumstances—Barab wasn't much of a swimmer—but it was especially nettlesome since Barab was wearing a business suit at the time. More successful at dealing with Ryan was another key hire in the early sixties, Steve Lewis, an artist who had taught sculpture at Temple University and who (thanks to his diplomacy, he says) would eventually become a vice president in charge of doll design.

OBLIVIOUS TO THE UPHEAVALS, BARBIE KEPT AMASSING clothes. In 1960, Mattel eliminated "Gay Parisienne," "Roman Holiday," and "Easter Parade" from her wardrobe. In their place, Charlotte Johnson concocted "Silken Flame," a knee-length white satin skirt with a red velvet bodice, "Enchanted Evening," a pale-pink floor-length gown with a rabbit fur stole, and "Solo in the Spotlight," a strapless black sequined dress with a tutu at the ankles.

Packaged with a rose and a miniature microphone, "Solo" was not the sort of thing one wore to a school dance. Its look was very Dietrich, evocative of the chanteuse she portrayed in Billy Wilder's *Foreign Affair*. One could imagine the Lilli doll wearing it, rasping out "Falling in Love Again" in some smoky Berlin cabaret. Patterned, Johnson said, on the outfit worn by a nightclub singer named Hildegarde, "Solo" hinted at Barbie's tainted genealogy, her emergence from the depths of an Axis-power cocktail lounge. As a counter to its sophistication, Johnson designed "Friday Night Date"— an outfit Pollyanna might wear to a church social—a blue corduroy jumper with a birdhouse appliqué that came with two aggressively wholesome glasses of milk.

Further evidence that Charlotte invented Barbie in her own image was "Busy Gal," a red linen suit that came with a sketch-filled portfolio labeled "Barbie Fashion Designer." Because neither Ruth nor Charlotte was a housewife, Barbie, from the outset, worked—at both dream and humdrum jobs. She served drinks to thankless travelers as an American Airlines stewardess and emptied bedpans as a registered nurse.

There was only one accessory Barbie lacked—a steady boyfriend. Consumer demand, however, overcame Mattel's reluctance to make a male doll, and in 1961 it brought out Ken.

Like Barbie, Ken was purchased in a bathing suit. His other essentials— a letter sweater, a tuxedo, and, because this was the era of Sloan Wilson, a gray flannel suit—were sold separately. Ken's blazers and trousers were intricately tailored; they looked like the fine, handmade suits that businessmen bought in the Orient for a fraction of what they would have cost on Savile Row. And, in fact, they were: the Japanese tailor who made Frank Nakamura's suits had a hand in designing them.

Making Ken's clothing was, however, far less of a problem than making Ken. At Mattel, a storm raged over his genitalia. Ruth and Charlotte, who wanted what Ruth termed "a bulge" in his groin, squabbled with the male executives, who didn't.

After the women vetoed a male doll that resembled Barbie in the crotch, three new versions were sculpted, with three degrees of what Charlotte called "bumps." "One was—you couldn't even see it," she said. "The next one was a little bit rounded, and the next one really *was*. So the men—especially one of the vice presidents—were terribly embarrassed. And he was a middle-aged man, you know—nothing to get so embarassed about. So Mrs. Handler and I picked the middle one as being the one that was nice-looking. And he said he would never have it in the toy line unless we painted Jockey shorts over it."

"None of us wanted a doll with a penis showing," Ruth amplified. "If the child took off the swimsuit, we felt it would be inappropriate with an adult boy to show the penis—so we all reached a conclusion that he should have a permanent swimsuit."

All except Charlotte, that is. She said: "Do you know what every little girl in this country is going to do? They are going to sit there and scratch that paint off to see what's under it. What else would they do?" Reluctantly, the men agreed. Ken got his "bump," but in a version modified to fit under trousers. "I had to work with the sculptor a little bit," Charlotte said, "because I realized when we were putting zippers in the fly—and the zipper on top of that bump—it got bigger and bigger."

Nevertheless, somebody at Mattel was disquieted by Ken's absent genital and tried to help him compensate. Barbie's clothes were usually accessorized with a matching purse, and purses—boxlike containers—are recognized by Freudians as symbols for female genitalia. Ken's first garments, by contrast, came with long, thin accessories—symbols for the penis he lacked. A long stick with a school pennant accompanied his "Campus Hero" outfit;

an electric shaver with a dangling cord accompanied his bathrobe; and his weekend "Casuals," khakis and a T-shirt, came with car keys. (A key is, of course, a male symbol, penetrating a female lock.)

By 1963, Ken's phallic props had become outrageous. He had a hunting outfit with an enormous rifle, a baseball outfit with a very long bat, and a doctor outfit with a pendulous stethoscope. He didn't motor around in a roadster like Barbie, he drove a *hot rod*. The cruelest comment on his genital deficiency, however, came in 1964, with "Cheerful Chef," a back-yard barbecue costume that included a long fork skewering a pink plastic weenie.

Barbie's cookout set had featured a spatula, a knife, a rolling pin, and a spoon. She never, ever had either a fork or a weenie. True, her "Suburban Shopper" outfit had been accessorized with vaguely phallic bananas, but they were popping out of her purse—a merging that subliminally suggests heterosexual intercourse. Similarly, her "Picnic Set" included a fishing rod, but its hook had pierced a plastic fish—a vulgar symbol for the female genitals—again evoking heterosexual penetration. The seeming deliberateness of these symbols makes it hard to interpret Ken's sad, solitary sausage as innocent. Likewise, the message on his apron—"Come and get it"—seems a bitter taunt about the genital he will never possess.

After Mattel issued wedding clothes for Barbie and Ken, children clamored for Barbie to have a baby. That, however, was where Ruth drew the line. Pregnancy would never mar Barbie's physique nor progeny compromise her freedom. Just as she does not depend on parents, she would have no offspring dependent on her. Still, Ruth reasoned, if buyers wanted a baby, there must be some way to sell them one. She eventually came up with "Barbie Baby-Sits," an ensemble containing an infant, its paraphernalia, and an apron clearly marked BABYSITTER. The set also came with books: *How to Get a Raise, How to Lose Weight,* and *How to Travel.*

"Barbie Baby-Sits" appeared in 1963, a year after the publication of

Helen Gurley Brown's best-selling *Sex and the Single Girl.* And whether it was Brown's influence or an effect of synchronicity, Barbie began to resemble Brown's happily unmarried woman. Ruth refused to give Barbie the trappings of postnuptial life; the doll would be forever independent, subservient to no one.

If Barbie wasn't already Brown's paradigm, her self-help books suggest that becoming it was her goal. The Single Girl, Brown wrote, "supports herself." She also keeps fit and roams the earth on her own; it's fun to meet men in new places. Hence Barbie's reading: *How to Get a Raise, How to Lose Weight,* and *How to Travel*—titles reminiscent of Brown's chapter headings—"Nine to Five," "The Shape You're In," and "The Rich, Full Life."

In 1963, Barbie also moved into her "sturdy, colorful chipboard" Dream House, a modest yet well-appointed dwelling, perfect for a Single Girl. "If you are to be a glamorous, sophisticated woman that exciting things happen to, you need an apartment and you need to live in it alone!" Brown orders. Roommates won't do, nor will living at home; but you don't have to take up residence in Versailles, either.

One can't help wondering whether Charlotte read *Sex and the Single Girl* while she was designing Barbie's 1963 wardrobe. "When a man thinks of a single woman," Brown writes, "he pictures her alone in her apartment, smooth legs sheathed in beige silk pants, lying tantalizingly among dozens of satin cushions, trying to read but not very successfully, for *he* is in that room—filling her thoughts, her dreams, her life." Sounds like Brown imagines him picturing Barbie—lying tantalizingly among the printed cushions on her pasteboard divan, smooth legs sheathed in the apricot silk pants that came with "Dinner at Eight," an outfit Charlotte introduced in 1963.

Barbie's similarity to Brown's brave, new, vaguely selfish and decidedly subversive heroine has more than whimsical ramifications. It makes Barbie an undercover radical. Brown was "the first spokeswoman for the revolution," say Barbara Ehrenreich, Elizabeth Hess, and Gloria Jacobs in *Re-*

Making Love: The Feminization of Sex, even though today Brown is "a woman whom many feminists would be loath to claim as one of their own." Long before feminism was a part of the American political vocabulary, they point out, droves of women bought Brown's book—an antimarriage manifesto and plea for women's financial liberation and sexual autonomy disguised as a breezy volume of self-help.

In choosing clothes, Brown urges: "Copycat a mentor with better taste than yours." And while Barbie didn't literally choose Charlotte, the designer certainly imposed her taste upon the doll. More significantly, the doll, to whom children looked up, was a sort of mentor to them. Just as *Sex and the Single Girl* spread Brown's gospel to adult women, Barbie and her paraphernalia conveyed it to their younger sisters.

In Brown's protofeminist philosophy, preoccupation with appearance was a pragmatic necessity, not a narcissistic luxury. Men desired a single woman because she had "time and often more money to spend on herself . . . the extra twenty minutes to exercise every day, an hour to make-up her face for their date." Brown's Single Girl did not live in the world of ideas, where a looker like Robert Browning would fall for a lump like Elizabeth Barrett; she lived in the material world, where beauty was the decisive weapon in the everlasting battle for men. The Single Girl was not an intellectual; introspection, Brown makes clear, was a waste of energy. But the Girl was encouraged to have a sort of cunning—a nonverbal sagacity; she expressed herself through a vocabulary of objects rather than words.

"Men survey women before treating them," John Berger wrote in *Ways of Seeing.* "Consequently, how a woman appears to a man can determine how she will be treated. To acquire some control over the process, women must contain it and interiorize it." A woman must cultivate the habit of simultaneously acting and watching herself act; she must split herself into two selves: the observer and the observed. She must turn herself, Berger says, into an "object of vision."

Brown's book taught women how to turn themselves into such an object. *Sex and the Single Girl* is a Berlitz phrase book to the vernacular of clothing and style, a guide to help women manipulate men by manipulating how they appear to men.

For some girls, Barbie no doubt functioned that way too. Not for all, but for many, I suspect. The relationship of the observed self to the observing self is much like that of a Barbie doll to its owner. When a girl projects herself onto a doll, she learns to split in two. She learns to manipulate an image of herself outside of herself. She learns what Brown and Berger would consider a survival skill.

Another developing feminist who understood the importance of a woman's appearance was Gloria Steinem. In 1963, the Viking Press published *The Beach Book*, her massive volume devoted not to gender inequalities but to looking good in a bathing suit. "Nothing is as transient, useless, or completely desirable as a suntan," she observed. "What a tan will do is make you look good, and that justifies anything."

Steinem, whose dust-jacket profile reveals that her "formative years were spent almost entirely in bathing suits," seems to have been in a particularly Barbie-esque stage of evolution in 1963. Decades before Jane Fonda, Marla Maples, and Barbie made exercise videos, Steinem prescribed a workout for her female readers—twenty arm pulls daily, executed while chanting: "I must . . . I must . . . I must develop my . . . Bust." The purpose of this regimen is revealed three pages later, in a diagram that teaches the reader how to "build" a bikini.

I doubt, however, that some of her exercises would pass muster with fitness experts. This one is particularly suspect: "Suck against the heel of your hand. This makes thin lips full, full lips firm, and fat cheeks lean."

Steinem had less need of arm pulls than many women. That was another thing she had in common with Barbie: her looks were good enough to land her a job as a *Playboy* Bunny. After weeks of wobbling around on spike heels, stuffing her bra with dry cleaner bags, and having her cottontail yanked by customers, she penned a behind-the-scenes exposé for *Show* magazine on the sordid, brutalizing, anything-but-glamorous working conditions at the Hefner hutch.

Significantly, Steinem's article, as Marcia Cohen has noted in *The Sisterhood: The True Story of the Women Who Changed the World,* "made the point that *Playboy* Bunnies were exploited, though it did not make the point that they were exploited because they were women"—an oversight Steinem acknowledges. "It was interesting," Steinem told Cohen, "that I could understand that much and still not make the connection."

Perhaps it was difficult for a woman whose looks had opened doors to realize that there were problems to having them opened that way. *The Beach Book* has an introduction by economist John Kenneth Galbraith, whom Gloria met in the Hamptons and who was captivated by her "terrific good looks." "If Gloria says it's otherwise," Galbraith told Cohen, "she's wrong." Galbraith's remarks make me think of *Barbie's New York Summer,* a young adult novel with Barbie as a character that Random House published in 1962. In it, Barbie's clever writing earns her a job at a magazine; she goes to Manhattan and is fawned over by rich, powerful men. "There are many chic women in New York," one tells her, "but . . . you are young and fresh and perfectly enchanting."

Galbraith strikes me as an apt introducer for *The Beach Book,* which is in large part about economics. The young Gloria—like the newly minted Barbie—was not unfamiliar with defining a lifestyle through things. She explains how one can change roles by changing outfits, very much the way Barbie does. Some beach looks include the "Ivy League" ("Women must wear tank suits and single strands of pearls"), "Muscle Beach" ("Alternate the coconut oil with the application of mascara . . . Chew gum"), and "Pure Science" (Carry "moss-filled Mason jars, a notebook, and a long-handled net"). If you're not going to wear high-status garments, though, you'd better be able to pass for a model; the Pure Science look "works only if you are very beautiful."

Steinem's book not only catalogues the status value attached to objects, it offers suggestions for condescending to the less fortunate. This seems odd for a woman who claims to have grown up in poverty. "One gets the sense talking to Gloria that she was born in the Toledo equivalent of the manger," Leonard Levitt once wrote in *Esquire*. But she has thought a great deal about the class implications of sun-altered skin tone and offers this hope to those who cannot tan: "With every office clerk able to afford a vacation at the shore, you may be able to make white skin worth more in status than a tan."

Well versed in the art of sunbathing, Barbie, in 1963, had not yet had her feminist consciousness raised—though, like Steinem's political awareness, it would evolve with time. ("Feminism didn't come into my life at all until 1968 or 1969," Steinem told me when I asked her about *The Beach Book*.) In Barbie's defense, however, she could hardly have pondered the condition of "women," having been for four years the only adult female doll on the market. This, however, changed when Mattel introduced her so-called best friend Midge.

Freckled of face, bulging of eye, Midge was from the outset a sorry Avis to Barbie's Hertz. Her debut commercial was a catalogue of tortures endured by homely teenage girls. Midge, the ad alleged, "is thrilled with Barbie's career as a teenage fashion model." But anyone who has ever been sixteen and female knows she was probably rent with feelings of inferiority.

"Barbie has introduced Midge to her boyfriend," the ad continues, "and the three of them go everywhere together." Terrific. Tagging along after Mr. and Miss High School. If plastic dolls could kill themselves, I'm sure Midge would have tried.

The following year things grew slightly more equitable; Mattel gave Midge a boyfriend (Allan) and dumped a younger sister (Skipper) on Barbie. Mattel's engineers also did something really hideous to Barbie's face, replacing her painted eyes with feline-shaped mechanical things that blinked. Now called "Miss Barbie," she looked like the offspring of an inter-species union, a cousin of Nastassia Kinski in *Cat People*.

Not surprisingly, as Barbie racked up other doll friends she also gathered competitors. Rival toymakers could scarcely witness Mattel's triumph without hatching plots to exploit it. Barbie's major challengers were Tammy, brought out by the Ideal Toy & Novelty Corporation in 1962, Tressy, brought out by the American Character Doll Company in 1963, and the Littlechap Family, introduced by Remco in 1964.

Named for an insipid movie character portrayed by Debbie Reynolds, Tammy looked as if she could have given Barbie a run for her money; but in hindsight it's clear that she never had a chance. Barbie may have appeared as if she belonged in the fifties, but her ethos was pure sixties; she was a swinging single with a house, a boyfriend, and no parents. Tammy, by contrast, came with Mom and Dad. She didn't have a boyfriend, she had a brother. "Basically, Tammy was a baby doll," explains vintage Barbie dealer Joe Blitman. Boring, sexless, and shackled to the moribund nuclear family, Tammy bit the dust in the mid-sixties when the divorce rate took off.

I must confess to feeling chills the first time I saw Tammy. There is something creepy about a doll with the body of an eight-year-old and the car, clothes, and trappings of a grown-up. If, as some psychoanalysts contend, anorexia is a perverse strategy to thwart the development of female secondary sex characteristics, Tammy is the model for such a weird infant-adult. At least Barbie embraced womanhood, however cartoonish her interpretation; she wasn't a female Peter Pan demanding car keys and the right to vote while shirking the burden of sexual development.

Tressy was possibly even more physically bizarre than Tammy; she had a tuft of hair in the middle of her head that could be yanked out and screwed back in, like a tape measure. When beehive hairdos went the way of the Hula Hoop, so did Tressy.

Like Tammy, Remco's Littlechap Family was cursed by its links to what *McCall's* in 1954 termed the "togetherness" movement, in which, as Betty Friedan put it in *The Feminine Mystique,* a woman "exists only for and through her husband and children." Daughter Judy Littlechap bore a striking resemblance to Jacqueline Bouvier Kennedy, which, when the doll was on the drawing board, no doubt seemed like a good idea. When it was released, however, after JFK's assassination, the doll's looks worked against it; they were a ghoulish reminder of a national tragedy.

Barbie's thorniest competitor in the sixties may have been Louis Marx & Co.'s Miss Seventeen—not because she was captivating, but because she didn't fight fair. Smarting from the Handlers' ascension, Marx dug out Barbie's Teutonic origins, acquired rights to the Lilli doll, rechristened it Miss Seventeen and launched it in America. Then on March 24, 1961, Marx's lawyers marched into U.S. District Court in Los Angeles and slapped Mattel with a patent-infringement suit.

At issue was Letters Patent No. 2,925,684, which Miss Seventeen wore boldly etched on her backside. It referred to a leg joint that permitted the doll to sit down with its legs together instead of spread apart—a useful feature, for taste reasons, on a sexy adult doll.

Given Marx's reputation for getting rich off cheap versions of stolen ideas, Miss Seventeen was the quintessential Marx product. If Barbie was tawdry, Miss Seventeen was downright mangy; as slutty as Lilli, but not nearly so healthy. Her plastic was jaundiced, and she seemed in need of a square meal—not because she was too thin but because she suffered from vitamin deficiencies. Her hair emerged from her head in irregular clumps; and while neither she nor Barbie could be said to have a penetrating gaze, her eyes were markedly out of focus, as if bleary from drugs. Miss Seventeen could easily pass for Miss Teen Runaway; if she were a person, she'd probably never make it to Miss Eighteen.

Marx alleged that Mattel had copied the "form, posture, facial expression

Fig.1

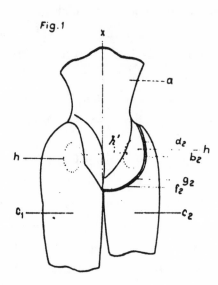

Fig.2

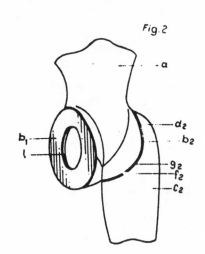

Fig.3

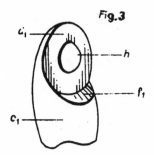

Fig 4

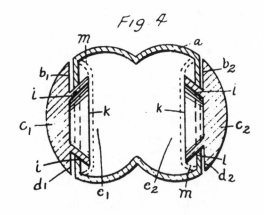

Fig 5

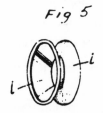

SKETCH OF LILLI LEG JOINT AS IT

APPEARS ON ITS PATENT REGISTRATION

and novel overall . . . appearance" of the *Bild* Lilli doll and "led the doll field and purchasing public to the belief that said 'Barbie' dolls were an original product . . . thereby perpetrating a fraud and a hoax upon the public."

Mattel countered by accusing Marx of conspiring with a bunch of Germans to compete unfairly by "marketing an inferior doll in the United States of confusingly similar appearance to" Barbie. It also accused Marx of knocking off Jack Ryan's Thunderburp cap gun mechanism, which also functioned as the guts of its Tommy Burst Detective gun.

What ensued was the toy world's *Bleak House.* Wily, indefatigable, both sides tossed accusations at each other like Molotov cocktails. Mattel, with mindboggling shamelessness, introduced as evidence a book of historic wooden dolls from the "collection of Miss Ruth Ellison, Springfield, Vermont" (cunningly unearthed by Jack Ryan's brother, Jim), and argued with conviction that Barbie, far from being knocked off from a German novelty item, had been inspired by Yankee folk art.

After two years of legal mudslinging, Judge Leon Yankwich dismissed both Marx's complaint and counterclaims and Mattel's counterclaims, "with prejudice as to all causes of action raised by said pleadings," and awarded no damages "or other affirmative relief . . . to any party, each party to bear its own costs and attorney's fees."

This is legal jargon for "A pox on both your houses." Neither company would be permitted to reintroduce the suit.

BETWEEN 1964 AND 1968, MATTEL GREW PRODIGIOUSLY, swallowing smaller companies like a whale ingesting plankton. By 1965, its sales exceeded $100 million—twice what they were in 1961. In 1967, it took over doll companies in West Germany and England and opened a plant in Mexico. In 1968, it gobbled up two toy companies in Italy and a toy distributor in Belgium, opened subsidiaries in Australia and Venezuela, and devoured Monogram Models, Inc., a domestic manufacturer of hobby kits. Its sales that year—including international sales—exceeded $200 million, double what they had been three years earlier.

But the United States to which Mattel sold toys in 1968 was very different from the one that had snapped up Barbie in 1959. It was no longer the tame, secure place it had been in the fifties. The rifts between young and old, black and white, Democrat and Republican grew larger and more painful. In four years, the civil rights movement made great strides through nonviolence, only to lose them all in the bloody assassination of Dr. Martin Luther King, Jr. Violence was a constant menace: a mugger on every urban street corner, a prowler in every suburban bedroom, a mean, gun-toting drifter in every rural Greyhound station. Sometimes the violence was random, like Charles Manson's 1969 attack on Sharon Tate. Sometimes it was focused, like Sirhan B. Sirhan's fatal assault on Robert F. Kennedy. And sometimes it just swept through a town, blind and angry, as it did through Watts in the summer of 1965.

Another liberation movement was also taking shape in the mid-sixties. In 1963, while Steinem was sunning herself on the beach, Betty Friedan published *The Feminine Mystique,* the groundbreaking book that identified the gender-based malaise afflicting millions of women. Naming the problem was the first step; on October 29, 1966, Friedan announced the formation of the National Organization for Women to combat it. Initially, the women's movement kept a low profile, but that changed in September 1968 when a group of demonstrators, led by activist Robin Morgan, stormed the Miss America Pageant. They threw bras, girdles, false eyelashes, and other objects beloved by drag queens into a "Freedom Trash Can" and crowned a live sheep outside the auditorium. In what must be construed as a dig at Barbie, some carried placards that read: "I Am . . . Not a Toy, a Pet or a Mascot."

That skirmish, however, was minor compared to the escalating controversy over the Vietnam War. By the summer of 1968, the friction between Americans who supported it and those who did not could no longer be ignored. Outside of the Democratic National Convention in Chicago, police clobbered and bloodied a crowd of antiwar demonstrators. And they did it in front of dozens of TV cameras.

The war tore popular culture apart. *Laugh-In,* which premiered in 1968, assaulted viewers with political realities; but other popular programs—*The Andy Griffith Show, The Beverly Hillbillies, Gomer Pyle, U.S.M.C.*—were so rooted in a fantasy of rural innocence that they remained vehicles of escape. "The typical George Wallace voter and the Bob Dylan fan lived in different worlds," Jim Miller wrote about 1968 in *The New York Times.* There was no common ground, no safe imaginary landscape in which to set the American Dream. This posed a particular dilemma for Mattel: you couldn't theme and miniaturize a center that wasn't holding.

Between 1964 and 1968, Mattel used various strategies to shield Barbie from the crossfire. She began by aping Jackie Kennedy, who initially seemed a risk-free role model. At first, all she copied were Jackie's clothes, beginning in 1962 with "Red Flare," a knock-off of the first lady's Inauguration outfit. Soon Jackie had an influence on Barbie's class pretensions. In 1966, Barbie lost interest in sock hops and the senior prom and collected outfits for tonier functions—"Debutante Ball" and "Benefit Performance." In her English riding outfit, she affected Anglophilia and a love of tweed. But in 1968, Mattel dropped Jackie as swiftly as it had embraced her. She had married Aristotle Onassis, and Mattel was not about to link its Golden Girl to some stubby, shriveled Mediterranean type with alleged links to international organized crime.

As real life grew more politically polarized, Barbie turned away from it, retreating into a self-contained fantasy world. The titles of her clothes became almost completely self-referential. Where initially outfits had been named for activities—"Goin' Fishin'," "Friday Night Date," "Sorority

Meeting," and "Garden Party"—they were now named for their fabric or pattern—"Knit Hit," "Swirly Cue," "Snug Fuzz," and "Bouncy-Flouncy." It was as if Mattel didn't dare admit where a real college student might wear such clothes—to march in Washington against the war, to drop acid at a Jefferson Airplane concert, or to light up a joint while occupying the president's office at Columbia University.

The doll's activities also ceased to be grounded in reality. This pattern began in 1966 with "Color Magic" Barbie, a doll whose hair and clothing changed color when a "magic" solution was applied to it. It is plausible to tint hair with a chemical; millions of women do it. It is also plausible to dye one's clothes. But only in fantasy would a woman change the color of her dress *while she was wearing it.*

Perhaps sensing the degree to which Barbie was out-of-it, Mattel gave her vaguely with-it relatives and friends. Francie, a cousin, appeared in 1966, followed by Casey and Twiggy (based on the real-life model) in 1967. In 1969, Barbie also got black friends—Christie and Julia (the latter based on a TV character played by Diahann Carroll).

Meanwhile, Barbie's original pals were whisked off the market. Midge vanished in 1967; and, after a humiliating 1966 incarnation as "Ken a Go Go," which required him to wear a fright wig and play a ukelele, Ken disappeared, returning with a new face in 1969. Mattel designer Steve Lewis said Ken vanished because he wasn't selling. But a few Ken dolls were, during those years, still on sale in Canada; collectors speculate that his draft status figured in his departure.

As for Barbie's new friends, their principal distinction was their body type; more boyish than bovine, they could wear the trendy, so-called Mod clothes imported from London. "Mod" was not arbitrary, but a systematic effort to throw off the codified fashions of the 1950s—fashions that had made Barbie's name. It parodied historical styles, mixed blazing colors and metallic textures, and reflected, often with wit, the disapproval that its young adherents felt for the established culture. It was, say fashion historians Arian and Michael Batterberry, "a sort of ecstatic vision of Imperial Rome and Byzantium conceived by Moreau and Bakst and brashly adapted to the beat of rock-and-roll."

It also had an element of androgyny. Boys wore velvet and had long hair; girls wore bell-bottoms and didn't. Nor could Mod have happened without the canonization of those girlish guys from Liverpool, the Beatles. John, George, Paul, and Ringo offered "a vision of sexuality freed from the shadow of gender inequality because the group mocked the gender distinctions that bifurcated the American landscape into 'his' and 'hers,' " say Barbara Ehrenreich, Elizabeth Hess, and Gloria Jacobs in *Re-Making Love*. "To Americans that believed fervently that sexuality hinged on *la différence*, the Beatlemaniacs said, No, blur the lines and expand the possibilities."

Barbie's body, which we will examine more carefully in a later chapter, did not blur anything; it was *la différence* incarnate. It was the body of Dior's New Look—cinched waist, accentuated breasts—that had hit the market in 1947. By the mid-sixties, it had begun to look as stuffy and dated as Jackie Kennedy's pillbox hat.

The reason, one suspects, for the gender-blurring was the increasing popularity of the birth control pill, which had been approved for sale in 1960. Once women had the option of turning off their fertility, they could behave as rakishly as men. In the age of the pill, sex did not automatically lead to marriage and babies; it generally led to more sex. So in 1966, the Barbie team made a decision. The times they were a-changin'. And Barbie, to some degree, would have to change with them.

CHAPTER FOUR

THE WHITE
GODDESS

Let us leave Barbie poised for metamorphosis and shift the narrative to a living room in La Jolla, California—a modest, middle-class room with nubby green wall-to-wall carpeting, a nut-brown sectional and a black-and-white television in the corner. There is a large picture window through which one can make out a hazy strip of Pacific Ocean. The year is 1963 and I—a milk-white, painfully thin only child with long, anemic braids—am sitting alone on the carpet surrounded by my Barbie paraphernalia.

Almost invariably, when I told women my age that I was writing about Barbie, they said: "Why *you*? *I* should be writing that book. I own twenty thousand Barbies." Or, "I threw up after dinner for a year because of Barbie." Or, "I am a model or a stylist or a fiction writer or a you-fill-in-the-blank because of Barbie."

And they are, of course, right. Barbie left a personal impression on many members of my generation. But like my friends I have a story to tell, and this seems to be the right moment to tell it.

At thirty-seven, I am a five-foot-six, 123-pound, tolerably fit woman whose knees and elbows are considerably more prominent than her breasts. At the

SUNSPELL, ONE OF MATTEL'S GUARDIAN
GODDESSES, TOSSING OFF HER DRESS AND
VANQUISHING EVIL GEOFF SPEAR

same age, my mother was, by most people's definitions, a beauty: five feet ten, 132 pounds, and possessed of breasts that in their size and shape resembled Barbie's. They didn't droop or sag; nor did their size—38-C—interfere with her ability to win at sports. Even in her forties she could swim faster and hit a softball harder than people half her age. No doubt you assume that I will write about how her perfection placed me in competition with her and, by extension, all women; how I ached to have 38-C breasts; and how every month when *Vogue* arrived I pored over pictures of Verushka begging, "Dear God, please make me look like her." Nothing, however, could be further from the truth.

When I was eight years old and my mother was forty-six, she had a mastectomy. Her experience with cancer did not have the happy ending that Ruth Handler's did. It was a prelude to chemotherapy, more operations, and, six years later, death. This was before the age of reconstructive surgery, political activism, and the life-affirming defiance that one sees among breast cancer patients today. The illness was shrouded in secrecy, almost shame.

As her health deteriorated, her remaining breast mocked her. It hovered there—flawless—next to her indignant red scar. What it said to me was: You do not want Barbie's breasts; the last thing on earth you want are Barbie's breasts. I associated them with nausea, hair loss, pain, and decay. I associated them with annihilation. I believed myself blessed when nature didn't provide them.

True, at sixteen, when I had my first serious beau, I felt vaguely shabby that his gropings were so meanly rewarded; but the shabby feeling quickly passed. I was alive and hoped to remain so. In my mind, small breasts would make this possible; they seemed somehow less vulnerable. Of course not every little girl's mother has a mastectomy, but many do. Since 1980, 450,000 women have died of breast cancer. In the decade of the nineties, an estimated 1.5 million women will be diagnosed with the disease, and one-third of them will die.

These grim statistics suggest that daughters of breast-cancer patients are far from an insignificant minority. But I suspect, as a consequence of the disease's historical invisibility, the experiences of breast-cancer daughters have often been ignored by so-called body image experts. When I heard *Beauty Myth* author Naomi Wolf say on National Public Radio, "We were all raised on a very explicit idea of what a sexually successful woman was supposed to look like," I wanted to shout that another "we"—millions of breast-cancer daughters—had had a very different experience. When Wolf said "the official breast" was "Barbie's breast," I muttered aloud, "Speak for yourself, lady." Not all women respond in a crazed, competitive, Pavlovian fashion to pictures of models or the body of a doll. And it's demeaning to suggest that they do.

My Barbie play was as idiosyncratic as my childhood. I remembered nothing about it until four years ago when my father got my dolls out of storage and shipped them to me. Tucked away since 1968, the vinyl cases seemed innocuous, yet I kept finding reasons not to open them.

I wonder if archeologists hesitate, mid-dig, before making their discoveries, if they falter outside tombs the way I fumbled with the clasp of Ken's mildewed sarcophagus. When, after several tugs, the latch finally gave, I dropped the case, bouncing Ken onto the floor. I reached for him, then froze. He was wearing Barbie's low-cut, sequined "Solo in the Spotlight."

Nonchalant, he gazed at me, radiating what Susan Sontag has called the "androgynous vacancy" behind Greta Garbo's "perfect beauty." If Mattel had intended to model him on the Swedish actress, it couldn't have done a better job.

My Midge, by contrast, was laid out spartanly in her original carton; a mere sidekick, she didn't have a fancy case. At least she looked comfortable, wearing what I would have worn for twenty years in storage—Ken's khaki trousers, navy blazer, and dress shirt.

Then there was Barbie—blond ponytail Barbie—wearing tennis whites

KEN BOTTO. "RED CHAIR." 1982

and a sweatshirt in her glossy red valise. Her cruel mouth, still haughty, brought back memories. I remembered a fight after which my mother grudgingly bought me fat-cheeked, blotchy Midge. I remembered a second fight after which she bought me perfect Barbie and Ken. And I remembered Midge's ordeal. Midge didn't seduce Ken—that would have been too obvious. She became his platonic pal, introducing him to a new pastime: looking more Barbie-like than Barbie.

I was tempted to slam the cases, to squelch the memories, but I rummaged farther. My dolls had not been cross-dressed in a vacuum. It had happened during the years of my mother's illness; years of uncertainty, of sleepovers at friends' houses when she was in the hospital; years which, until I opened the boxes, I had forgotten. But as I picked through the miniatures, why I did what I did became less of a mystery.

My Barbie paraphernalia was a museum of my mother's values. Arrayed together, the objects were a nonverbal vocabulary, the sort of language in which John Berger urged women to express themselves. Except for "Solo," which a friend had given me, the language was hers.

A chemist who fled graduate school long before completing a Ph.D., my mother was a casualty of the Feminine Mystique. She had stopped work to become a fifties housewife and hated every minute of it. She didn't tell me, "Housework is thralldom," but she refused to buy Barbie cooking utensils. She didn't say, "Marriage is jail," but she refused to buy Barbie a wedding dress. What she did say often, though, was "Education is power." And in case I missed the point, she bought graduation outfits for each of my dolls.

Nor did she complain about her mastectomy. I sensed the scar embarrassed her, but I never knew how much. Then I unearthed Barbie's bathing suit—a stretched-out maillot onto which my mother had sewn two clumsy straps to keep the top from falling down.

That sad piece of handiwork spoke to me in a way she never had. It spoke not of priggishness or prudery, but of the anguish she had felt poolside and why she rarely ventured into the water. It spoke of how she felt herself watched—how all women feel themselves watched—turning male heads before the operation and fearing male scrutiny after it. It spoke of pain and stoicism and quiet forbearance. It broke her silence and my heart.

When things of aesthetic power—say, the Vietnam Veterans Memorial—have emotional resonance, the resonance feels right. But I cannot tell you how strange it was to ache with grief over a bunch of doll clothes. Or to find in a Barbie case a reliquary of my mother.

I forced myself to study Ken masquerading as Steichen's portrait of Garbo; Midge looking like a refugee from a boys' boarding school; even Barbie looking more Martina than Chrissy. (Barbie wore a tiny tennis skirt, but it was under *Ken's* sweatshirt.) I concluded that I'd been one messed-up kid.

But as I explored the mess, I came to realize that, given my environment, it would have been far flakier not to have cross-dressed the dolls. It wasn't just my mother's message that a woman's traditional role was loathsome; it was all the weirdness and fear floating around the idea of breasts. I don't think Midge's sartorial inspiration was Una Lady Troubridge or Radclyffe Hall. I think it was terror. Femaleness, in my eight-year-old cosmos, equaled disease; I disguised Midge in men's clothes to protect her. If her breasts were invisible, maybe the disease would pass over them. Maybe she'd survive. I even shielded Barbie, permitting her to show her legs but armoring her chest. Only Ken was allowed the luxury of feminine display; he had no breasts to make him vulnerable.

Seeing Barbie ignited a brushfire of ancient emotions; no longer could I dismiss the doll as trivial. Freud, of course, understood that dolls weren't trivial; in his essay on "The Uncanny," he writes about the creepy or "uncanny" feeling dolls or automata provoke in people when such dolls are too lifelike. He also understood that if commonplace or familiar things—like, say, Barbies—trigger the recollection of a repressed memory, they can send shivers down one's spine.

In German, "the uncanny" is *das Unheimliche*—that which is weird or foreign. The word is the opposite of *das Heimliche*—that which is familiar, native, of the home. Once "homely" objects, my dolls had become uncanny: they preserved, as if in amber, the forgotten terrors of my childhood. Freud explains: "If psycho-analytic theory is correct in maintaining that every affect belonging to an emotional impulse, whatever its kind, is transformed, if it is repressed, into anxiety, then among instances of frightening things there must be one class in which the frightening element can be shown to be something repressed which *recurs*."

He calls this class of scary things "the uncanny." Consequently, Freud writes, "we can understand why linguistic usage has extended *das Heimliche* ['homely'] into its opposite *das Unheimliche*, for this uncanny is really nothing new or alien, but something which is familiar and old-established in the mind and which has become alienated from it only through the process of repression."

In his essay, Freud pushes the idea of the uncanny much farther than I do. He describes the fantasy of being mistakenly buried alive as "the most uncanny thing of all"—remarking that psychoanalysis has revealed that fantasy to be a transformation of another, originally nonterrifying fantasy qualified "by a certain lasciviousness"—that of intrauterine existence.

Thus the womb, "the former *Heim* [home] of all human beings," is the ultimate *unheimlich* place. This might also suggest why, while not literally a return to the womb, my profound reconnection with my mother—experienced as an adult through my childhood dolls—seemed uncanny.

I was eight when I got my Barbies, well past the age of appropriating them as what psychoanalyst D. W. Winnicott termed "transitional objects." But Mattel's research shows that today kids get Barbies earlier, usually about age three. Thus, Barbies, in the psyches of toddlers, can function as transitional objects—which warrants a closer look at Winnicott's concept.

During the months following birth, a baby doesn't grasp that its mother is separate from itself. Embodied by her ever-nurturing breast, the mother is an extension of the child; she can be magically conjured up by the child whenever the child wants—or so the child believes. As the child develops, however, it must face the fact that this just isn't so—not, for the child, a happy idea. It isn't just the physical weaning, having to give up a stress-free means of satisfying hunger. It's also the trauma of becoming independent, of losing the blissful, boundariless connection to Mom.

This, says Winnicott, is where transitional objects come in. They are, for a child, his or her first "not me" objects. The child imbues them with elements of the self and the mother; and they symbolize, for the child, that relationship, which is coming to an end.

There aren't hard and fast rules about transitional objects: They can be as stereotypical as Linus's security blanket in *Peanuts* or as idiosyncratic as a piece of string. Nor are there rules about the age at which children appropriate them. Sometimes a baby will attach itself to a toy in its crib; sometimes an older child—such as Linus—will endure the ridicule of schoolmates rather than renounce his object. But the objects, Winnicott has pointed out, aren't fetishes; having them, for kids, is normal behavior.

Significantly, though, the transitional object "is not just a 'not me' object, it's also a 'me' object," said Ellen Handler Spitz, who has written on the phenomenon in *Art and Psyche*. "If she loses it and is put to bed without it, she may have a tantrum and be devastated. Like the transitional object, the Barbie doll leads the child into the future by enabling her to detach, to some extent, from the mother. At the same time, because the doll is a little woman, it represents the relationship with the mother." A transitional object can also be a child's bridge to future aesthetic experiences. This is because the child often sucks, strokes, and mutilates it into "a highly personal object," the way an artist fashions artwork out of clay.

LEGALLY SPEAKING, THE BARBIE DOLL *IS* A WORK OF ART. Mattel copyrighted Barbie's face as a piece of sculpture, not because the doll was intended to be a unique object, but because it wasn't. The manual processes in Barbie's creation—the sewing-on of hair, the painting of lips— might permit a variation or two; thus hair and makeup were not copyrighted. But the duplication of the doll's body was mechanical and, therefore, uniform; hence the registration of the sculpture.

In 1936, when critic Walter Benjamin investigated the idea of *Art in the Age of Mechanical Reproduction,* he focused principally on photographs, which in his view satisfied the masses' craving "to bring things 'closer' spatially and humanly, which is just as ardent as their bent toward overcoming the uniqueness of every reality by accepting its reproduction."

In the case of Barbie, however, the reality is the reproduction. Human icons—Elvis, Garbo, Madonna—can only be possessed through film or audiotape; there either was or is an "original" somewhere that forever eludes ownership. But Barbie herself was meant to be owned—not just by a few but by everybody. Issued in editions of billions, she is the ultimate piece of mass art.

Benjamin was writing at the dawn of the age of mechanical reproduction, two decades before the post–World War II boom in synthetics that made Barbie possible. He wrote before the era of plastic, the revolutionary material that did for objects what film did for images. Plastic is a key to understanding Barbie: Her substance is very much her essence.

Hard, smooth, cool to the touch, plastic can hold any shape and reproduce the tiniest of details. It is not mined or harvested; chemists manufacture it. Nor does it return to nature: you can throw it away, but it will not vanish— poof—from the landfill. Time may alter its appearance, as it has with some of the earlier Barbies—dolls with white arms on coral torsos with oily, apricot-colored legs.

To a poet or a child or anyone given to anthropomorphizing, such dolls are victims of vitiligo, the disease from which Michael Jackson claims to suffer. But to a chemist, they are evidence of an inadequate recipe. Never mind the beads of moisture on their mottled thighs, old dolls, a chemist will tell you, don't sweat. But their "plasticizer" (the substance used to make plastic pliable) may begin to separate from their "resin" (the plastic base—polyvinylchloride in Barbie's case). Or their dyes might fade.

In the environmentally conscious nineties, it's hard to remember a time when plastic was considered miraculous. In the fifties, "Better living through chemistry" was the slogan of the plastic pocket protector set, not an ironic catch phrase coined by users of hallucinogenic drugs. Science was inextricably tied up with patriotism. The Soviets launched *Sputnik* in September 1957; we countered four months later with a satellite of our own. Can-do, know-how—these were American things, as were those big acrylic polymers and giant supermolecules. It had been our manifest destiny to tame a big continent; we drove big cars; even on the molecular level, we placed our trust in big.

With the introduction of credit cards, "plastic" became a synonym for money. Diner's Club issued the first universal credit card in 1950, American Express followed in 1958, and by 1968, the best career tip for a youth like Dustin Hoffman in *The Graduate* was simply: "Plastics."

Plastic, Roland Barthes wrote, "is the very idea of its infinite transformation; as its everyday name indicates, it is ubiquity made visible." It is also democratic, almost promiscuously commonplace. In the past, imitation materials implied pretentiousness; they were used to simulate luxuries—diamonds, fur, silver—and "belonged to the world of appearances not to that of actual use." Plastic, by contrast, is a "magical substance which consents to be prosaic"; it is cast, extruded, drawn, or laminated into billions of household things.

But if Barbie's substance is the very essence of the mid-twentieth century, her form is nearly as old as humanity, and it is her form that gives her mythic resonance. Barbie is a space-age fertility symbol: a narrow-hipped mother goddess for the epoch of cesarean sections. She is both relentlessly of her time and timeless. To such overripe totems as the Venus of Willendorf, the Venus of Lespugue, and the Venus of Dolni, we must add the Venus of Hawthorne, California.

But wait, you say, Barbie is no swelling icon of fecundity: thick of waist, round of shoulder, pendulous of breast and bulging of buttock. How can you link her with Stone Age, pre-Christian fertility amulets? The connection rests on her feet, or the relative lack of them.

The Venus of Willendorf is a portable object of veneration. Her legs, like those of other Stone Age "Venuses," taper into prongs at the ankles. For her to stand up, the prong or prongs must be plunged into the earth, an act that, as she is a representation of the Great Mother, completes her. Mother Nature, Great Mother, Mother Goddess, Mother Earth—by any name, the female principle of fecundity is "chthonian," literally "of the earth."

In this context, Barbie's itty-bitty arched feet can be interpreted as vestigial prongs. Their suitability to the wearing of high heels is a camouflage, diverting the modern eye from their ancient function. No one disputes that Barbie has the trappings of a contemporary woman, but, either deliberately or coincidentally, they are arrayed on a prehistoric icon. When I raised the issue with Mattel employees, most responded cryptically with a remark like: "I've heard that said."

VENUS OF LESPUGUE,

COLLECTION OF MUSÉE DE

L'HOMME, PARIS

Sleek, angular fertility idols are not without precedent. The best-known were produced in the Cyclades, Aegean islands off the coast of Greece, between 2600 and 1100 B.C. The artist who fashioned the Venus of Willendorf conceived of female anatomy as a landscape of dimpled knolls; the Cycladic artists, by contrast, translated breasts and bellies into schematized geometric forms. Like Barbie's, the shoulders of Cycladic dolls are wider than their hips and their bodies are hard and smooth. They are an example of what art historian Kenneth Clark terms a "crystalline Aphrodite"—a stylized descendant of the Neolithic "vegetable Aphrodite." Why Cycladic sculptors streamlined the dolls, however, remains a mystery; scholars, says art historian H. W. Janson, can't "even venture a guess."

Over the years, "dolls"—anthropomorphic sculptures of the human figure—have been used as often in religion as in play. Archeologists who unearth such figures must puzzle out whether they were intended for the temple or the nursery. When first discovered, the ancient Egyptian figures known as *Ushabti* were believed to be dolls; scholars now classify them as funereal statues—miniature versions of a master's slaves buried with the master to serve him after death. Likewise, the Barbie-shaped "snake goddesses" produced in Crete around 1600 B.C. look like dolls but were in fact religious icons.

Then there are dolls that defy classification. Traditionally, Hopi Indian parents give their children kachina figures— cult objects representing various gods—to play with on ceremonial occasions. The dolls teach them the fine points of their faith. Like the kachinas, Barbie is both toy and mythic object—modern woman and Ur-woman—navelless, motherless, an incarnation of "the One Goddess with a Thousand Names." In the reservoir of communal memory that psychologist Carl Jung has termed the "collective unconscious," Barbie is an archetype of something ancient, matriarchal, and profound.

In Barbie's universe, women are not the second sex. Barbie's genesis subverts the biblical myth of Genesis, which Camille Paglia has described as "a male declaration of independence from the ancient mother-cults." Just as the goddess-based religions antedated Judeo-Christian monotheism, Barbie came before Ken. The whole idea of woman as temptress, or woman as subordinate to man, is absent from the Barbie cosmology. Ken is a gnat, a fly, a slave, an accessory of Barbie. Barbie was made perfect: her body has not evolved dramatically with time. Ken, by contrast, was a blunder: first scrawny, now pumped-up, his everchanging body is neither eternal nor talismanic.

Critics who ignore Barbie's mythic dimension often find fault with her lifestyle. But it is mythologically imperative that she live the way she does. Of course Barbie inhabits a prelapsarian paradise of consumer goods; she has never been exiled from the garden.

Mattel attributes the success of its 1992 "Totally Hair" Barbie, a woolly object reminiscent of Cousin It from *The Addams Family*, to little girls' fascination with "hairplay"—combing, brushing, and generally making a mess of the doll's ankle-length tresses. But since not all Barbie owners become cosmetologists, one has to wonder what "hairplay" is really about. I think it may be a modern reenactment of an ancient goddess-cult ritual.

VENUS OF WILLENDORF,
COLLECTION OF
NATURHISTORISCHES
MUSEUM, WIEN

Witches traditionally muss up their hair when they are preparing to engage in witchcraft. As late as the seventeenth century, civilized Europeans, historian Barbara Walker tells us, actually believed witches "raised storms, summoned demons and produced all sorts of destruction by unbinding their hair." In Scottish coastal communities, women were forbidden to brush their hair at night, lest they cause a storm that would kill their male relatives at sea. St. Paul, one of history's all-time woman-haters, was scared of women's hair; he thought unkempt locks could upset the angels.

The toddler brushing Barbie's hair may look innocent, but who knows, perhaps she is in touch with some ancient matriarchal power. In 1991, a survey of three thousand children commissioned by the American Association of University Women revealed that girls begin to lose their self-confidence at puberty, about the time they give up Barbie. At age nine, the girls were assertive and felt positive about themselves, but by high school, fewer than a third felt that way. Perhaps this could have been avoided had the girls simply hung on to their Barbies. Forget trying to be Barbie; even gorgeous grown people would be hard-pressed to pass for an eleven-and-a-half-inch thing. But maybe they should build a shrine to the doll and light some incense.

There is a remarkable amount of pagan symbolism surrounding Barbie. Even the original location of Mattel—Hawthorne—has significance. The Hawthorn, or May Tree, represents the White Goddess Maia, the mother of Hermes, goddess of love and death, "both the ever-young Virgin giving birth to the God, and the Grandmother bringing him to the end of his season." Barbie's pagan identity could also account for Ken's genital abridgment; cults of the Great Mother were ministered to by eunuchs. And it would explain why the housewives in Dichter's study took an immediate dislike to Barbie: "The white goddess is anti-domestic," Robert Graves writes in *The White Goddess: A Historical Grammar of Poetic Myth.* "She is the perpetual 'other woman.' "

Even if it wanted to, Mattel could not assert ignorance of pagan symbolism. This isn't merely because Aldo Favilli, the Italian-born, classically educated former sculpture restorer at Florence's Uffizi Gallery who has run Mattel's sculpture department since 1972, ought to know a thing or two about iconography. In 1979, the company test-marketed two "Guardian Goddesses," "SunSpell," "the fiery guardian of good," and "MoonMystic," "who wears the symbols of night." Identical in size and shape to Barbie, they came with four additional outfits—"Lion Queen," "Soaring Eagle," "Blazing Fire," and "Ice Empress"—sort of Joseph Campbell meets Cindy Crawford. But even stranger than their appearance was what they did. To "unlock" their "powers," you *spread their legs*—or, as their box euphemizes, made them "step to the side." Then they flung their arms upward, threw off their street clothes and controlled nature. Freezing volcanoes, drying up floods, blowing away tornadoes, and halting a herd of stampeding elephants are among the activities suggested on their box.

The goddesses took Barbie's crystalline hardness one step further. They wore plastic breastplates and thigh-high dominatrix boots—outfits created by two female Mattel designers that evoke Camille Paglia's characterization of the Great Mother as "a sexual dictator, symbolically impenetrable." Yet despite their literal virginity, their powers were metaphorically linked to sex. To set the dolls' mechanism, their thighs had to be squeezed together until they clicked. To release it, their legs had to be parted; the box features a drawing of two juvenile hands clutching each foot. Vintage doll dealers speculate that the goddesses were removed from the market because their mechanism was too delicate. But between their lubricious leg action and pantheistic message, they strike me as having been too indelicate.

IF I HAD TO LOCATE THE POINT AT WHICH I BEGAN TO SEE the ancient archetype within the modern toy, it would be at the home of Robin Swicord, a Santa Monica–based screenwriter whom Mattel commissioned in the 1980s to write the book for a Broadway musical about the doll.

Swicord is not a New Age nut; she's a writer. And even after mega-wrangles with Mattel's management—the musical was sketched out but never produced—she is still a fan of the doll. "Barbie," she said, "is bigger than all those executives. She has lasted through many regimes. She's lasted through neglect. She's survived the feminist backlash. In countries where they don't even sell makeup or have anything like our dating rituals, they play with Barbie. Barbie embodies not a cultural view of femininity but the essence of woman."

Over the course of two interviews with Swicord, her young daughters played with their Barbies. I watched one wrap her tiny fist around the doll's legs and move it forward by hopping. It looked as if she were plunging the doll into the earth—or, in any event, into the bedroom floor. And while I handle words like "empowering" with tongs, it's a good description of her daughters' Barbie play. The girls do not live in a matriarchal household. Their father, Swicord's husband, Nicholas Kazan, who wrote the screenplay for *Reversal of Fortune,* is very much a presence in their lives. Still, the girls play in a female-run universe, where women are queens and men are drones. The ratio of Barbies to Kens is about eight to one. Barbie works, drives, owns the house, and occasionally exploits Ken for sex. But even that is infrequent: In one scenario, Ken was so inconsequential that the girls made him a valet parking attendant. His entire role was to bring the cars around for the Barbies.

In other informal interviews with children, I began to notice a pattern: Clever kids are unpredictable; they don't cut their creativity to fit the fashions of Mattel. One girl who wanted to be a doctor didn't demand a toy hospital; she turned Barbie's hot pink kitchen into an operating room. Others made furniture—sometimes whole apartment complexes—out of Kleenex boxes and packing cartons. And one summer afternoon in Amagansett, New York, I watched a girl and her older brother act out a fairy tale that fractured gender conventions. While hiking in the mountains, a group of ineffectual Kens was abducted by an evil dragon who ate all but one. He remained trapped until a posse of half-naked Barbies—knights in shining spandex—swaggered across the lawn and bludgeoned the dragon to death with their hairbrushes.

When the dragon devoured the Kens, the brother dismembered them. "More boys would buy Barbies if you could put them together yourself," he told me, adding that he enjoys combining the body parts in original ways. "That was the beginning of the downfall of Barbie in our house," his mother told me. "Once we saw one with three legs and two heads, it was hard to just let her be herself."

I also learned to ask children what their doll scenarios meant to them, rather than to make assumptions. Last summer, for example, I was playing on my living-room floor with a six-year-old, under the watchful eye of her parents—he a black television executive, she a white magazine writer. The girl had brought her own blond Barbie, and the doll—like the girl—was quite a coquette. Her "play" consisted of going on dates with five of my male dolls: a blond Ken, a G.I. Joe, and three members of Hasbro's Barbie-scaled New Kids on the Block. She completely ignored Jamal, a black male doll made by Mattel, leaving him sprawled facedown on the rug—troublingly evocative of William Holden at the beginning of *Sunset Boulevard.*

I was not, it soon became evident, the only one who was troubled. When Jamal had been neglected for what seemed like eons, the girl's mother finally grabbed him and asked, "Wouldn't Barbie like to go out with Jamal?" The child looked exasperated. "But she can't, Mommy," she said. "That's *Daddy.*"

Scholars agree that for children, "play" is "work." Jean Piaget has grouped children's play into three categories: games of mastery (building with blocks, climbing on jungle gyms), games with rules (checkers, hide-and-seek), and games of "make-believe," in which play involves a story that begins "What if . . ." Make-believe play is concerned with the manipulation of symbols and the exercise of imagination—and it is into this category that Barbie play falls.

To some scholars, toys and games are the Lego bricks in the social con-struction of gender. "When kids maneuver to form same-gender groups on the playground or organize a kickball game as 'boys-against-the-girls,' they produce a sense of gender as dichotomy and opposition," University of Southern California sociologist Barrie Thorne writes in *Gender Play.* "And when girls and boys work cooperatively on a classroom project, they actively undermine a sense of gender as opposition."

But the role of make-believe play is less clear than that of games of mas-tery or games with rules because it involves entering the logic (and occa-sionally illogic) of the child's imaginary world. Children sometimes use Barbie and Ken to dramatize relationships between the adults in their lives, especially if those adults are a source of anxiety. In Sarah Gilbert's novel *Summer Gloves,* the female narrator's daughter mutilates her Midge doll and practically glues her Ken to her Barbie. This seems odd until the mother comments: "I married a Ken and he's about to run off with a Midge. And they may good and well deserve each other, the bores."

Children's therapists even use Barbie and Ken—or the Heart family, Mattel's Barbie-sized domestic unit—to help their young patients commu-nicate. "A lot of them act out their own problems with the Heart family," Yale University psychologist Dorothy G. Singer told me. "One child whose parents were going to be divorced would constantly lock Mr. Heart out of the dollhouse—make him sleep in the garden."

Singer is the author of *Playing for Their Lives: Helping Troubled Children Through Play Therapy,* and, with her husband, Yale psychologist Jerome L. Singer, of *Make Believe: Games and Activities to Foster Imaginative Play in Young Children.* She says that although some children use Barbie for cre-ative play, it's not because the doll has—as Mattel's commercials contend—"something special." "Imaginative kids take some toys and make them into anything they want," she told me. "But you have to ask: Where does that imagination come from and how does it start? What we found in our research is that if the parent sanctions that kind of play—starts a game, helps—then by the time the child is four or five, [he or she] doesn't need the parent. They now have ideas for scripts and they can make any world that they want."

Not every parent is quite so willing to disappear. In her short story "The Geometry of Soap Bubbles," Rebecca Goldstein dramatizes the efforts of a mother—Chloe, a member of the classics department at Barnard College—to teach the art of make-believe to her daughter, Phoebe. In defiance of her colleagues' "finer sensibilities," Chloe presents the child with an array of Kens and Barbies, "having felt the drama latent in their flesh." Then she uses the dolls to act out mythological tales. In one scenario, Ken, "clad in psychedelic bathing trunks," becomes "the shining god Apollo"; Barbie, the clairvoyant princess Cassandra. In another, a corybantic adaptation of Euripides's *Bacchae,* Ken portrays Dionysus. Unfortunately, Chloe's strategy works too well: Instead of playing with the dolls, the daughter, who prefers math problems, asks her mother to play with them "*for* her."

Even when mothers don't intervene actively, they can influence what their children do with the doll. During her daughter's Barbie years, Ann Lewis, Democratic party activist and sister of Massachusetts Representative Barney Frank, spent her nights doing political work. One evening, before going out, she noticed that her daughter had dressed Barbie in a floor-length formal gown. "Where's Barbie going?" Lewis asked. "To a meeting," her daughter replied.

This is not to say that when daughters emulate their mothers in Barbie play, it's always a constructive experience. Mothers who believe in restricted roles for women transmit messages of restriction: of opportunities, behavior, even body size. "There are a lot of mothers who don't want their kids to be fat when they go to the country club and put on bathing suits," Singer told me. "I have in my own practice now a child whose mother is forcing her to diet. She goes to Weight Watchers for Children . . . and this kid eats this crazy stuff. She's a little plump but not in any way overweight or looking obese."

Sometimes mothers blame Barbie for negative messages that they themselves convey, and that involve their own ambivalent feelings about femininity. When Mattel publicist Donna Gibbs invited me to sit in on a market research session, I realized just how often Barbie becomes a scapegoat for things mothers actually communicate. I was sitting in a dark room behind a one-way mirror with Gibbs and Alan Fine, Mattel's Brooklyn-born senior vice president for research. On the other side were four girls and an assortment of Barbie products. Three of the girls were cheery moppets who immediately lunged for the dolls; the fourth, a sullen, asocial girl, played alone with Barbie's horses. All went smoothly until Barbie decided to go for a drive with Ken, and two of the girls placed Barbie behind the wheel of her car. This enraged the third girl, who yanked Barbie out of the driver's seat and inserted Ken. "My mommy says men are supposed to drive!" she shouted.

Her two playmates looked stunned. Fine and Gibbs looked stunned. Even the girl with the horses looked stunned. Fine finally shrugged his shoulders and said: "And they blame it on *us*?"

CHAPTER FIVE

THE BOOK OF RUTH

As a feat of engineering, the 1967 Twist 'N Turn Barbie is a marvel. Steve Lewis and Jack Ryan devised a doll that swiveled on a compound angle at its hips and neck. A compound angle is not perpendicular to the vertical axis of the doll; it is askew, and the resulting tilt gives the doll a human-looking *contrapposto*. A delicate new face with eyelashes made of real synthetic hair added the final touch. Lewis remembered the meeting at which he unveiled the prototype: "Everyone sat back and there was great silence. And one of the VPs, who is still in the toy business but not with Mattel, said, 'That is the most beautiful doll I have ever seen.'"

The doll's promotion was less attractive, however. In the Twist 'N Turn kickoff commercial, a swarm of girls stampeded to a toy store to trade in their old Barbies for a discount on the new one. So much for projecting a personality onto a beloved anthropomorphic toy, so much for clinging to Barbie as a transitional object, or, as in the case of the toy in Margery Williams's *The Velveteen Rabbit*, cherishing Barbie because she had been "made real" through wear.

Futurist Alvin Toffler condemned the trade-in as proof that "man's rela-

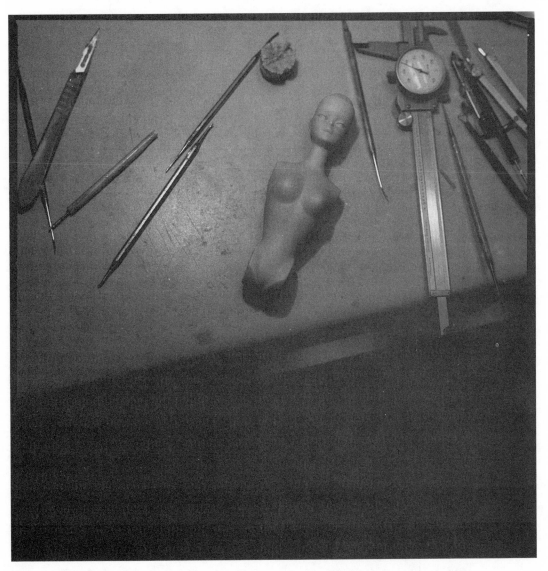

SCULPTOR'S WORK SPACE, TOP SECRET

MATTEL DESIGN CENTER SYLVIA PLACHY

tionships with things are increasingly temporal." But he missed what was, for women, a more alarming message. It wasn't worn sneakers or crushed Dixie cups that the kids were throwing away; it was women's bodies. Older females should simply be chucked, the ad implied, the way Jack Ryan discarded his older wives and mistresses. Ryan, inventor of the Hot Wheels miniature car line that Mattel would introduce the following year, brought automotive obsolescence to Barbie.

In 1968, Mattel plunged Barbie deeper into social irrelevance. It gave her a voice—so she could declare her membership in the Silent Majority. "Would you like to go shopping?" the doll twittered. "I love being a fashion model. What shall I wear to the prom?" This may be what Tricia Nixon said when you pulled the loop at the back of her neck, but in my experience a young woman in 1968 had broader concerns.

In a world where the under-thirties had pitted themselves against the over-thirties, Barbie betrayed her peers. She had a passing familiarity with youthspeak—"groovy" modified an occasional outfit or product—but no affinity with youth culture. Barbie existed to consume at a time when young people were repudiating consumption. They moved to communes and wore lumpy, distressed work clothes. Synthetic materials fell into disrepute, and Barbie's very essence—not to mention her house, beach bus, sister, and boyfriend—was plastic. For Barbie to have endorsed the values of the young would have been to negate herself.

Between 1970 and 1971, the feminist movement made significant strides. In 1970, the Equal Rights Amendment was forced out of the House Judiciary Committee, where it had been stuck since 1948; the following year, it passed in the House of Representatives. In response to a sit-in led by Susan Brownmiller, *Ladies' Home Journal* published a feminist supplement on issues of concern to women. *Time* featured *Sexual Politics* author Kate Millett on its cover, and *Ms.*, a feminist monthly, debuted as an insert in *New York* magazine. Even twelve members of a group with which Barbie had much in common—Transworld Airlines stewardesses—rose up, filing a multimillion-dollar sex discrimination suit against the airline.

Surprisingly, Barbie didn't ignore these events as she had the Vietnam War; she responded. Her 1970 "Living" incarnation had jointed ankles, permitting her feet to flatten out. If one views the doll as a stylized fertility icon, Barbie's arched feet are a source of strength; but if one views her as a literal representation of a modern woman—an equally valid interpretation—her arched feet are a hindrance. Historically, men have hobbled women to prevent them from running away. Women of Old China had their feet bound in childhood; Arab women wore sandals on stilts; Palestinian women were secured at the ankles with chains to which bells were attached; Japanese women were wound up in heavy kimonos; and Western women were hampered by long, restrictive skirts and precarious heels.

Given this precedent, Barbie's flattened feet were revolutionary. Mattel did not, however, promote them that way. Her feet were just one more "poseable" element of her "poseable" body. It was almost poignant. Barbie was at last able to march with her sisters; but her sisters misunderstood her and pushed her away.

Celebrities who in the sixties had led Barbie-esque lives now forswore them. Jane Fonda no longer vamped through the galaxy as "Barbarella," she flew to Hanoi. Gloria Steinem no longer wrote "The Passionate Shopper" column for *New York*, she edited *Ms.* And although *McCall's* had described Steinem as "a life-size counter-culture Barbie doll" in a 1971 profile, Barbie was the enemy.

NOW's formal assault on Mattel began in August 1971, when its New York chapter issued a press release condemning ten companies for sexist advertising. Mattel's ad, which showed boys playing with educational toys and girls with dolls, seems tame when compared with those of the other transgressors. Crisco, for instance, sold its oil by depicting a woman quaking in fear because her husband hated her salad dressing. Chrysler showed a marriage-minded mom urging her daughter to conceal from the boys how much she knew about cars. And Amelia Earhart Luggage—if ever a product was misnamed—ran a print ad of a naked woman painted with stripes to match her suitcases.

Feminists followed up in February 1972 by leafleting at Toy Fair. They alleged that dolls like Topper Toy's Dawn, Ideal's Bizzie Lizzie, and Mattel's Barbie encouraged girls "to see themselves solely as mannequins, sex objects or housekeepers," reported *The New York Times*. The first two dolls were perhaps deserving targets. Dawn's glitzy lifestyle was devoid of social responsibility, a precursor, as collector Beauregard Houston Montgomery has put it, of the "disco consciousness of the 1970s." And Bizzie Lizzie, who clutched an iron in one hand and a mop in the other, was a drudge. But if feminists had embraced Barbie when she stepped down from her high heels, her seventies persona might have been dramatically different. She was on the brink of a conversion. If they hadn't spurned, slapped, and mocked her, she might have canvassed for George McGovern or worked for the ERA. She might have spearheaded a consciousness-raising group with Francie and Christie, or Dawn and Bizzie Lizzie. But Barbie could not go where she was not wanted. "Living" Barbie lasted only a year. She went back on tiptoe and stayed there.

Perhaps because of this bitter legacy, "feminist" seems to be an obscene word at Mattel. "If you asked me to give you fifty words that describe me, it wouldn't be on the list," said Rita Rao, executive vice president of marketing on the Barbie line. Yet when Rao discusses her career, she recounts experiences that might have made another woman join NOW, like her 1964 job interview at Levi Strauss where she was told, "We don't hire women"; and in 1969, her applications to various stock brokerage firms that, except for one to Dean Witter, were turned down for the same reason.

First hired in 1966, Rao left Mattel in 1970, returned in 1973, left again in 1979 to start her own company, and returned in 1987 as a vice president.

Mattel must be a good place for a woman to work, she jokes, because she keeps coming back. "I know Ruth Handler absolutely doesn't think of herself as a feminist," Rao explains. "She's antifeminist, if anything. [But] when there's a woman at the top, it's illogical to say that a woman can't be capable. So even though she didn't really promote women or move them forward, her very being there made a statement."

Ruth Handler is almost too original for modifiers like "feminist" and "antifeminist" or even "good" and "evil." "Swashbuckling," "intrepid," "one-of-a-kind"—these are adjectives for Ruth. Conventional propriety has never seemed to weigh heavily upon her. It isn't so much that she sees herself outside the law, but that she is a law unto herself. This no doubt helped her to cope with breast cancer; unashamed, she diagnosed the shortcomings of existing mastectomy prostheses and founded a company to make better ones. But it may also have contributed to her being found guilty of white-collar crimes that, in the words of the judge who sentenced her, were "exploitative, parasitic, and . . . disgraceful to anything decent in this society."

Barbie's fate in the early seventies was very closely linked with Ruth's. Barbie's values were Ruth's values, and the risk Ruth took by introducing Barbie had paid off handsomely. But in 1970, Ruth's luck changed. "I had a mastectomy and the world started to fall apart," she said.

Back at work two weeks after the operation, Ruth had her hands full. While Elliot handled Mattel's creative side, Ruth attended to its business and financial aspects, which, ten years after the company went public, had expanded well beyond toys. In 1969, Mattel acquired Metaframe Corporation, a manufacturer of hamster cages, aquariums, and other pet supplies. Not satisfied with small animals, in 1970 it moved to larger ones—lions, tigers, and bears—by acquiring the Ringling Bros. and Barnum & Bailey Circus. It bought Audio Magnetics Corporation, a manufacturer of audiotape, and Turco Manufacturing, a maker of playground equipment, and it formed Optigon Corporation, a distributor of keyboard musical instruments. It even got into the movie business, forming Radnitz/Mattel Productions, Inc., which produced the Academy Award–winning *Sounder.*

Mattel's goal in diversifying was to retain some sort of equilibrium. Toys are a volatile, seasonal business; by acquiring stable companies with stable sales, Mattel hoped to offset the capriciousness of the toy market. It also began accounting practices that would even out its earnings vacillations, such as "annualization," the deferring of some of its expenses until late in the year when most of its sales took place. Before beginning its diversification, it brought in two key outsiders: Arthur Spear, an MIT engineering graduate who had headed manufacturing operations at Revlon; and Seymour Rosenberg, a financial expert who had earned a reputation as an acquisitions wizard at Litton Industries.

Despite all this, 1970 was as bad a year for Mattel as it was for Ruth. Its Talking Barbies were silenced when its plant in Mexicali, Mexico, where they were made, burned. And when its Sizzler toy line—a subsidiary of Hot Wheels—failed to generate as much revenue as Mattel had predicted, the company simply overstated its sales, net income, and accounts receivable, and instigated a "bill and hold" accounting practice—invoicing clients for orders that, because the clients had the right to cancel and often did, were not shipped. The inclusion of these "bill and hold" sales increased reported pretax earnings by about $7.8 million. Had Mattel made a miraculous recovery—which, given the unpredictability of the industry, was not impossible—its borrowing against future sales might have gone unnoticed. But as the company weathered bad quarter after bad quarter, the gap between the business it reported and the business it did widened.

By 1972, it could no longer disguise its losses. It reported a $29.9 million loss on sales of $272.4 million; and Wall Street, which had embraced Mattel as a glamour stock, began to suspect that something was rotten in Hawthorne. In August, Seymour Rosenberg, executive vice president, left;

his acquisitions had been losers and his accounting practices were getting Ruth into hot water. Meanwhile, Mattel's bankers, worried about their short-term financing, had been having independent discussions with operations manager Arthur Spear. In December, they refused to deal with Ruth any longer; she was permitted to retain the title of president, but forced to relinquish control of the company to Spear.

In February 1973, Mattel's internal drama became public farce. The company issued contradictory press releases within three weeks. The first predicted a strong recovery; the second said: Forget the first; we just happened to have overlooked a $32.4 million loss. When, as a consequence of the announcement, Mattel stock plummeted, its shareholders filed five class-action lawsuits against the company, various current and former officers, and Arthur Andersen & Co., its independent accounting agency. The Securities and Exchange Commission also began an investigation.

Ruth, forced to resign as president (but allowed to continue with Elliot as cochairman of the board), was publicly repudiated, stripped of her power. Shaken, she lost faith even in Barbie.

"There's a group of people in this company that says Barbie is dead," former Mattel executive Tom Kalinske recalls Ruth telling him in 1973. "Last year we had our first decline ever since the introduction of Barbie. People are saying that Barbie's over, finished, and that we ought to get on to other categories of toys." Shocked, Kalinske responded, "That's the most ridiculous thing I've heard. Barbie's going to be here long after you and I are gone." Moved by his enthusiasm, Ruth made him marketing director on the line.

"Ruth was an incredible woman . . . a great marketing person and a great finance person," Kalinske told me at Toy Fair in 1993. "But she had these years of success where everything went correctly for her. Every quarter, earnings would be up, sales would be up—and it just kept going that way for years and years. Then she had a quarter where that didn't occur. So she ended up relying on some inside financial and sales people who basically advised her, 'Don't worry about this. . . . This is a momentary problem, a calendarization problem.' Well, needless to say, after three quarters of it not getting any better, she had committed fraud—or the company had, and as the leader of the company she had. So there were extenuating circumstances, but nevertheless she was responsible for having reported sales and earnings that didn't exist."

Ken Handler sees it differently. "[My mother] was hated because she was a strong, powerful woman," he told me. "Men that work in these kinds of organizations . . . bring a tremendous amount of unresolved sexual energy to the workplace. These men were not able to sit back and take that much strength from a woman. And my mother wasn't very diplomatic always; she could be very tough. So they resented her deeply, and they conspired against her in her absence."

Whatever the true cause of the nightmare, it dragged on. On September 6, 1974, Mattel requested that trading in its stock on the New York and Pacific stock exchanges be suspended; it had "discovered" enormous misstatements in its financial reports for fiscal 1971 and 1972. Then, on October 2, 1974, Mattel consented to the SEC's request that it make people outside the company a majority of its board of directors—an unprecedented move that, when Mattel agreed to it, overturned the traditional stockholders' right to a voice in the selection of their company's directors.

Mattel also agreed to appoint a special counsel and a special auditor to investigate its financial statements. On November 3, 1975, when the special counsel filed a report confirming that Mattel had cooked its books, the company settled its shareholder suits out of court for more than $30 million. Ruth and Elliot got the boot, but, as part of the settlement, they agreed to contribute two million shares of Mattel stock and to reimburse the company for $112,000 in attorney's fees. Rosenberg also agreed to pay back $94,000 in attorney's fees, cancel his severance agreement, and contribute $100,000 cash.

On February 16, 1978, Ruth Handler and Seymour Rosenberg, comptroller Yashuo Yoshida and two other employees were indicted by a federal grand jury for conspiring to violate federal securities, mail, and banking laws by preparing false financial records. The crimes spelled out in the indictment are chilling. It says that the bogus data was used to inflate the market price of Mattel stock, which in turn was used to acquire bank loans. Then the stock was sold by the defendants for their own benefit. In 1972, Rosenberg allegedly realized $1.9 million by selling 80,300 shares of Mattel stock, and Ruth, acting as a trustee for her children, took in $383,000 from the sale of 16,600 shares. The two were also accused of hiding real data from Arthur Andersen and of altering royalty statements, inventory records, and tooling costs. And in one of its most unsettling passages, the indictment stated that to increase 1970 profits, Rosenberg and Ruth actually discussed withholding $2.6 million of Mattel's contribution to its employee profit-sharing trust, though it doesn't say whether the two implemented their devious plan.

"I . . . will exert every ounce of strength at my disposal to prove my innocence," Ruth vowed when indicted, but ten months later she pleaded no contest. In December 1978, U.S. District Court Judge Robert Takasugi sentenced her to a forty-one-year prison sentence and a $57,000 fine, both of which he suspended. He did, however, require that she devote five hundred hours per year for five years to community service and pay $57,000 in "reparations" to fund an occupational rehab center for convicted felons. Ruth does not seem to be the sort of woman to run away from a fight. But she did.

"I did fight it for years and years," she told me, "but what happened is I went into retirement in 1975 and I hated it. I was as low as a person could get emotionally, psychologically. And I was having trouble finding a breast prosthesis. So I got into the business. In 'seventy-six, I was designing the product and in 'seventy-seven, I was marketing the product—running

around the country doing promotions. And my lawyers kept calling and saying, 'You have to appear in court.' I'm on a crusade to correct the world—
to change the world as it relates to the mastectomy—and every time I turned
around they wanted me."

Ruth and her staff, mostly women who had lost breasts to cancer, held fitting sessions at department stores. They played tapes of Ruth on television,
opening her shirt and asking interviewers if they could tell which breast was
real. "We were dignifying the fitting process," she said. "Women would see
dozens of other women milling around waiting to be fitted, and they'd have
their own little jam sessions. . . . They'd talk to each other and it became a
party to these gals, a fun experience. By the time they got fitted, they were
walking with their chest out; they were feeling each other; they were laughing. Imagine women going around and feeling each other's breasts—publicly—and laughing and kidding around."

But, she continued, "I had to come home to this other life of fighting the
lawyers. . . . So one day I said, 'Do something. Get it changed. . . . There's
got to be another way.' "

Her lawyers suggested that she plead nolo contendere, but warned that it
was the equivalent of pleading guilty, except that it couldn't be used against
her in subsequent civil suits. "I won't plead guilty," she told them, "I'd like
to plead nolo contendere. . . . I'll accept [the court's] version of guilty, but
I want to say when I plead that I'm innocent." You can't do that, one lawyer
said, but a second thought it was possible. "And sure enough they looked it
up and there was a precedent," Ruth said. "I could plead nolo and at the
same time protest that I'm innocent *and get away with it.*" Which she did.

Ruth's biography is so much larger than life that over the course of our
interviews, I felt as if I were in a TV movie—some sort of courtroom drama,
or HBO's *Barbarians at the Gate.* The tone and direction, however, changed
from scene to scene. Ruth was a sentimental Frank Capra heroine one
minute, a John Waters character the next. Part Leona Helmsley, part Joan

of Arc, Ruth is an almost impossible blend of acquisitiveness and idealism.

Words often came to Ruth in the form of slogans and catchy product names, which gave our talks the flavor of a TV commercial. She is proud of her three best-selling prostheses—the "Nearly Me Three," her "classic best breast"; the "So-Soft," an all-silicone breast for "women who need the softer, more hanging look"; and the "Rest Breast," an all-foam breast that can be worn while swimming. Nor did she manufacture breasts merely as a service; as early as 1977, Nearly Me, a privately held company (no messy filing with the SEC), which she sold to Kimberly-Clark Corporation in 1991, did a million dollars' worth of business.

"There are breasts and there are breasts," she told me between bites of an egg salad sandwich at Beverly Hills' Hillcrest Country Club in 1992. "Some breasts are much softer and some breasts are much firmer. Some have a tendency to lift up and be full; others have a tendency to lift up and hang down. It depends on the muscles and the age and the construction and the body."

Ruth tends not to look at the whys of things; but she misses no detail when it comes to the hows. She figured out what male prosthesis makers had overlooked: breasts, like feet, come in "rights" and "lefts," as must prostheses. To implement her discovery, Ruth formed Ruthton, the precursor of Nearly Me, with Peyton Massey, a Santa Monica–based prosthesis maker. "After he gave me all the reasons why it wouldn't work, he agreed that he would do it," she told me. "We cleared out an old storeroom at his place . . . and he sculpted the breasts and I did all the other stuff to make it happen."

Ruth was unhappy with Massey's materials—the early prostheses had "a very peculiar odor," she recalled—so she brought in a half-dozen retired Mattel toy and doll designers to revise them. She wanted the breasts to be "lightweight" and to have "a swoop on the top and a fullness on the bottom." She also wanted "some kind of a 'skin' to wrap around—to hold all of this together." Within a couple of hours, the toymakers determined that Ruth's needs could be met by a model with a foam back, a silicone front, and a polyurethane "skin."

"Thirty years of working at Mattel had trained me to know what is needed if you want to design a product," she explained. It also taught her how to sell one. In January 1977, she arranged her first department store promotion at Neiman Marcus in Dallas. Her goal was to get out of Los Angeles and see how the breasts played in a less trendy part of the country. The merchandise manager was at first taken aback. But after Ruth delivered her pitch face-to-face, Neiman Marcus opened its doors.

"I don't want all the stores," Ruth told the merchandise manager. "Pick the one in your most affluent Jewish neighborhood, because there's a high degree of breast cancer among Jewish people . . . and get me some publicity."

"Some publicity" quickly turned into appearances on talk shows across the country. While her staff sent handwritten invitations to mastectomy victims near each host store, she stripped off her shirt for *People* magazine and invited a *New York Times* reporter to feel her breasts. Nearly Me became a phenomenon. Although some mastectomy patients in the mid-eighties chose to have their breasts surgically remade, their numbers weren't large enough to affect her business. "I was negative as hell on breast reconstruction at the beginning," she explained. "Because they reminded me of the early prostheses. They didn't match the other side. Women showed me . . . their own breast down here and the artificial breast up here—hard as a rock up here." She gestured to a spot near her shoulder. "I saw hundreds of those. Out of place. Crazy locations. If when you put a brassiere on, the two sides don't match, what the hell have you got?"

For most of the sixteen years that Ruth ran Nearly Me, she traveled two weeks out of every four. During the five years after her sentencing, however, she had to give community service at home—taking poor kids to her beach house in Malibu and setting up the Foundation for People, an agency that enabled white-collar felons to help blue-collar felons learn skills and get jobs.

"After I got the swing of it, I turned that into a positive thing and we formed a positive group," she said. "We rented a floor in an old rundown hotel and I got my personal decorator to do the whole floor for free. . . . I think white-collar offenders in most cases have been punished enough by the time they get to the sentencing. The humiliation is worse than going to jail. And the comedown from where they've been is so great—it's like you've already shot the guy, now stab him. What you need to do to help society take care of itself is say, 'Okay, buddy, it's your turn now to turn society around—to devote your money to it and help it.' "

Ruth's foundation enjoyed great success in the early eighties but was later disbanded. When Michael Milken and Ivan Boesky were sentenced, public sentiment turned against the idea of permitting white-collar criminals to elude jail.

WHILE RUTH REHABILITATED FELONS AND CANCER PA-tients, the plastic doll she invented helped Mattel recover from its near collapse. If Barbie was distraught during Ruth's run-in with the law, she didn't show it. There was no Day-in-Court Barbie or Barbie-for-the-Defense. She kept active; her "Busy" incarnation had clawlike hands; she could pick up such leisure-time paraphernalia as a phone, a TV, a record player, a serving tray, and a suitcase. She kept fit; her "Live Action" and "Walk Lively" versions twitched and strutted. And in an incarnation that featured the Twist 'N Turn face with a dead-on stare, she celebrated her sixteenth birthday.

Mattel also kept up its jibes at the women's movement. In 1968, feminists protested the Miss America Pageant; in 1972, the company introduced an official Miss America doll. A year later, it came out with "Barbie's Friend

Ship," a plastic airplane-cum-carrying case that featured—lest girls get any inflated ideas about taking the controls—a painted-on male pilot. A similar plane was issued with "Big Jim," a boys' line of Schwarzenegger-bodied, flannel-shirted, fire-fighting, construction-working, alligator-wrestling male dolls, so cartoonlike in their virility that they resembled the Village People, the ultramasculine gay disco recording artists. The cockpit of Big Jim's plane, however, was designed to hold Big Jim.

Then, in 1975, Skipper grew up, or, in any event, sprouted breasts. Growing Up Skipper, as the pre- and post-pubescent doll was called, required two wardrobes: one innocent, featuring strapless Mary Janes and knee socks; the other sophisticated, featuring grown-up, seventies platform shoes. It also required from its owner a taste for the macabre: Even in the Mattel catalogue the child photographed with it looks wide-eyed and aghast. The doll squeaks and lurches as its bosoms pop out, then, after another turn of its arm, snaps back into flatness. Growing Up Skipper slipped into production while men managed the Barbie line. Earlier Barbie products had reflected a sort of sly, knowing, conspiracy-of-women approach to the mysteries of femininity. But Growing Up Skipper is a male interpretation of female coming-of-age, focusing not on the true marker of womanhood—menstruation—but on a tidy, superficial change.

Steve Lewis defended the doll as "educational," but because it sidesteps what Joan Didion termed "that dark involvement with birth and blood and death," it doesn't teach biology. Rather, it is about signaling one's grown-up status to men through clothing. For many real-life females, becoming a woman is a messy, bloody, harrowing event. It is also nonreversible; only a small minority of anorexics and athletes manage to turn it back. But for the doll, the transition is a lark; no muss, no fuss, and an open invitation to retreat. I was heartened, however, to learn that not all the men who worked on Growing Up Skipper approved of it. "That thing was grotesque," said Mattel chief of sculpture Aldo Favilli.

Although there were complaints about Growing Up Skipper, they were, for the most part, drowned out by the furor over another 1975 product, Baby Brother Tenderlove, an anatomically correct male doll. In Louisville, Kentucky, a group of women stormed into a toy store and castrated the dolls; in response, some retailers placed stickers over the penis in the doll's photo on the box. The National Organization for Women, former Mattel publicist Beverly Cannady recalls, applauded Baby Brother Tenderlove; but columnist Ellen Goodman didn't, and Cannady wound up debating her on the Phil Donahue show. Other detractors were even more direct: Tom Kalinske received death threats.

Nineteen seventy-six was a more benign year for Barbie, as were the rest of the seventies. The world was no longer the raw, politicized place it had been a decade earlier. Young people who had turned away from plastic again embraced it. Infected with a sickness called "Saturday Night Fever," they left their homes at sunset, glistening with the brave unnatural shimmer of polyester. Physically energized, mentally narcotized, they spun on Lucite dance floors that exploded in brilliantly colored light. Their hearts beat, their limbs shook, their eyes slit to the throb of plastic disco records: "Get down. Boogy oogy oogy." "I'd love to love you, baby." They were transported, hypnotized, borne aloft, their dreary daytime lives checked like an overcoat at the door. It was a narcissistic opiate; any *zhlub* could be a star.

Although the idea of disco was democratic—a sound system and lights were all one needed to experience it—big-city discotheques maintained their mystique through exclusivity. Poor, ugly, and obscure people rarely mixed with the voluptuaries at Manhattan's Studio 54; an imperious blond doorman kept the masses at bay. In *Interview,* a magazine he founded in 1969, Studio 54 habitué Andy Warhol recorded the dull chat of his fellow habitués—Liza, Truman, Bianca, Halston. Celebrity became a cult, with stars its priests, boring conversation its liturgy, and the guarded discotheque its temple.

By 1977, Barbie had earned a place in that temple. Ruth intended the doll to represent Everygirl; and for a while, she did. But after eighteen years in the public eye, she was as famous as the wraiths who haunted the notorious Fifty-fourth Street *boîte de nuit*. No matter that she stood less than a foot tall, Barbie, like Ruth, had become bigger than life.

Perhaps in recognition of her increased stature, Mattel, in 1977, issued an eighteen-inch version of the Barbie doll. The larger edition was not, however, her most dramatic change. Mattel resculpted the face on both large and small models and anointed Barbie a "SuperStar." It also equipped her with the trappings of stardom—a hot pink Star 'Vette, a Star Traveler Motorhome, and a "salon of the stars" Beauty Boutique.

Barbie's new face, fashioned by doll sculptor Joyce Clark, was the face of disco. The doll appears in the 1977 catalogue against a black background, as if on the edge of a cavernous dance floor. Light glints off her glossy magenta boa, her burnished gold hair, her luminous diamondlike ring. Gone is the haughty smirk of her early years. Seemingly stupefied by the disco beat, SuperStar Barbie's mouth is set in a broad smile.

The revamped Barbie changed the relationship between the doll and the little girl who owned it. Barbie could still function as an object onto which the child projected her future self; but because the doll had the trappings of celebrity, the girl's imagined future had to involve being rich and famous. Nor did the doll's paraphernalia indicate how she came to hobnob with the stars. Did she earn her money as an actress or a model? Did she inherit it? Or was she running some nefarious business and being paid off the books? (Did Hollywood madam Heidi Fleiss play with this doll?)

In 1978, Mattel established Barbie's persona as a cover girl with a mechanical contraption called Fashion Photo Barbie. This play set came with a toy camera and a Barbie doll that struck fashion poses when the child "focused" the camera. The brainchild of Derek Gable, a British engineer who had been recruited to join Ryan's team in 1968, Fashion Photo Barbie is very much a boys' action toy masquerading as a girls' play set. Like Growing Up Skipper, it reflects a masculine understanding of the female experience; a little boy could take the role of fashion "photographer" as easily as a little girl could. But when a girl operates the toy, she can pretend to be either the model or the photographer; thus the toy encourages her to internalize a sense of herself-as-object; to split herself, in John Berger's words, into "the surveyor" and "the surveyed."

In the middle-seventies, feminist film theory began to focus on the "male gaze"; mainstream cinema, the argument went, presumed a male spectator and objectified women accordingly. "In a world ordered by sexual imbalance, pleasure in looking has been split between active/male and passive/female," Laura Mulvey wrote in "Visual Pleasure and Narrative Cinema," a 1975 essay that has generated mountains of scholarly rebuttal, qualification, and elaboration. "The determining gaze projects fantasy onto the female figure, which is styled accordingly. In their traditional exhibitionist role women are simultaneously looked at and displayed, with their appearance coded for strong visual and erotic impact so that they can be said to connote *to-be-looked-at-ness*."

Fashion Photo Barbie comes with preprinted "photographs" of Barbie in various fashion poses that the child can remove from the camera when the "photo session" is over. These teach—for children willing to be taught—a code of feminine erotic styling, of "to-be-looked-at-ness." They define what looks are acceptable, just as—for women who are willing to accept such definitions—photos of models in magazines do.

But Fashion Photo Barbie is not just about passivity. Little girls are not required to project themselves onto Barbie; they can view the doll as wholly other. Nor do they have to play with the "acceptable" photographs. Fashion Photo Barbie offers a girl power not only over an image of an adult, but over an adult celebrity. When the child adjusts the lens, Barbie responds instantly; her body pivots and her head snaps to the side. Peering through the viewfinder, the girl can interiorize the "male gaze." She is Richard Avedon, David Bailey, Deborah Turberville. She can play at controlling—and therefore defining—feminine erotic style. She can also explore less socially approved themes in her fashion photo-play: voyeurism and the erotization of her own gender.

Curiously, Fashion Photo Barbie came out the same year as *The Eyes of Laura Mars*, a movie starring Faye Dunaway as a female fashion photographer who has premonitions of horrible homicides. Mars's photos sell clothing through staged sex and violence; the shots used in the film were, in fact, taken by Helmut Newton. Set in a sort of disco inferno—its soundtrack pounds like a migraine—the movie credibly depicts the decadent, druggy inhabitants of the seventies fashion scene, many of whom wind up dead. This is not to imply that Fashion Photo Barbie sucked children into that scene; but it does make one wonder: Just how *did* kids play with that toy?

Barbie's SuperStar status also had an impact on the company she kept. She didn't drop Ken or Skipper, but she did start hanging out with Mattel versions of real-life celebrities. They included Debby Boone, Charlie's Angels Cheryl Ladd and Kate Jackson, and, in clothes befitting a male hoodlum, Kristy McNichol. Missing Angel Farrah Fawcett evidently declined to be cast in plastic, but that didn't stop Barbie from stealing her hairdo in 1981.

Barbie was also seen with Donnie, Jimmy, and Marie Osmond. Not exactly the Laura Mars type, Marie was a Mormon, and her mother demanded that Mattel engineer the doll's outfits so that Mormon "garments"—sacred, baggy, one-piece underwear—could be worn beneath them. Traditionally emblazoned with religious symbols over each breast and a slit in the crotch, the "garments," however, were not issued with the doll. Marie's mother also forced Mattel to bring out a thirty-inch Marie doll with dress patterns. A rabid advocate of home sewing, she hoped such a doll would inspire girls to use a needle and thread.

Although Barbie helped reverse Mattel's losses in the late seventies, she was never the darling of its top management. Arthur Spear, who became chairman of the board in 1978, was committed to reducing the company's involvement with toys. In 1979, it acquired Western Publishing, the producer of Golden Books, for $120 million. With its Ringling Bros. subsidiary, it expanded Circus World, a theme park near Orlando, Florida. It entered the electronics business with Intellivision, a $300 home video game system, and dumped its unprofitable acquisitions, such as Metaframe.

The press, for the most part, applauded Spear. "Under Mr. Spear, Mattel has pulled out of its earnings slump [and] reduced its long term debt from $118 million to about $20 million at the end of the 1979 fiscal year," *The New York Times* wrote. "His austere, no-nonsense style of management has brought a measure of order to a company that was run haphazardly for years," *Fortune* said, noting that Spear was a teetotaling nonsmoker who worked out daily on an exercise bicycle.

But *Business Week* remained skeptical. After "years of murky legal and financial battles," Mattel's hottest new toy, the magazine insinuated, had a certain appropriateness. The toy was "Slime"—green, runny glop that came with its own plastic garbage can.

CHAPTER SIX

SOME LIKE IT BARBIE

In 1980, Americans banished Jimmy Carter from the White House. They had had enough of greasy peanuts and off-the-rack suits. They craved chintz and glitter, Galanos and glen plaid. It was time to chuck the Birkenstocks and sell the six-year-old Toyota. There was Armani to be worn and a new BMW to be driven. Owing a trillion dollars hadn't slowed the country. Debt was good; greed was good; Barbie was good.

When the Reagans moved into 1600 Pennsylvania Avenue, they brought their Veblenesque appetites with them. Like Barbie, they were Californians, and their tastes bore the stamp of sun and surf and celluloid. Never had Barbie been more West Coast—her "Sun Lovin'" Malibu incarnation actually had tan lines—or more in tune with the times. "She's got the billion dollar look," said Mattel's 1981 catalogue about its "Golden Dream" Barbie. She was even prepared for escalating tension between haves and have-nots; in 1979, Mattel issued a Barbie "Fur & Jewels Safe" complete with security alarm.

In her 1979 "Kissing" version, Barbie—head tilted, lips puckered— waited as if in the wings of a theater to make her comeback. And when, at

BARBIE HEADS SYLVIA PLACHY

the 1981 Inaugural youth gala, the Beach Boys sang, "I wish they all could be California girls," it was as if they had beckoned her onstage. In the eighties, Mattel's talented female managers contributed to Barbie's revival, but she also got a boost from the *Zeitgeist*.

Barbie finally reflected, in a slightly skewed looking glass, the progress racial and ethnic minorities had made during the seventies. Styled by Kitty Black Perkins, an African-American designer whom Mattel hired in 1975, Black Barbie made her debut in 1980. Barbie had had black friends since the late sixties, but by 1979, Mattel determined that America was ready for the dream girl herself to be of color. Because the new doll was likely to be scrutinized, Mattel fashioned her with sensitivity: her hair is short and realistically textured; her face, if not aggressively non-Caucasian, is at least different from blond Barbie's; and her dress, while corporate, is livened up with jewelry evocative of African sculpture.

Hispanic Barbie, who appeared the same year, is another story. Decked out in a peasant blouse, a two-tiered skirt, and a mantilla, the doll looks like a refugee from an amateur production of *Carmen;* she even has a rose pinned at her neck. Mattel's designers could hardly be unacquainted with Hispanics: there are millions in southern California, and some even work for the company. Yet rather than dress her in an authentic folk costume or normal clothes, Mattel clad her in what it labeled "fiesta-style"—an adjective one expects to find imprinted on a plastic bag of tortilla chips.

"Little Hispanic girls can now play with their very own Barbie," the catalogue reads, and the contrast between the company's noble intentions—the box was printed in English and Spanish—and its actual product is puzzling. Unlike Mattel's international Barbies, aimed at adult collectors for whom authenticity is not a high priority, this doll was meant for real children, whose parents must, to a degree, have felt patronized by it.

The complexities of marketing dolls of color—as well as the way mainstream toy companies have interpreted ethnicity over time—will be examined later. But even in their imperfect executions, the mere existence of Black Barbie and Hispanic Barbie in 1980 was a landmark. Like the coronation of Vanessa Williams as Miss America in 1983, the dolls commented on the evolution of popular taste. Slowly (with the speed of a glacier, critics might say), standards of so-called beauty were changing.

Besides the country's collective twist to the right, Barbie benefited from another trend. Baby boomers who had played with the original doll were beginning to breed, and those who had once enjoyed Barbie gave her to their daughters, often when they were as young as two years old. This led to the invention in 1981 of My First Barbie, which was intended to be easier to dress. It had straight arms and rounded hands—some collectors refer to them scornfully as "fins"—since the doll's original sharp fingers could stab out a toddler's eye.

By 1983, the titles of Barbie's outfits began to lose the self-refer-

OFFICE OF MATTEL

COO JILL BARAD

SYLVIA PLACHY

entiality that had characterized them since the late sixties. It was safe to name them for activities again: "Holiday Hostess," "Horseback ridin'," "Ski party!" There was no danger Barbie would wear these to, say, demonstrate for the Equal Rights Amendment, which, by 1980, had failed. Shoppers who had used their charge cards surreptitiously in the seventies came out of the closet; far from requiring a place to hide, they needed the storage space. It was déjà vu time at Mattel. The company produced a Dream Store reminiscent of Barbie's 1963 Fashion Shop and a Barbie Loves McDonald's plastic hamburger stand, which, among other things, heightened brand recognition among preschoolers.

Eating was a key part of the eighties ethos; the decade's emblematic fauna—young urban professionals—lived to consume. True, fast-food rarely passed between their lips. They preferred pricy, affected fare—white truffles, sun-dried tomatoes, the uncooked bellies of tuna. But their children, who had not yet learned to distinguish sashimi from a dead pet guppy, cheerfully chowed down beneath the Golden Arches.

In contrast to the fad diets they had embraced in the seventies—Pritikin, Scarsdale, Beverly Hills—people in the eighties trained their bodies to burn fat instead of cutting calories. Being fit meant being able to eat conspicuously. "The only way to keep ahead—to eat significantly, impressively, competitively—was to keep in shape," Barbara Ehrenreich observed about the decade in *Fear of Falling: The Inner Life of the Middle Class.* "In a very real sense, eating was what one got in shape *for.*"

So it's not surprising that Barbie Loves McDonald's was followed in 1984 by Great Shape Barbie, a doll that came with a leotard, leg warmers, exercise shoes, and (presumably) a health club membership. Of course Barbie didn't need to take an aerobics class; she already had the consummate eighties body. It had "definition," the goal toward which every gym rat sweated, and, metaphorically, the essence of the eighties persona. "To achieve definition was to present a hard outline to the world," Ehrenreich

writes, "a projection of self that was not sensitive and receptive—as thera-
pies in the seventies had aimed at—but tough and contained." Few projections of self could be harder than Barbie's—her "skin" is, in fact, a
carapace. In the eighties, it wasn't just Barbie's curves that women sought
to emulate, it was the toughness of her vinyl. During Barbie's first years,
Bud Westmore, Universal Studio's makeup wizard, modeled Barbie on real-
life actresses; her blond hair, for instance, was matched to Kim Novak's. By
the eighties, however, the tables had turned: real-life women were modeling
themselves on the doll.

But transforming flesh—a pliant, yielding, organic substance—into plastic is not easy. The formula for this conversion—"No pain, no gain"—seems
to have inspired the Great Shape dolls; indeed, their description in Mattel's
catalogue reads like an instruction manual for a dominatrix. Under a picture
of a contorted Barbie is the directive: "Make her do scissor lifts." Under
Ken, who is frozen, doglike, on all fours: "Make him do push-ups." And over
Skipper, who appears to be trying to drag herself across the floor with a broken leg: "Make her do back extensions." The dolls are even packaged with
a booklet of diagrams to make sure they do their "exercises" correctly.

In projecting her future persona onto a Great Shape Barbie, a little girl
can learn to split herself not only into "the surveyor" and "the surveyed,"
but into "the trainer" and "the trainee." By internalizing the sadism of an
aerobics instructor, a little girl can, in her own exercise regimen, turn that
sadism upon herself. But let us not rush to blame Barbie for making children obsessed with exercise. Not until 1992 did Barbie come out with her
own workout video. Let us place the onus where it belongs—on drill
sergeant and recovering Barbarella Jane Fonda. Besides, slothful children,
of the sort that I once was, could happily—perhaps even sadistically—move
Great Shape Barbie through her miniature workout without feeling the
faintest urge to perform one of their own.

Significantly, the Great Shape dolls contained no mechanism to cause them to exercise by themselves. This was a breakthrough. Led by Judy Shackelford, who had joined Mattel in 1976 and was named its first female vice president in 1978, the Barbie marketing team let the doll go back to being a doll. Although her 1981 Western incarnation winked, Barbie had finally ceased to be an action toy. Girls, Shackelford observed, didn't want gimmicky doll bodies engineered for dynamic obsolescence; they preferred inert figures with fancy clothes and combable hair. Girls "didn't care if Barbie winked or not," Shackelford told me. "Guys cared. They said, 'God, look at that doll wink.' " Of Western Barbie, she confided: "It was the ugliest Barbie doll we ever did."

Instead of reworking the doll, Shackelford implemented a market "segmentation strategy," which she thinks helped Barbie achieve record sales. She did this by "segmenting the market," introducing dolls with different themes and then "creating whole worlds around them." Beginning about 1980, Mattel issued separate dolls for each of the major play patterns. There was a "hairplay" doll that came with styling paraphernalia; a "lifestyle" doll that came with sporting equipment; and a "glamour" doll that came with a gaudy dress. The strategy benefited Mattel in two major ways: because the costumes were sold on dolls, Mattel could charge more for them, and the variety encouraged girls to own more than one doll.

Shackelford got into the toy and novelty business as an entrepreneur, where her unusual combination of talents—Ruth Handler's business sense and Elliot Handler's art background—served her well. After graduating from Southern Illinois University with a degree in art, she moved to New York and taught grade school. "I was in this smock going from room to room with my paintbrushes—not my idea of a career," she said. So she took one of her art lessons, turned it into a toy, and sold the idea to a toy company, which led to more ideas for more companies. Later she went into manufacturing, inventing and producing an inflatable boot-tree designed to hold the knee-high footwear worn with miniskirts. But when hemlines fell, sales slowed, and to recoup her $100,000 investment, she wound up loading the trees into a truck and selling them herself across the country.

Shackelford learned the toy business from industry veterans, but not in a formal seminar. "When I started designing toys, I was twenty-four years old, and the only way I could get an appointment was to get one at four o'clock for cocktails," she said. "It was me and my partner—who was very voluptuous, like Barbie." When they showed a design, they'd ask for criticism, and the male executives would share what they had learned on the job. "I got stories from back in the 1940s. People were telling me what toys worked, why they didn't work," she explained. "And I was like a sponge. You pick all this stuff up. And suddenly you begin to perceive what 'market niching' is—you don't know the right words for it, but you begin to see." Working at Mattel was, for her, the culmination of this apprenticeship; she felt she "knew how to drive" but had finally gotten into "a really good car—one that didn't shake and you were sure wasn't going to run out of gas halfway there."

Working her way west after the boot-tree fiasco, Shackelford took a job with the Chicago-based toy design firm of Marvin Glass & Associates, which, until its demise in 1988, was preeminent in its field. Like Barbie marketing director Rita Rao, who left Mattel in 1979, Shackelford does not describe herself as a "feminist." But she does acknowledge a commitment to hiring and promoting women. She feels Mattel, for purely practical reasons, offers great opportunities to women: "They have more girls' volume than any other toy company . . . and no matter what anybody says about the marketers, you can't have that much girl product run by nothing but men. You need a balance." Yet given her own history, when it came to advancement in a male-run field, she could hardly pretend that a woman's appearance meant nothing.

Perhaps even more than Shackelford, Jill Elikann Barad, who joined Mattel in 1981 and was made its CEO in 1992, understands the value of appearance—and how to create a look that sells. While still an undergrad-

MATTEL COO JILL BARAD AND FRIENDS,
1994 <u>PEOPLE WEEKLY</u>, COPYRIGHT © 1994
BY MARK SENNET

uate at New York's Queens College, she traveled around the East Coast as a beauty consultant for Love Cosmetics. A drama major who graduated in 1973, she briefly flirted with an acting career, landing a nonspeaking part as Miss Italian America in *Barbarella* producer Dino De Laurentiis's film *Crazy Joe;* but she renounced greasepaint for Coty Cosmetics—ascending, in a record three years, from a lowly trainer of department store demonstrators to brand manager of its entire line. Nor did marriage to Paramount executive Thomas Barad detour her rise. When she relocated to Los Angeles in 1978, the Wells, Rich, Greene ad agency put her in charge of its Max Factor account. Even her application to Mattel—made after taking time off to have a baby—stressed her beauty know-how: she approached the company with a plan to sell cosmetics to children.

Barad was not, however, permitted to realize her vision immediately. Slime was still an important product at Mattel, and Barad's first assignment was to sell it in its then-current incarnation, A Bad Case of Worms, which featured, besides the popular green glop, brown vinyl crawlers. The modified Slime also functioned as an activity toy. If you threw it against a wall, it would stick and wriggle down. Barad rose to the occasion but ultimately confronted her boss, Tom Kalinske, and asked for greater responsibility on an aspect of girls' toys. He assigned her to work with Shackelford on Barbie. While she was pregnant with her second child she was promoted to marketing director, and what can be described as the doll's golden era began.

A chief element in positioning the new Barbie was her promotion. In 1984, after a campaign that featured "Hey There, Barbie Girl" sung to the tune of "Georgy Girl," Mattel launched a startling series of ads that toyed with female empowerment. Its slogan was "We Girls Can Do Anything," and its launch commercial, driven by an irresistibly upbeat soundtrack, was a sort of feminist *Chariots of Fire.* Responding to the increased number of women with jobs, the ad opens at the end of a workday with a little girl rushing to meet her business-suited mother and carrying her mother's briefcase into the house. A female voice says, "You know it, and so does your little girl." Then a chorus sings, "We girls can do anything."

The ad plays with the possibility of unconventional gender roles. A rough-looking Little Leaguer of uncertain gender swaggers onscreen. She yanks off her baseball cap, her long hair tumbles down, and—sigh of relief—she grabs a particularly frilly Barbie doll. (The message: Barbie is an amulet to prevent athletic girls from growing up into hulking, masculine women.) There are images of gymnasts executing complicated stunts and a toddler learning to tie her shoelaces. (The message: Even seemingly minor achievements are still achievements.) But the shot with the most radical message takes place in a laboratory where a frizzy-haired, myopic brunette peers into a microscope. Since the seventies, Barbie commercials had featured little girls of different races and hair colors, but they were always pretty. Of her days in acting school, Tracy Ullman remarked in *TV Guide* that she was the "ugly kid with the brown hair and the big nose who didn't get [cast in] the Barbie commercials." With "We Girls," however, Barbie extends her tiny hand to bookish ugly ducklings; no longer a snooty sorority rush chairman, she is "big-tent" Barbie.

Although the ad, and, by extension, the whole career Barbie series, is not without problematic and contradictory content, it is such a departure from the doll's fatuous, disco positioning in the seventies that one's jaw tends to drop. And one wonders: How on earth did it happen?

One factor was the Barbie group at Ogilvy & Mather, the ad agency that had, in the seventies, acquired Carson/Roberts. By 1984—a year after Sally Ride's landmark space flight, the same year as Geraldine Ferraro's historic bid for the U.S. vice presidency—Mattel urged O&M creative director Elaine Haller and writer Barbara Lui to, in Lui's words, "express where women were and where they wanted their daughters to be at the time." Upon hearing that, Lui told me last year, she remembered her own childhood on Manhattan's Upper West Side. "My mother's words came to me," she said.

"My name is Barbara—I was called Bobbie at home—and my mother used to say, 'Bobbie, you can do anything,' " which, with a few revisions, became the doll's new slogan: "We girls can do anything, right, Barbie?"

And in 1985, it seemed "we girls" actually could. For the first time since the sixties, Barbie, in her Day-to-Night incarnation, was positioned *as* a career woman *by* career women who knew what it took to achieve in the business world. (Not in an idealized world, but in the one that really existed.)

What they came up with was Day-to-Night Barbie, a yuppie princess, equipped to charge, network, and follow the market. Her attaché case contains a credit card, a business card, a newspaper, and a calculator. Although her suit is baby-blanket pink rather than boardroom blue, it is tastefully cut and covers her knees. Her outfit, however, does more than look good during the day. Turn it inside out, and it is a fussy, glittery evening dress.

To decode the meaning of Day-to-Night Barbie, one must turn to the work of Joan Rivière, a female Freudian psychoanalyst, who in 1929 published an essay about a pattern she had begun to notice among her professionally accomplished female analysands. Many powerful women, Rivière discovered, were uncomfortable with their masculine strivings; to conceal them, they overcompensated, decking themselves out like caricatures of women. One woman, after giving a successful lecture, flirted idiotically and inappropriately; she also delivered her presentation in cartoonishly feminine clothes. Others exaggerated different aspects of femininity, and one even dreamt that she had been saved from a precipitous fall by wearing a mask. "Womanliness therefore could be assumed and worn as a mask," Rivière wrote, "both to hide the possession of masculinity and to avert the reprisals expected if [a woman] was found to possess it—much as a thief will turn out his pockets and ask to be searched to prove he has not the stolen goods."

In her book *Female Perversions: The Temptations of Emma Bovary*, psychoanalyst Louise J. Kaplan uses the term *homeovestism* for this strategy of cloaking one's cross-gender strivings by disguising oneself as a parody of one's own sex. It is the reverse of transvestism, in which one acts out one's cross-gender impulses by wearing the clothes of the opposite sex. Nor is homeovestism practiced exclusively by women. A male homeovestite, for instance, might mask his feminine urges by dressing up like Norman Schwarzkopf. In literature, Scarlett O'Hara seems a convincing example of a female homeovestite. She is as aggressive and tenacious as any biological male, but she conceals it behind fluttering eyelashes and an affected fragility. Of course, the only people who know they are homeovestites are the homeovestites themselves. It is, I suppose, possible for a woman to tart up like a Gabor sister and not know she is a caricature. But if a high-powered female executive wears enough makeup for a Kabuki performance, negotiates in a purr, tosses her hair coquettishly, unbuttons more than two buttons on her clinging silk blouse, and generally vamps around the conference table, she may well be a homeovestite.

Day-to-Night Barbie strikes me as a teaching implement for homeovestism. Clearly, the doll is meant to be a serious professional; her case contains the tools for executive achievement, where the idea of possessing a "tool," a colloquialism for the penis, implies a sort of phallic empowerment. Her nighttime outfit, however, is about hiding those "tools." Like the thief who turns out his pockets, the doll disguises herself by exposing herself. Her shoulders are bare; her toes are uncovered; her translucent skirt flutters around her legs. She is fluffy, girlish, vulnerable. By day, a virago; by night, Little Bo Peep.

Mattel issued Day-to-Night ensembles for other vocations as well. By rearranging her costume, any female achiever—teacher, dress designer, TV news reporter—can masquerade as Marla Maples or Donna Rice. Ken also has a Day-to-Night incarnation, but his seems to reflect cross-class rather than cross-gender strivings. By day, a TV sports reporter; by night, a Wayne Newton impersonator.

Although Kaplan categorizes homeovestism as a "perverse strategy," it strikes me as both cynical and pragmatic. Masculine business clothing has always been power-coded; something as subtle as the width of a pinstripe can signal an executive's status. But for women, the coding is less easy to decipher. Whether one likes it or not, there is a strong power-pulchritude nexus in business; making it to the top in a fashion or entertainment field involves not just the bottom line, but the hemline, neckline, hairline, etc. Of course too much glamour can be as bad as not enough. It interferes with a woman's ability to be taken seriously. But if one has to err, Barbie teaches, better soignée than sorry.

Barbie's 1986 astronaut incarnation certainly weighs in on the side of glamour. When Barbie first blasted off in 1965, she wore a baggy gray spacesuit. By 1986, you wouldn't catch her in that kind of *shmatte*. She comes with a hot pink miniskirt, a clear plastic helmet, sleek pink bodysuit, even silver space lingerie. "I thought Barbie would *dress* if she were on the moon," said Carol Spencer, the outfit's designer.

She-Ra, Princess of Power, is another Mattel toy from this period that explores the link between female strength and female beauty. Promoted with the slogan, "The fate of the world is in the hands of one beautiful girl," She-Ra, a five-and-a-half-inch action figure, was introduced as the sister of Mattel's He-Man in 1985, the same year as Day-to-Night Barbie. He-Man by then required no introduction. On the market since 1982, he and his fellow Masters of the Universe, based on a popular children's television show, were by 1984 second in sales only to Barbie.

She-Ra inhabits a world called Etheria, a curious mix of Middle Earth and Rodeo Drive. From what the catalogue terms its "plush rug and free-standing fireplace" to its "clothes tree for shields, swords and capes," She-Ra's Crystal Castle is a sort of Valhalla 90210, populated by sturdy, breast-plated females reminiscent of the biker Valkyries in Charles Ludlum's Wagnerian satire, *Der Ring Gott Farblonjet*. There is a villain named Catra

("Jealous Beauty!" the catalogue calls her), a secret agent named Double Trouble (who literally has two faces), a boyfriend named Bow, and several assorted allies including Castaspella, an "enchantress who hypnotizes." Because of their long, combable hair and their sparkling outfits the figures were introduced as "fashion dolls," but this group doesn't just change its clothes. Children can use the dolls to act out a struggle between females for the title of "most powerful woman in the Universe."

Although She-Ra is not outfitted for the boardroom, the doll, perhaps even more than Day-to-Night Barbie, seems to be an instructional tool for corporate achievement. She-Ra's state of nature is a state of perpetual war. All the inhabitants are armed, and some of them are dangerous. Women are designated as jealous, manipulative (spell-casting), and Janus-faced. And of all the weapons each doll possesses, perhaps the most potent is her beauty.

While She-Ra was not a flop—in the first of her two years on the market, she generated about $65 million in domestic sales—she never approached Barbie. Some say this is because the dolls were too robust. "They looked like lady wrestlers," observed collector Beauregard Houston Montgomery. But I suspect She-Ra's short life was predicated on metaphor. No matter what she wears, Barbie is a female fertility archetype. She-Ra, by contrast, lacked Barbie's pronglike feet; she and her pals could not plunge their toes into the earth, they merely stood solidly upon it. They had no totemic link to the power of the Great Mother. Their abundant hair and radioactive eye makeup are not enough. If Barbie is pure physical yin, they are, alas, rather yang.

Barad was inspired to create She-Ra and her world after a conversation with her sister, who had disparaged toymakers for inflicting silly, frilly playthings on American daughters. "It seemed time to offer little girls a role model who also had strength and power," Barad told *Working Woman* in 1990. And to play out the other early-eighties fantasy—"having it all," where "all" referred to children and a career—Barad invented the Heart

Family, a Barbie-sized couple that, unlike Barbie and Ken, were married and had a brood of plastic children.

The She-Ra state of war, however, far more than the Heart household's domesticity, reflected the atmosphere at Mattel during the dolls' development. By 1984, CEO Arthur Spear's diversification strategy had proved disastrous. Mattel was on the brink of bankruptcy. It had begun the year burdened by a staggering $394 million loss from the previous year. Like the executives at Warner Communications' Atari division, Spear had been seduced by the seeming boundlessness of the home video game market. To him, the country's craving for the likes of Pac-Man and Space Invaders looked insatiable. Inspired by Atari's gargantuan profits—from 1979 to 1980 Atari's sales increased from $238.1 million to $512.7 million—Mattel in 1980 introduced Intellivision, a competitor to Atari's home video system that in 1981 did, in fact, initially do well. The company's electronics division was also at work on a line of home computers.

But in 1983, when the home video game market crashed, Mattel crashed with it. Desperate to stay afloat, it began unloading its subsidiaries—Western Publishing, Circus World, Monogram Models—even its own electronics division. Ironically, all the companies whose stability was intended to offset the toy world's volatility were undergoing upheavals. And toys—particularly Barbie—were thriving.

It could be said that Barbie saved Mattel. Lured by her track record of profitability, venture capitalist E. M. Warburg, Pincus & Company, junk-bond king Drexel Burnham Lambert Inc., and merchant banking firm Riordan & Joseph supplied the toymaker with $231 million in capital in July 1984. It was, given her penchant for hanging out with celebrities, a classic Barbie moment. Her white knight at Drexel was none other than Michael Milken himself. The deal, however, was a huge gamble for Mattel's management and a reflection of its desperate straits. It had to risk losing control of the company to gain the funds to continue operating. The group was given a 45 percent voting interest in the toymaker; if, however, Mattel couldn't pay dividends on a new preferred stock held by the investors, each of their shares would inflate to 1.5 votes—giving them a controlling interest of 51 percent.

By December 1984, Mattel had rebounded, reporting an 81 percent increase in its fiscal third-quarter profit. This enabled it to pay off the dividends it owed on its preferred stock and, in 1985, to float another $100 million in junk bonds.

With Mattel's future resting on Barbie's slight shoulders, the Barbie team, like the warriors in Etheria, fought bitterly to rebuff her competitors—particularly a "full frontal attack," as Shackelford put it, from a doll called Jem. In the fall of 1985, Shackelford learned from undercover sources that Hasbro was planning to launch a new rock star fashion doll at Toy Fair in February. "All we needed to know was the theme," she said. "Within five minutes, we had a war council. Within an hour, we thought of what we were going to do." By the time Toy Fair rolled around, Mattel brought out an MTV version of Barbie—Barbie and the Rockers—with greater fanfare than Hasbro had prepared for Jem. Mattel even beat Hasbro at shipping its dolls to stores. But the thing that really killed Jem, doll experts say, was her size—twelve and a half inches—which made her too tall to wear Barbie's clothes. "If you're going to go up against General Motors," says doll dealer Joe Blitman, "you'd better be the same size."

Despite Barbie's constant triumphs in the marketplace, Spear stubbornly refused to place his faith in her. To attempt to reverse Mattel's fortunes, he launched new product lines—including Captain Power, a gimmicky electronic superhero that responded to cues in a Mattel-produced television cartoon program. In 1987, when Captain Power fizzled and Mattel reported a $113 million loss, John W. Ammerman, who had been in charge of its international division, replaced Spear as CEO.

Ammerman began his tenure with a machete; he slashed the payroll by

22 percent and refinanced $110 million of costly junk-bond debt. Heads rolled both at home and abroad: he closed ten factories—including those in Taiwan, the Philippines, and Paramount, California, Mattel's last domestic plant—leaving open only nine, all in countries with the lowest labor costs. It was during this upheaval and the unstable years before—a time that broke or battered other Mattel executives—that Barad flourished. "The company was going to hell," one executive told *Working Woman,* and Barad "not only survived it, she rose up out of the ashes."

Shackelford resigned in 1988. Rita Rao, who had left when Shackelford (and other people at Shackelford's and Rao's level) was made a vice president in 1978, returned. Until the dust settled, Barad removed herself from marketing to product development, a relative backwater. Then in 1988, she returned to lead the Barbie team. Supporters of Barad—and there are legions—suggest she made her way upward through a combination of brilliance and charm; detractors include guile as well.

In 1988, under Ammerman's guidance, Mattel's financial course did, in fact, reverse. It reported $35.9 million in earnings. The growth continued in 1989 with earnings of $79.6 million, more than double that of the previous year. Some of this rise can be attributed to the introduction of Holiday Barbie in 1988, a doll that pushed Mattel's market segmentation strategy a step farther, testing the waters to see if the mass market would spend more money on a deluxe version of the doll. "My motivation in doing it was to see if we could break a price barrier," Rita Rao explains. "Barbie pretty much has always been a ten-dollar doll, and it was kind of deemed an unspoken rule that you couldn't go past that. And I felt that in the long term for the company we had to . . . break through that barrier. And . . . to do it in a big way." Not only was Holiday Barbie successful, but "it opened the door for us to do Birthday Barbies and Talking Barbies and other things that were at the higher price point."

In 1989, Barad became president of the girls' and activities toys division;

then, in 1990, president of Mattel USA. She was elected to the board of directors in 1991. Soon she began to be lionized in the press—for her achievements, her youth, her beauty. Male colleagues were awed by her fluency in the language of clothes. "Her sense of product was exquisite," Tom Kalinske told me. "I think she still thought like a little girl. She had this way of looking at a hundred different ideas and saying, 'This one won't work because . . .' or 'This one will—and why don't you put a little more hair on it?' "

One year she told Kalinske, " 'We've got to put Barbie in an all-gold lamé gown,' " he recalled. "And I said, 'It's a really expensive fabric. Why can't we just put her in pink again?' " She said, 'Because gold lamé is really the "in" fabric.' Well, it wasn't at that particular moment, but by the time we brought the doll out, it was. Now how the hell do you know that?"

Even Ruth Handler, who does not compliment idly, praises Barad. As she and I thumbed through snapshots of Barad and herself receiving an award at a United Jewish Appeal function that had taken place shortly before our interview, she called Barad "terrific" and "smart."

Like She-Ra and the gang from Etheria, who had personal mythologies and wore talismans that represented their magical powers, Barad created a myth to explain her success and designated a piece of jewelry as its symbol. Each day, on her chic and impeccably accessorized ensembles, she pins a golden bee. "The bee is an oddity of nature," she explains in her official Mattel bio. "It shouldn't be able to fly but it does. Every time I see that bee out of the corner of my eye I am reminded to keep pushing for the impossible."

Given Barad's schedule, booking an interview with her meant "pushing for the impossible." Things kept cropping up—like her being named, on July 23, 1992, Mattel's CEO, the second-highest-ranking officer in the $1.6 billion company. (She has since been named COO.) Consequently, in September, after having finally secured an appointment, I was not surprised when she canceled. Her reason, however, floored me: she had been stung by a bee and was suffering a severe allergic reaction.

Happily, Barad rallied, and a few days later, with publicist Donna Gibbs adhering to my side like a Secret Service agent, I traversed the wide blue-carpeted halls of Mattel's executive enclave. Without relinquishing the trappings of corporate power—big desk, panoramic view—Barad had created a cozy atmosphere within her sprawling office. The place was thick with potted palms. Upscale collector baby dolls by artist Annette Himsteadt, whose company is owned by Mattel, were sprawled in eerily human positions on a couch. And refulgent in their sequins, the 1992 Empress Bride and Neptune's Fantasy Barbies—outfitted by Bob Mackie—twinkled on her desk.

Barad directed me to a conference table whose legs were planted on a thick Chinese carpet. The deep red rug sat atop wall-to-wall carpeting, and I felt myself sink into it. If Barad had deliberately coded her office to create a sense of softness and femininity, she couldn't have been more effective. Radiant amid the fronds, she was clad in a yellow silk suit with bold color splashes that resembled, on closer inspection, jungle animals. She wore shiny yellow slippers that seemed too perfect to have touched pavement. Nor had she abandoned her trademark bee. I had, of course, seen photos of her, but that did not prepare me for the perfect hair, seamless manicure, and makeup striking enough for television. She made the Barbies look unkempt.

As Andy Warhol's likeness of Barbie beamed down at us from the wall, Barad told how she had met the artist at a publicity party for She-Ra, and, after he revealed his fascination with Barbie, commissioned a portrait of the doll—a bold gesture, it struck me, in keeping with her philosophy of "pushing for the impossible." Inspired, I, too, decided to push, intrepidly asking if, as one of the country's top female executives, she defined herself as a feminist.

OFFICE OF MATTEL

COO JILL BARAD

SYLVIA PLACHY

"No," she said in a cool voice. "The fact is, I really don't know what that means. There are negative implications and positive implications. I'm very female. And I believe there are many dimensions to being a woman—and in my life I have been blessed with experiencing so many of those dimensions, whether it's being a mother, being a wife, being a friend, being an executive. Being so much. And I want kids to be able to realize all the different sides of being a woman too.

"I've been able to do that through toys," she continued. "Baby dolls teaching mothering and nurturing—the soft tender moments. Barbie saying, 'What's it gonna be like when I grow up?' Or Princess saying, 'I'll protect you.' Or the Heart Family—the whole family situation. It was very much not just a belief in me—but in all the people here in girls' toys—that we were going to explore all the parts of being a girl."

Barad shares with Ruth Handler the ability to disarm an interlocutor. I won't say our interview was exactly a pajama party, but something about that doll-packed room lent itself to girl talk. I found myself experiencing ancient feelings that I thought I had left behind in high school—a consciousness of myself as an owlish drudge dutifully recording, for the minutes of a club meeting, the wisdom of the homecoming queen. I was shaken by the terrible power of childhood archetypes. I felt like *Midge*.

Soon we were agreeing passionately that Barbie was "forever," as an icon, anyway. But I wondered if her sales could sustain their phenomenal growth. Was there a saturation point? In 1992, the average American girl owned seven Barbies; would twenty soon be the norm?

Barad likened a child's interest in Barbies to a woman's interest in clothes. "I don't know about you," she said, glancing at my outfit so disconcertingly that I checked to make sure I hadn't spilled something on it, "but I would imagine every year you buy something to put in your wardrobe that's new—that makes you feel like it's a fresh year, or it's the beginning of a season, or you have an event that you didn't have before." I nodded.

Kids are the same, she feels. "They really do go on to what's the latest, what's new, what's exciting."

I asked her if she viewed children as noble savages or beasts to be civilized. She rejected both extremes and talked about "magic . . . that keeps the child in all of us alive." I asked why no rival doll had ever successfully challenged Barbie—as if I, Midge, didn't know. "I think you've got heritage going," she explained. "We've got the marketing and product design talent. There really is no hole that somebody's going to come in and fill. And anytime someone comes after us frankly only makes us smarter and better. You've got to stay on your toes."

I lumbered flat-footedly out of the interview, wallowing in my Midge-hood. Something Camille Paglia told me sprang to mind: "Barbie truly is one of the dominant sexual personae of our time." What did it mean, I wondered, to identify with the personae of the supporting cast? If Barbie were Ur-woman, did that make me Ur-sidekick?

Barad has grumbled about accusations that she used her looks to advance herself—"I've seen very handsome men in business," she told the *Los Angeles Times*. "Does anyone ever say it's because he was so handsome that he got ahead?"—but after listening to her polished, diplomatic responses, I was sure that she hadn't. It did, however, cross my mind that she may have used her looks to camouflage her nonreliance on them—and, so briefly as to be almost unnoticeable, Day-to-Night Barbie flashed before my eyes.

But even with her record sales, the Barbie of the late eighties was not the vibrant virago of the early eighties. "We Girls Can Do Anything" gave way to "We're into Barbie," a slogan that suggests turning inward, away from active engagement with the world. "The viewpoint of people changed," Barbara Lui explained, "and the 'mommy track' came on, and women didn't believe anymore that they could do anything. We're in an era—perhaps we're leaving it now—where people did not give themselves goals that were as tough."

Lui did not get that idea out of the air; though whether it was true or not remains a subject of debate. "The supermom is fading fast—doomed by anger, guilt, and exhaustion," *Newsweek* reported in 1988. "A growing number of mothers" believe "that they can't have it all." Yet in her book *Backlash,* Susan Faludi points out that the survey on which *Newsweek* based the article revealed nothing of the sort. It found that 71 percent of mothers at home would prefer to work and 75 percent of the working mothers would go on working even if their financial needs could be otherwise met. Faludi also reports that *Good Housekeeping*'s 1988 "New Traditionalist" ad campaign, which featured born-again housewives happily recovering from the horrors of the workplace, was based on neither hard facts nor even opinion polls. The two opinion studies by the Yankelovich organization, which had allegedly buttressed *Good Housekeeping*'s position, had, in fact, showed no evidence that women were either leaving work or wanted to leave.

This is not to cast Barbie as a New Traditionalist. Even in retrograde times, she has never stayed at home against her will. The jobs on her 1989 résumé—physician, astronaut, veterinarian, fashion designer, executive, Olympic athlete—are impressive; a little girl could do worse than identify with such a doll. Her move away from demeaning stereotypes can also be documented. Compared with, say, the 1973 Barbie Friend Ship, in which Barbie is forced to play scullery maid to a painted-on pilot, the 1990 Flight Time Barbie, developed in 1989, is herself an aviatrix. But Flight Time Barbie is also a Day-to-Night doll, and her after-hours outfit, vastly more girlish than what she wore in 1985, undercuts her authority. In five years, her homeovestite behavior has intensified, suggesting that her achievements have left her fraught with anxiety.

What Flight Time Barbie wears at night is a Christian Lacroix–inspired "pouf" skirt that barely covers her plastic derriere. Susan Faludi draws a convincing parallel between the juvenilizing bubble skirts that Lacroix introduced in 1987 ("for women who like to 'dress up like little girls,' " he says) and the New Look that Christian Dior fobbed off on women forty years earlier. Both were fussy, ruffly, waist-cinched fashions that exaggerated female curves to the point of caricature and looked goofy on all but the adolescent and acutely svelte. Both came after a period of relative sartorial sanity: the dull but practical "Dress for Success" formula John Molloy coded in the seventies, and the dress-for-comfort system women coded for themselves during World War II. Both also followed a time when women had enjoyed opportunities for professional realization—when male soldiers returned from the war, women who had taken the men's jobs gave them back; just as, when unemployment soared after the 1987 stock market crash, women were urged through "mommy-track" propaganda to relinquish limited spots in the workforce to men.

Flight Time Barbie's Day-to-Night transformation parallels the fashion industry's late-eighties campaign to convince mature career women that it would be in their professional interest to dress like teenage cupcakes. The doll follows the established strategy of disguising her cross-gender strivings through exposure, except that she reveals more flesh than she did in 1985. It is as if the masculinizing necktie she wears in the cockpit is strangling her, and she must rip it off, the way that *Mademoiselle* in 1987 instructed fashion votaries to say "Bye-bye" to that relic of Molloyism, "the little bow tie." Or perhaps her excesses have another source: certainly the idea of a cockpit, where "cock" is a colloquialism for the penis, could have exacerbated her homeovestite panic, pushing her over the sartorial edge.

To be sure, Barbie is a toy, and in market research sessions, as Barbie's first advertising copywriter Cy Schneider has pointed out, children, presented with choices that can be characterized as "tasteful, gaudy, gaudier, or gaudiest," invariably choose "gaudiest." But Barbie is also a reflection of her times—or a reflection of how market researchers and professional prognosticators interpret them. And perhaps therein lies the paradox. Mattel hangs on every prediction of such national surveys as the Yankelovich

Youth Monitor, as well as its own market research. And it is not alone in this: few major companies make a move without consulting trained, high-tech prophets, even though futurists themselves acknowledge that the very act of anticipating the marketplace can influence it.

"When I as a futurist share our assumptions with the wide bunch of CEOs who are our clients, it's halfway to a self-fulfilling prophecy," explains Laurel Cutler, worldwide director of marketing planning for Foote Cone Belding, Inc., and vice chairman of FCB Leber Katz, who has been spotting trends for corporations for the last twenty-five years. "Because if you get enough people in enough different places thinking along the same lines, they start reinforcing each other and giving each other the support to proceed along those lines. There's one company that makes a fortune from predicting what the 'in' colors will be—in fashion, paint, wallpaper, and so on. But if you say, 'red, orange, and russet' to enough people in enough places early on—well, you see what I mean by halfway to a self-fulfilling prophecy."

Although women's sphere did contract in the late eighties, Barbie was not long bound by its constraints. Mattel had factories and branches all over the world, and by 1989, the world was on the verge of a radical change. When the Berlin Wall fell on November 9, Barbie, that coruscating cheerleader of consumption, gained a new mission. Capitalism had defeated its frumpy totalitarian foe. Czechs and Magyars, Poles and Latvians, Estonians, Lithuanians, Romanians, Ukrainians—all the citizens of the former Soviet bloc—were starved for style. They craved a model of free-market femininity, and Mattel moved in 1991 to provide them with one. As twilight fell on the Reagan decade, Barbie's star rose in the East.

CHAPTER SEVEN

PAPER DOLL

Before Barbie strides bravely into her fourth decade, let us roll the film back to her first. We have been considering her as a toy, an object, a distillation of the feminine principle. But she is also an invented personality. In recent years, to Mattel's chagrin, novelists and poets have imagined all manner of dark, rich, textured lives for her. She has, however, had a blander, authorized existence, too. With the 1961 debut of *Barbie* magazine, the Barbie Fan Club's official publication, Barbie took shape as a character in stories by Bette Lou Maybee and Cynthia Lawrence, two Carson/Roberts copywriters who were then in their thirties. Barbie also lent her name to Mattel's "Queen of the Prom: The Barbie Game," which, while not a narrative, can nonetheless be examined as an authorized text that sheds light on Barbie's world.

The strange thing about the stories and the game is that the values of one contradict the values of the other. The stories and novels, which were published in book form by Random House between 1962 and 1965, were revolutionary: In them, Barbie doesn't model herself on Mom, a self-abnegating slave in financial thrall to Dad; she finds a female mentor who points the

BARBIE COLLECTORS' CONVENTION, 1992

SYLVIA PLACHY

way to independence. The books also found large audiences. Issued simultaneously and packaged together, each of the first three books—*Here's Barbie, Barbie's New York Summer,* and *Barbie's Fashion Success*—sold about 80,000 copies (at $1.95 apiece) in their first year of publication. *Here's Barbie* sold best—88,656 copies as of June 1963. What is more, Barbie either kept pace with or outperformed other juvenile series. For an intraoffice presentation, Random House approximated that in 1962, one hundred thousand new Nancy Drew books were sold with 45,000 sales per new title, and 40,000 new Cherry Ames books were sold with 20,000 sales per new title.

Then there was the best-selling Barbie Game, which promoted a different agenda—exploiting men for financial gain and competing for them based on physical appearance. To appreciate why the Barbie novels were, for many girls, windows onto a wider world, one must reexperience the claustrophobia, cosseting, corseting, girdling, and cantilevering that underwired women in the late fifties. One must, in other words, roll the dice and plunge oneself into the mindset of the Barbie Game.

My friend Helen—I am not so pitiless as to call her by her real name—claims to have been horribly scarred by the game. She cannot forget the time that, in two hours of play, she was unable to get a boyfriend—not even Poindexter, the dud, the nerd, the untouchable. Helen had achieved almost everything she needed to win. She was "popular"; the Drama Club had elected her its president. She had a formal dress—indeed, the game's most expensive one, Enchanted Evening, a regal pink gown with a rabbit fur wrap. She had earned more money than the other players. But without a boyfriend, Helen was a washout. She couldn't even attend the prom, much less be crowned queen.

This cruel moment did not occur in 1961 when Helen was seven and Mattel first issued the game. This happened last summer, at one of the gatherings I convened to observe various adult female friends playing the game—just as I had been watching children play it. My purpose was not, as one sore loser accused, "to relive the worst moments in a girl's life," but to see whether women who grew up reading *Ms.* and discussing "sisterhood" could devolve into back-stabbing, predatory, cartoon mantraps out of Clare Boothe Luce's *The Women.* (They could.) I was also curious whether contestants' careers would influence their style of play. Would, say, lawyers and doctors compete more ruthlessly than painters and novelists?

Careers, I discovered, had little impact. After the first bottle of champagne (and the first groans over such instructions as "You are not ready when he calls. Miss 1 turn.") nearly everyone got a sort of crazed glint in her eye. An odd coincidence, however, was that although success in the game relied primarily on luck, people's real-life achievements—or shortcomings—were often reflected on the board. Helen, for instance, is a highly accomplished professional, but anguishes over her lack of a beau. Consequently, she was shaken by the eerie playing out of this difficulty. "I'm not telling my mother about this," she said. "But I am telling my therapist."

Touted on its box as "A fun game with real-life appeal for all girls," Queen of the Prom is set not in "real life" but in a precursor of She-Ra's state of nature—with a few Potemkin tract houses scattered about to create the illusion of a middle-class suburb. Or, more accurately, an upper-middle-class suburb. At a time when gum was ten cents and two could dine in a fashionable Manhattan restaurant for under twenty-five dollars, I doubt many youngsters from blue-collar families could afford to drop thirty-five to sixty-five dollars on a prom dress, as players are required to do. In the game, Dad does not sully his manicured nails on an assembly line. He plays the market; one "Surprise" card entitles a player to a ten-dollar present in celebration of Dad's "extra large stock dividend." Like Nancy Drew, who solved cases with her widower father, players of the Barbie Game have a close relationship with Dad; he turns up often in the "Surprise" cards as a source of cash. Having no money of her own, Mom, however, is virtually invisible.

The box promises competition in three areas—Shopping, Dating, and School Activities—evidently the only races that matter. The message is: Don't waste your time on academic, athletic, or artistic achievement—and especially, don't look inside yourself. Be outer-directed.

Significantly, the sketch illustrating School Activities does not show a classroom, a library, or a laboratory, but two stylish women standing around with sodas. They appear to be displaying themselves, which, according to sociologist Winni Breines, author of *Young, White and Miserable: Growing Up Female in the Fifties,* was a big part of what a teenage girl was expected to do. "The commodification of one's look became the basis of success," Breines writes. "Even the post-war dating system, in which dates were commodities that validated an individual's worth, was based on display, on being seen, since unseen, one's value could not be measured." High schools were a key place to be seen, which was "one of the main attractions of attending school."

In the game, the greatest rewards come not from skill or learning but from physical appearance. The largest sum of money a player can earn at one time is ten dollars for a modeling job, as opposed to, say, one dollar for washing dishes. Players are taught not to expect to profit from brainwork. One space in the "Earning Money" section invites the player to write a story for a magazine, only to jeer at the player's presumption: "Sorry—no sale."

It isn't as if looks alone are commodified; so are men. A player rolls the dice, lands on a potential boyfriend's face, and if she wants to win, she grabs him—even if he disgusts her. In the abridged version, boyfriend cards are predealt to players along with their allowance. It's easy to come away thinking: A boyfriend is a dress is a dollar.

If a player lands on a space with two arrows, she can move in either direction, except at the "School Entrance." School is neither optional nor pleasant; all but one square inside it promises misery. The lone desirable square grants straight A's to the player who lands on it—then, as a reward, instructs the player to hasten to any "Stop and Shop" space on the board. The subtext here: Achievement is never for its own sake; it is only meaningful as a stepping-stone to acquiring objects, particularly those that will enhance one's looks.

Nearly every square on the board is a land mine, especially for women who have grown up with feminist assumptions. Yet the game is strikingly efficient at reinforcing behavior—the way repeated electric shocks can persuade a laboratory rat to perform tricks against its will. Frequent landings at the "soda fountain," for instance, a square where players without boyfriends must surrender a dollar, have, in my observation, caused even committed lesbian feminists to stalk men—at least for the duration of the game.

To be fair, Mattel at almost the same time introduced a "Keys to Fame" game that encouraged little girls to try their hands at careers. But Queen of the Prom was the game that took off; it is the one boomers remember—especially for the splashy, eye-catching fifties graphics that belied its grim economic message. While playing it recently, I often brooded on the invisibility of the mother. Did little girls perceive Mom's absence as a victory in the war for Dad? Did they associate it with her status as a non-wage-earning entity? Or did they realize that they, too, could be headed in Mom's direction—a glistening prom queen one minute, a shadow the next?

I also thought of Ernest Dichter's market research on Barbie—the way he urged Mattel to exploit mothers' dark, unarticulatable fear that without a stern tug in the right direction, their boyish daughters would grow up into unmarriageable brutes. In Queen of the Prom, as in the card game Old Maid, to be ugly, frowzy, or manless is to be shut out forever from success.

To a degree, the three Barbie short-story collections and eight Barbie novels that Random House published are set in a similar world—the world of proms and boyfriends and "school activities." But Barbie Millicent Roberts, as the fictive character is called, reflects the biases and experiences of the young, independent women who told her stories. In 1962, a year before Betty Friedan identified "the problem that has no name" in *The Feminine Mystique*, Cynthia Lawrence dramatized it in her novel *Barbie's New York Summer.* In it, Margaret Roberts, Barbie's housebound mother, lurches from sacrifice to sacrifice; if she isn't renouncing some pleasure to accommodate her husband, George, she is torturing herself for Barbie. Flabbergasted by her masochism, Barbie finally blurts, "Mother, don't you ever want anything for yourself?" To which Mrs. Roberts, after weirdly taking stock of her living-room furniture, replies: "I have you till you're grown and I have Dad. You're the one who has an exciting career ahead of you."

Far from patterning herself on Mom, Barbie models herself after autonomous professional women. She has a string of glamorous female mentors who introduce her, and, by extension, millions of little girls (by 1966, the Barbie Fan Club had a million members), to the idea of economic self-sufficiency. These women have men in their lives, but they aren't dependent on them. Their autonomy is portrayed as desirable; none attended the Joan Crawford school of executive gorgonhood. Paula Foxx, a West Coast swimsuit designer who, in Bette Lou Maybee's *Barbie's Fashion Success,* invites Barbie to intern with her company, slips into the Roberts "family circle as naturally, as warmly, as any ordinary woman might have done." She is "not some cold, frightening creature that oozed sophistication."

Barbie's mother welcomes Foxx—even though Foxx's mode of existence implicitly calls Mrs. Roberts's into question. Instead of seeking self-validation by creating Barbie in her image, she goes the stage mother route. She admires Foxx for recognizing "what a pretty and talented daughter I have," where "I have" is a significant detail. Barbie is her possession—like the living-room furniture—and she enjoys having its quality discerned.

Like the world depicted on *Father Knows Best,* Barbie's cosmos is a comforting place for children. Justice prevails. Conflicts resolve. Life isn't random; actions have a cause and effect. Barbie's relentlessly nonethnic parents don't drink, fight, gobble tranquilizers, or have extramarital dalliances. Nor does Willows, the generic midwestern town where Barbie lives, teem with heroin addicts or teenage runaways. Barbie does not stew over nuclear war—or class or race war, for that matter. Asians, African Americans, and Hispanics apparently do not live in Willows, though an Italian-American family turns up in one of the later stories.

Significantly, Barbie cannot bear family conflict—in her own or anybody else's. Wherever she goes, she hatches plots to reconcile parents with their estranged children, and she is not above resorting to deception to patch up domestic rifts. Were Barbie neither fetching enough to model nor deft enough to design clothes, she could have a big future in family therapy.

Although the Barbie who emerges in Maybee's and Lawrence's fiction is slim, smart, and adept at winning national talent competitions, she manages to escape total obnoxiousness through a couple of humanizing imperfections. One is her sexual insecurity: Never mind that she looks great; she fears that other women look better and will divert male attention away from her. In Bette Lou Maybee's "Barbie's Big Prom," published in *Barbie* magazine's inaugural issue, she smolders with jealousy during the visit of her cousin, an orange-haired hussy from New Orleans. Barbie's other refreshing flaw is her petulance; she is moody, afflicted with "rare streaks of being just plain ornery," which today might be diagnosed as premenstrual huffs.

Issues of friendship and "popularity" arise as frequently in Barbie's fictive world as they do in high school. Barbie has male and female friends, but in the early stories her relationships with members of her own gender are rocky. Perhaps as a consequence of her chronic sexual jealousy, Barbie's sidekicks are invariably less comely and clever than she. Midge is "a round berry" with an impulsiveness that clouds her judgment, so eager in Cynthia Lawrence's "My Friend the Pioneer" to impress a certain boy that she lies about her wilderness skills, endangering Barbie and herself. Then there's Jody Perkins, an astrology nut whose greatest aspiration is to marry money. "There are more important things to dream about than being rich," Barbie reprimands. "Name one," Jody counters.

Lawrence's *Barbie Solves a Mystery,* in which Barbie's sleuthing straightens out the life of a prominent Willows-born fashion designer, cries out for comparison with Nancy Drew. And the two gumshoes have more in common than their golden hair. Ned Nickerson, Nancy's beau, is as much of a dishrag as Ken—indeed, Ned is so ineffectual that Nancy's car runs faster than his. The "man" in Nancy's life is, of course, Carson Drew, her widowed father, whose stunning inability to solve cases without his daughter has curiously never impaired his professional standing. Barbie, by contrast, does not turn to her father when Ken proves inadequate; she dates other boys. There is little incestuous tension in the Barbie novels. Mr. and Mrs. Roberts are very much a separate unit.

Barbie and Nancy have personality differences, too. In *Rascals at Large, or the Clue in the Old Nostalgia,* Arthur Prager suggests that for prepubescent girls, identifying with Nancy "is within reach. . . . She is pretty but not beautiful." Identifying with Barbie is harder, but, because of her humanizing imperfections, not impossible. Nancy also has a richer spectrum of sidekicks with whom less-conventional girls can identify, ranging from necktie-wearing George to frilly Bess, who quakes at the sight of spiders.

This is not to say Barbie doesn't have a supporting cast—by far the strangest of which is "Big Bertha," a self-hating size fourteen who develops an unwholesome fixation on Barbie in Lawrence's "The Size 10 Dress." Humiliated during a hygiene class "weigh-in," Big B. waddles off to the doctor, who places her on a diet. As Bertha suffers a cruel withdrawal from cream pies, Barbie, who has no trouble extending herself to blubbery girls, cheers her on. Then a funny thing happens. Bertha not only slims down, she transforms herself into Barbie—affecting the same ponytail, the same clothes, even the same *laugh.* Barbie tries to be tolerant; after all, Bertha's mom is dead and, consequently, unavailable for fashion guidance. Naturally

Bertha would want to model herself on the most tasteful girl in school. But having a doppelgänger freaks her out, and in the great tradition of small-town Protestants who have not been psychoanalyzed, she is seized by "emotions so strange that she could not understand them herself."

Perhaps if Barbie had watched *All About Eve* she might have had a clue. But deliberately oblivious to the murky forces that might underlie Bertha's behavior, Barbie addresses its surface manifestation—she helps Bertha personalize a dress that Bertha had copied from one of hers—and curing the symptom evidently vanquishes its cause. Darkness dissolves quickly in Willows. At the sewing-class fashion show, Barbie and Bertha hold hands in a "warm spotlight"—which, given the possible homoerotic subtext to Bertha's reinventing herself as the object of her fixation, is a curious resolution. But such undercurrents remain buried in commercial fiction, and the story's moral, seemingly, is this: It's okay to want to be like Barbie, but you shouldn't try to *be* Barbie.

Although Barbie's refusal to look inward—a common limitation of characters in commercial fiction—is exasperating in "The Size 10 Dress," it is less annoying in *Barbie's New York Summer,* a novel that charts the same superficial terrain as Sylvia Plath's relentlessly introspective novel, *The Bell Jar.* Both Plath's character Esther Greenwood and Barbie Roberts are small-town girls who have earned guest editorships at fictional Manhattan magazines—*Ladies' Day* and *Teen Journal,* respectively. Plath herself was awarded a guest editorship at *Mademoiselle,* Joan Didion won *Vogue*'s Prix de Paris—such internships were, in the fifties, a commonplace stepping-stone in a writing career. They also had a Cinderella quality: "Look what can happen in this country," Plath's heroine comments with irony. "A girl lives in some out-of-the-way town for nineteen years, so poor she can't afford a magazine, and then she . . . wins a prize here and a prize there and ends up steering New York like her own private car."

Because Barbie's story is told in a young adult novel and not in a literary one, it is considerably less raw than Esther's. But there are similarities. Both are frustrated by commitments to oafish boyfriends back home—"calm, steady" Ken Carson, who cannot reach the "cloudland" where Barbie lives, and Buddy Willard, a plodding figure whose genitalia, while not nearly as deficient as a Ken doll's, will live in infamy for having reminded Esther of "turkey neck and turkey gizzards." Both are squired around Manhattan by exotic New York men—Esther by United Nations interpreter Constantin something-or-other (a name Esther cannot pronounce, because it is "full of S's and K's") and Barbie by Pablo Smith, a rich Brazilian who aspires to be a playwright. Both also had female mentors keen to mold them—*Ladies' Day* editor Jay Cee for Esther and *Teen Journal* chief Cornelia Desmond for Barbie.

Esther is, however, a few years older than Barbie, and the thrill of being a protégée has worn off. "Why did I attract these weird old women?" she laments. "They all wanted to adopt me in some way, and, for the price of their care and influence, have me resemble them." One wonders if with time Barbie, too, will grow disenchanted with her Pygmalions.

For both Barbie and Esther, clothes represent a great deal more than protection against the elements. One reason Barbie applied to *Teen Journal* was to get "a whole New York wardrobe, free." Like a Berlitz student mastering a foreign accent, she scrutinizes stylish Manhattan women and shortens her dresses so she will resemble them. Esther also judges by appearance, coolly decoding messages of sexual availability and social status in other women's outfits. Consequently, when Esther hurls all of her clothes off the roof of her hotel, it is a forceful declaration of her madness—a rejection of the feminine language she has taken pains to learn. In both novels, fashionability is, for women, the outward manifestation of mental health: Barbie, who is allegedly sane, collects clothes; Esther, who is growing flakier by the minute, flings them into the street.

In the same way that Esther—seasoned, jaded—is critical of her mentors, she is also violently ambivalent about her mother. When Esther, who by this time is in a mental hospital, describes her mother "begging [her] with a sorrowful face to tell her what she had done wrong," it is hard not to think of Mrs. Roberts and her eerie, masochistic relationship to Barbie. If the conventions of the genre had permitted Barbie to look inward, would she, too, have been revolted by her mother's manipulative self-denial? Certainly Barbie's flight from a future resembling her mother's suggests a horror of it, and, by extension, of her. "I hate her," Esther shouts in response to her therapist's inquiry about her mother. "I suppose you do," the therapist replies. Is this what lies ahead for Barbie?

Yet the struggle to become independent and separate from one's mother is not a problem unique to Barbie; it is, for all girls, a core aspect of prepubescent development. In *The Reproduction of Mothering: Psychoanalysis and the Sociology of Gender*, Nancy Chodorow, building upon observations of psychoanalyst Helene Deutsch, describes detachment strategies that could have been inspired by the Barbie novels: "A girl . . . tries to resolve her ambivalent dependence and sense of oneness [with her mother] by projection and by splitting the good and bad aspects of objects; her mother and home represent bad, the extrafamilial world, good. Alternately, she may try in every way to be unlike her mother. (She may idealize a woman teacher, another adult woman or older girl, or characters in books or films and contrast them to her mother.) In this case her solution again involves defensive splitting along with projection, introjection, and the creation of arbitrary boundaries by negative identification (I am what she is not)."

Of course there is no way Cynthia Lawrence, who published *Barbie's New York Summer* in 1962, could have been literally influenced by the *The Bell Jar*; it was published pseudonymously in England in 1963 and did not appear in America until 1971—having been delayed by Plath's mother's vigorous campaign to suppress it. Yet within the circumscriptions of its genre, *Barbie's New York Summer* actually does address the problems of a talented young girl learning to define and achieve her goals. It is also filled with sophisticated jokes, including an interior monologue in which Barbie, while modeling for a photographer, expresses outrage at being treated like a doll or mannequin. "I felt like a piece of merchandise," she grumbles. Lawrence also slyly freezes Barbie in sexy stills from popular culture—such as this image inspired by Marilyn Monroe standing over a subway grate in *The Seven Year Itch:* "A sudden gust of wind caught [Barbie's] full skirt and made it flutter like a flag. She clamped it down with her palms as Pablo laughed."

Nor do Barbie's Boswells interpret her character identically. What stands out in the fiction of Bette Lou Maybee—whose family, she told me, immigrated to America before the Revolution—is Barbie's fierce democratic tendencies. Life is portrayed as a meritocracy: Rich kids who exploit their parents' wealth or social position do not get ahead, they get their comeuppance. In *Barbie's Hawaiian Holiday*, a novel unfortunately dated by its phonetic renderings of Chinese-accented English, Maybee rages against monarchism and the evils of an inflexible class system. In one scene, the woman with whom Barbie and her family are staying rhapsodizes about how King Kamehameha and his troops united Hawaii by driving a rival chieftain's army off a steep bluff. "It was probably Clara's British background that made her think so highly of monarchies," Maybee writes in Barbie's voice. "Even when these were achieved at the cost of pushing people off cliffs."

Barbie, Midge and Ken (1964), Lawrence and Maybee's last anthology, contains their most openly subversive stories. "She's a Jolly Good Fellow" and "Go Fly a Kite" are about girls whose opportunities have been limited because of their gender. In "She's a Jolly Good Fellow," Willows High School's first female class president—who ascends from the vice presidency when the male president abdicates—overcomes gender-based prejudice. And in "Go Fly a Kite," Skipper and a female friend defiantly enter a boys' kite-making contest. They don't win, but they don't embarrass themselves either. Instead, Maybee introduces a young boy who actually helps Skipper construct her kite—an underage avatar of the seventies "Sensitive Male."

I asked Maybee, who is currently retired on the West Coast, if she and Lawrence had intended their stories to open windows for girls. "I was born in the wrong part of the century myself, and probably there was some ventilating," Maybee said. "I never fitted into the whatever-women-were-supposed-to-be kinds of roles. And ["Go Fly a Kite"] was probably out of one of my childhood experiences." The novels, I learned from Maybee, were produced under acute deadline pressure; she worries there may have been stylistic flaws because there wasn't enough time to rewrite. But the authors definitely did incorporate their experiences in their stories. Lawrence, who grew up in New York, wrote *Barbie's New York Summer;* Maybee, who was raised in Seattle and lived on the West Coast, wrote novels set in San Francisco and Hawaii. And while Paula Foxx, the mentor figure and swimsuit designer in Maybee's *Barbie's Fashion Success,* was not literally modeled on beachwear manufacturer Rose Marie Reid, there are elements of Reid in her personality—a reflection of Maybee's having written advertising copy for Reid's company. In *Sex and the Single Girl,* Helen Gurley Brown elevated Reid as a paradigm of female financial independence: a "swimsuit wizardess . . . off and running at the success steeplechase." If one accepts Brown's book as a progressive tome, this makes Reid an equally progressive role model.

After speaking with Maybee, I was baffled: How could Mattel—maker of the Barbie Game—place its imprimatur on these lively, seditious books? Further investigation, however, suggested a possibility: No one at Mattel had actually read them. Not one of the hundreds of letters exchanged between the toymaker and Random House—preserved in the Random House archive at Columbia University—alludes to the content of the books. There are dozens of memos about the correct placement of the trademark symbol on various title pages. There are multiple complaints from Ruth Handler that the books didn't have enough pictures. There is even a lengthy exchange about where the Handlers should stay when they visited Manhattan in August 1963; this includes a letter from the manager of the New York Hilton, who, presenting himself as a friend of Random House editor Robert Bernstein, recommends its Tower Suites, which then ran between $175 and $250 a day. There are royalty statements—and rejoinders from Mattel saying that the royalties are both insufficient and not reported often enough. But never do issues of plot or character or tone or appropriateness emerge in the correspondence.

This is not to say that such issues were not discussed by the executives on, say, the telephone. Lawrence, Maybee, and Random House editor Louise Bonino conferred about the content; Bonino required a "screen treatment" for each book, Maybee told me, "to psyche out whether we were Johnny One Note or we could actually write this novella." But Mattel seemed to view the books not as texts but as products—or vehicles for selling products. In December 1964, Mattel instructed Random House to have its illustrator depict Barbie in renderings of the doll's actual clothes, sending along its toy catalogue for reference. And while this may reflect excessive sentimentality on my part, I was shaken by the brutal way Mattel announced its phase-out of Midge. In a letter dated August 31, 1965, Mattel sales promotion manager Bernard L. Gottlieb ordered Robert Bernstein to purge her "from your thinking."

The later Barbie books—*Barbie's Hawaiian Holiday, Barbie Solves a Mystery, Barbie and Ken, Barbie in Television, Barbie, Midge and Ken, Barbie and the Ghost Town Mystery, Barbie's Secret,* and *Barbie's Candy-Striped Summer*—did not live up to the promise of the original three. Sales plummeted; the last three sold barely twenty thousand copies. Compiled by Lawrence in 1964, *Barbie's Easy as Pie Cookbook*—which includes recipes for "Pineapple Egg Nog," "Crispy Liver Steaks," and "Swedish Prune

Pudding"—did, however, find a following and is still popular with collectors; it was issued in a modified version to delegates at the 1992 Barbie-doll
collector's convention.

One reason for the demise of the Barbie series was that just as Midge had
been scrapped, so were Lawrence and Maybee. Recorded in correspondence
from July 1963, the decision to retire them came after Bernstein lunched
with them in Los Angeles and Lawrence had the temerity to suggest that
they might get an agent. Why would they want to give away ten percent of
their royalties, Bernstein countered, when the publisher was paying them
the most money that it possibly could? Rather than wait for an answer,
Random House brought in new authors—seemingly without bothering to
ascertain if they could write. So sloppy is the language in Eleanor Woolvin's
1965 opus, *Barbie and the Ghost Town Mystery*, that one wonders if anyone
even proofread it. In a scene that cries out for a translator, Barbie, Skipper,
and two male consorts follow a stray donkey through an abandoned desert
town. Woolvin writes, "With the donkey's *noisesome* [italics mine] voice to
guide them, it was not too difficult." Does that mean the donkey had bad
breath?

With Woolvin's byline on the title page of the last three books, it's not
surprising that the series bit the dust. Even children, I think, know when
quality has fallen off. But edited by Gloria Tinkley, Cy Schneider's secretary, and written by Carson/Roberts copywriters Vel Rankin, Barbara
Charlebois, and Nancy Joffe, *Barbie* magazine soldiered on through the sixties. In addition to fashion pieces and promotions for the doll, it featured
educational articles on foreign countries and on famous women in history—
predictable characters like Florence Nightingale and Helen Keller, sur-
prises like Mary McLeod Bethune, an African-American educator. Re-
designed in 1970, it limped into the Me Decade with a new name—*Barbie
Talk*—but did not make it through the seventies alive.

Barbie's fictional persona, however, transcended the death of the magazine. In 1983, while the "We Girls Can Do Anything" campaign took shape on the West Coast, Mattel approached *Muppet Magazine* publisher Donald E. Welsh and editor Katy Dobbs to create a fresh fanzine for the doll. By the winter of 1984, *Barbie, The Magazine for Girls*—thirty-two glossy full-color pages of fashion, hair care, recipes, and gift ideas—was born.

It was not, however, an easy delivery. Because the new magazine's target audience was younger than the original's—six- to seven-year-olds instead of eight- to eleven-year-olds—it couldn't feature long stories about Barbie; kids that age couldn't read them. Instead, Barbie's life unfolded in a "photodrama," a narrative made from pictures of real dolls over which comic-strip-style talk balloons had been superimposed. Integrating images and text would seem simple enough, but for the writer and photographer of the original drama, it wasn't. The feature came out so disastrously that Mattel had to pulp its half-million-dollar maiden printing and try again. (Highlights of the aborted drama: Barbie giggles while trying to run over Ken in her pink Corvette and lunches in the snow at an outdoor McDonald's—the photograph of which has been printed backward so that the menu looks as if it were written in Russian.)

Within months, though, the photodrama, written by the editors and realized by photographer Donal Holway, became a cult sensation. When in 1986, the magazine spent $1,500 for miniatures of original furniture by designers associated with the then-chic "Memphis" style—Ettore Sottsass, Flavio Albanese, Saporiti and Felice Rossi—*House & Garden* took note in a piece called "Barbie Goes Milano." A kitschy, self-conscious send-up of 1950s suburbanism that defined itself in opposition to modernism, "Memphis" was well suited to the campy tone of the photodrama. Sottsass originally intended the style as "an ironic gesture," Stephen Bayley observed in *Taste: The Secret Meaning of Things*, but through overexposure in magazines like *House & Garden* it became "just another style of rich man's chic."

Holway was equally attentive to details of clothing and real estate. In "Barbie Goes to Brazil," Barbie's glitzy record producer wore a tiny, non-Mattel-issue Rolex, and the "windows" of his office showed a real view from atop Rockefeller Center. Like Lawrence's and Maybee's stories, many of the photodramas dealt with Barbie's domestic life; but they also jump-started girls' imaginations: the tale that began in the record company office took Barbie to Carnaval in Rio de Janeiro—a swirl of dolls in wild costumes, including men in apparent drag. It even had captions in Portuguese.

Although Mattel never formally codified rules for the dramas, it had guidelines. No attempt was made to provide continuity with the original novels. George and Martha Roberts, that Friedan-era prototype of marital inequity, were erased forever. "We couldn't show Barbie's family except for Skipper," explained Karen Tina Harrison, *Barbie* editor until 1989. "She has no family. These stories are episodic. They have no background. Barbie has no biography to be passed on. Barbie simply is. No one knows where she came from or how she got there." As to the way she could be portrayed, drudgery—or even, say, seeing patients in her physician incarnation—was out. "Only glamour could befall Barbie," Harrison said.

Barbie's Italian counterpart was not, however, similarly constrained. Its photodramas were described by Welsh Publications editorial director Katy Dobbs as operatic. This meant that on one occasion, Barbie, in a fit of jealous rage, slugged a rival female doll with her handbag. Another time, Barbie and Ken were spelunking and a huge Styrofoam rock fell on Ken, leaving him covered with blood. "We can't do anything like that," she said. Inevitably, though, staging even a tame photodrama involves implicit carnage; in order for a doll to be photographed seated, its legs must be broken. Dobbs sighed: "You have to wipe out so many dolls to do a crowd scene."

Barbie also introduced little girls to real-life superstars—frequently on the eve of a scandal. Vanessa Williams squeaked into the magazine shortly before her lesbian porn shots were unearthed. Likewise Drew Barrymore, then about the same age as *Barbie*'s readers, was portrayed as a wholesome preteen—not as the drug-addicted boozer she later declared herself to be. Nor has profiling celebrities always been fun. "We gave Drew this dress to wear and her mother took one look at it and snarled, 'Barrymores don't wear green,'" Harrison recalled. "So we convinced her it was teal, and the kid wore the dress. Of course we had to give [the kid] everything she touched, but that's standard."

After Harrison left, the magazine became less about whimsy and more about selling products. Current photodramas are not geared to whisking kids off on flights of fancy, but to showing them predictable scenarios that they can play out with Mattel-authorized miniatures. Dramas are set in Mattel-issue settings; the pictures function like illustrations in toy catalogues. From a marketing standpoint, this may be a more effective way to promote merchandise, and Barbie sales, in the 1990s, have certainly skyrocketed. But it seems dry and joyless, stultifying to children's imaginations—not what Barbie, in her most positive, door-opening sense, should be.

Maybe it was a reflection of the difference between West Coast and East Coast style—or between the styles of marketing and journalism—but Katy Dobbs, who is based in New York, was the first top-level Barbie person who leaped to define herself as a "feminist." "I take my daughter to marches," Dobbs told me. "We're pro-choice." Then she related feminism to the doll, which her six-year-old little girl has played with for years: "I think Barbie is about options—options in fantasy, options in play patterns, options in opportunities. . . . There's more to her than just the pink and the plastic. Because every little girl brings to her a different orientation and [to attack her] is sort of taking away the individuality of what each little girl brings. I think Mattel does a really good job of offering her in many different ways for different kinds of girls. I mean, somebody's going to buy Marine Corps Barbie—not me."

Dobbs's chaotic Madison Avenue office was the antithesis of Jill Barad's plush inner sanctum, yet Dobbs appeared unrattled by the turmoil. There were, not surprisingly, Barbie and Muppet images everywhere, but also a plastic Mickey Mouse atop her desk and a Mickey video playing on a TV monitor—to which, because of a temporary child-care crisis, her toddler son was glued. He soon developed an interest in the interview, however, and plopped himself on his mother's lap, where he assiduously applied himself to unbuttoning her sweater.

As Dobbs continued her narrative—deftly closing the buttons her son had opened—I was struck by the total un-Mattel-ness of the operation. Except for Dobbs, most of the staff appeared to be in their twenties, and the office felt like that of a campus newspaper. When *Barbie* magazine was started, Dobbs, too, was virtually fresh out of school, after having spent a deracinated childhood as a military brat whose father was from Alabama and whose mother was from Zagreb, Croatia. She feels her career is representative of her baby-boom contemporaries. "When I first came to New York, all I did was go to book parties—eat shrimp—and hang out at Studio [54]," Dobbs said, "because I was at Condé Nast covering entertainment. Then I got married and had kids and now I'm doing this."

But even with its deliberate turning away from seamy reality, putting out the magazine has its somber moments. Beverly Cannady, whose first job at Mattel in the sixties was answering Barbie's mail, observed a poignant pattern to the way kids related to the doll. The magazine has always existed to promote Barbie as a commercial product; but kids look to her as an oracle— a vivid, godlike presence in the landscape of childhood. And sometimes, with aching candor, they'd beg Barbie to help stabilize their parents' rocky marriages or mitigate tragedies in their lives.

Many letters to Barbie, in fact, have such a Miss Lonelyhearts quality that they are too gloomy to print. To ask kids to send in their three wishes is to invite heartbreak. "It's like when you blow out your birthday candles, you go: 'Wait. Should I go personal or global here? Should I go for me or for world peace?' " Dobbs told me. "So a lot of them start out with 'Clean up the world, make peace, [then they'll add] my mommy and daddy not get divorced.' " Karen Tina Harrison was so touched by some of the unpublishable letters that she saved them and occasionally responded to them. One note that accompanied a strangely anguished self-portrait simply said: "My name is Tequila. I am 8 years old. With brown eyes. Black long hair. Brown skin."

Although many big-time models like Christy Turlington currently sport navel rings, body modification has been banned from the magazine; even showing a model with pierced ears enrages some mothers. I wanted to press Dobbs about other forbidden topics, but she had an excellent pretext to avoid my question. Her son's diaper had become, well, noisome, requiring her immediate attention.

As I left her office, Bret Mirsky, the magazine's editor in 1992, presented me with a set of back issues that, except for their graphics, were virtually identical to the those of the sixties. True, there were small differences: In 1963, 1968, and 1970, the magazine featured articles on becoming an airline hostess; by 1990, Barbie was the pilot of the plane. And in the old magazines, pages with educational material—articles on history and geography—seemed to outnumber pages with ads. But even the child-star drug scandals had counterparts in the past. Drew Barrymore's prepubescent coke addiction paled next to the fate of Anissa Jones—"Buffy" on CBS's *Family Affair*—who, in 1969 and 1971, was profiled in both *Barbie* and *Barbie Talk*. Jones died at eighteen in 1976 from an overdose of cocaine, Quaaludes, and barbiturates that Oceanside, California, coroner Robert Creason called "the largest drug combination of any case I have ever encountered."

The similarity between *Barbie* then and *Barbie* now was startling. It suggested that the transformations allegedly wrought by feminism had been either merely cosmetic or nonexistent. It was even more uncanny to learn that Western Publishing had resurrected "Queen of the Prom: The Barbie Game" and issued it with two new board games—"Barbie's Dream Date" and "We Girls Can Do Anything."

Although one six-year-old I browbeat into playing We Girls Can Do Anything with me described the game as "BOOOOR-ing," I enjoyed it. Players make "career moves" and endure "career setbacks" to become musicians, actresses, pilots, fashion designers, physicians, or ballerinas. The game's bright fuschia graphics and lurid photos of actual dolls, however, are somewhat garish; grown-ups may require sunglasses to stare at the board. Unlike the Mattel games from the sixties, which featured stylish line drawings of Barbie and her crowd, the new ones are illustrated exclusively with photographs. This no doubt helps young children recognize products, but it does not enhance nascent taste.

Nor is the revised Queen of the Prom identical to the original. Like the new *Barbie* magazine, the game is aimed at younger consumers—ages five and up. So the odious "Surprise" cards, which had to be read, are gone. Gone, too, are references to school or school clubs. Girls compete based on cars, clothes, looks, and boys. The collecting of female friends, although possible, slows a player down; a boyfriend is the only human trophy required to win. This suggests a certain prescience on the part of the game's makers: long before Thelma and Louise flickered subversively in a studio screening room, they sensed that female bonding was dangerous—and, consequently, to be quashed.

But compared with Barbie's Dream Date, the revised Queen of the Prom might have been written by the editors of *Ms.* This game isn't merely about winning approbation based on looks, it's about piling up expensive gifts from men. So similar is players' behavior to that of a call girl that it might more aptly be termed "The Hooker Game." Barbie's Dream Date is a race against time; each player's mission is to make Ken spend as much money as possible on her before the clock strikes twelve. When time runs out, players tally up their date and gift cards, and the one with the most cards wins. "If there is a tie, players with the same number of cards count their *date cards only*," the directions instruct. Like the floozy with the fullest Rolodex, "the girl with the most date cards wins."

Even in the vast contradictory morass that is Barbie history, the idea of We Girls Can Do Anything and the Hooker Game occupying adjacent shelf space is dumbfounding. Yet the more I inquired about the "We Girls" campaign, the more I learned that many male executives loathed it. "I can remember sitting in meetings with just people from the agency—and I won't name names—but the men were very resistant to the 'We Girls' ads," said Barbara Charlebois, who wrote for the original *Barbie* magazine and remained with Ogilvy & Mather after it acquired Carson/Roberts. "They really thought they were very offensive—well, you know how men are. Anything that's feminist or that says we girls can do anything or anything that says we girls are as good as you boys is very . . ." she trailed off, but I got the picture.

This perception, which, other sources confirm, extended to Mattel itself, made the contradictory threesome—We Girls Can Do Anything, Queen of the Prom, and the Hooker Game—comprehensible. Let 'em take one step forward, the message seemed to be, as long as they take two steps back.

I could end this chapter here, with Barbie sold into virtual white slavery for a dinner, a ski trip, and some bottles of perfume. But there is more to Barbie than that. Little girls know it; I have yet to watch kids play "Let's Fleece Ken" with real dolls—and I have watched a lot of kids at play. But because Barbie does, in fact, reflect the authentic condition of women, what shimmers in her rose-colored mirror is not always what one wants to see. Forget the new professions on Barbie's résumé; in this game, she practices the oldest one.

In December 1990, however, Marvel Comics rescued Barbie by providing an alternative to her sordid board-game identity. It began *Barbie* and *Barbie*

Fashion comic books, which, written by Lisa Trusiani and Barbara Slate, and edited by Hildy Mesnik, are sharp, sly, and very much in the tradition of Maybee's and Lawrence's novels. Even Diana Huss Green, the fierce Massachusetts-based watchdog of children's culture, gave them her blessing: In 1992, Parent's Choice, the organization she founded in 1978, singled the books out as reading material of quality.

Perhaps the most redeeming thing about the comic books is that they are hand-drawn. Although brand recognition may be one of their by-products, they do not exist to promote specific dolls. The constraining effect of photographs on children's imaginations has been overcome. Barbie exists as an open-ended construct, not a patented plastic one.

The uninitiated might dismiss *Barbie Fashion* as a pretext for Barbie to change clothes. But as conceived by Barbara Slate, the comics have dealt with such sophisticated concepts as divorce, homelessness, euthanasia of a dying pet, and the philosophy underlying pop art. Slate's comic "We Girls Can Do Anything," from June 1991, actually conveys the message of its title. While out driving, Barbie and Skipper pass a group of construction workers, one of whom is female; they watch two female police officers ticket a speeding motorist; and, when they get a flat tire, they actually fix it themselves. Nor is Barbie's comic-book persona so addicted to work that she treats people shabbily. In "Aunt Rose Comes First" (June 1992), Barbie's modeling agent, Eileen Plymouth (a crafty wordplay on Eileen Ford), gets Barbie a modeling job in Tahiti. When Barbie, who has a commitment to visit her aunt, won't go, Plymouth snarls: "This is business and business always comes first." But Barbie doesn't see it that way—and Barbie's contrarian vision is vindicated at the end.

In "The Volunteers" (February 1993), Skipper spends a winter holiday serving dinner at a homeless shelter. (To avoid pigeonholing the characters by religion, the holiday is unspecific.) Her experience has a sanitized quality; she encounters no unregenerate crack smokers or teenage mothers of six. But the idea of making homelessness visible—not erasing it through omission—is noteworthy. Skipper and Barbie interact not just with fashion dolls of color, but with people.

Given Barbie's universality—she can live anywhere or have any job—you'd think that writing for her would be a cinch. But there is one drawback: Mattel insists that she be infallible. Fortunately, Skipper and Ken are permitted to make mistakes, so at least someone's problems can be solved over the course of a story. "I have Ken being a feminist—being very considerate," Slate told me, "and I like to have him traveling, being the man-about-town. Because there's a reason why this guy is going out with the most fantastic girl in the world—he can't be stupid."

Slate's own background as a comic artist has always been controversial and, she says, feminist. She gained recognition in the seventies with a character called Ms. Liz, a wisecracking "liberated" woman who appeared in greeting cards, *Cosmopolitan,* and spots on the *Today* show. Ms. Liz flaunted her sexual emancipation and lampooned men whose sense of self derived from "supporting" the women in their lives. "Darling, of course I can live on your salary," Ms. Liz says on one greeting card, "but what will you live on?"

By 1986 Slate had a new female character—Angel Love, a young woman whose dealings with "drugs, sex and rock 'n' roll" were not G-rated. Nor were they morally simple. Featured in an eponymous DC comic book for twelve- to fourteen-year-old girls, Angel had a boyfriend who was doing "blow," a father who was suspected of child molestation, and an unmarried pregnant friend who was considering an abortion. The comic book was, however, short-lived—DC got tired of defending its volatile content.

Of course *Barbie Fashion* is considerably tamer than *Angel Love.* Barbie has not yet had to counsel Midge through the anguish of an abortion or coax Ken into rehab before his septum collapses. But Slate feels that the benefits of Barbie's name recognition dramatically outweigh the occasional drawbacks of writing for a character who cannot make mistakes. This is because girls aren't encouraged to read comic books. Given the traditional maleness of the comic-book market, the real wonder of Wonder Woman is that a female superhero has had any success at all. Without a brand-name attraction like Barbie, comic artists might as well write off reaching girls. "If they can't do it with Barbie, they can't do it with anybody," Slate said.

To be sure, the Barbie comic books have only a fraction of *Barbie* magazine's 600,000 subscribers, but girls *are* buying them. They are also being distributed in untraditional outlets, such as the Barbie section of FAO Schwarz. This is not a bad thing. Ever since Art Spiegelman's *Maus*, which dealt in pictures with the Holocaust, critics have taken a fresh look at comic books and started calling the ones they like "graphic novels." Which leads to another paradox in Barbie's ever contradictory career: Barbie, who epitomizes all that is stereotypically "feminine," is helping to masculinize—or, in any event, androgynize—the reading habits of young women.

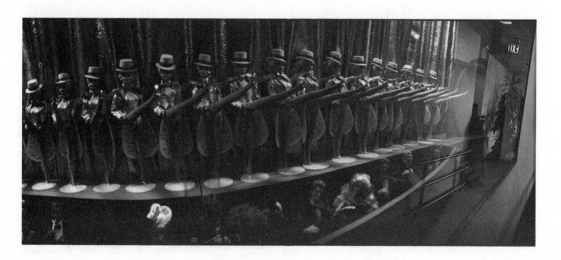

FAO SCHWARZ ROCKETTE BARBIE KICKLINE

SYLVIA PLACHY

CHAPTER EIGHT

BARBIE LIKE ME

The teenage doll that Ruth Handler invented had a lot in common with the teenage "dolls" created by the movie industry. But when people said the original Barbie looked like a star, they didn't mean Anna Magnani in *The Rose Tattoo* or Barbra Streisand in *Funny Girl*. They meant Donna Reed or Sandra Dee—actresses from whom conspicuous ethnicity had been purged; who weren't even Presbyterian or Methodist, but generic Protestant; who embodied a phantasmic, impossible "American" ideal.

In *An Empire of Their Own: How the Jews Invented Hollywood*, Neal Gabler tells how the studio moguls—all immigrants and outsiders—created an "America" that was more "American" than the country ever could be. They formed a "cluster of images and ideas—so powerful that, in a sense, they colonized the American imagination." And Americans, aping those images, ultimately became them. "As a result, the paradox—that the movies were quintessentially American while the men who made them were not—doubled back on itself," Gabler writes. "By creating their idealized America on the screen, the Jews reinvented the country in the image of their fiction."

To look at Mattel as a relative of the Hollywood studios is to make sense

SLADE THE SUPER AGENT, <u>SHINDANA TOYS</u>
<u>CATALOGUE</u>, 1977

of some of its contradictions. The daughter of a Polish Jewish immigrant, Ruth Handler coded with her fashion dolls the same sort of phantasmic "America" that Louis B. Mayer had coded in his movies. Barbie was, in fact, better suited than a human actress to exemplify an impossible ideal. There was no tribal taint in her plastic flesh, no baggage to betray an immigrant past. She had no navel; no parents; no heritage.

Yet even as Mattel grew rich off play sets that reflected white, middle-class values, its management was far from backward-thinking about race. This incongruity between public products and private politics is not without precedent in Hollywood. True, the studio moguls rejected Democratic politics in favor of a bland Republicanism that harmonized with their invented "America," but most screenwriters didn't. And Elliot Handler, who headed not only Mattel but also its creative team, can be said to have had a screenwriter's social conscience.

As early as the 1940s, Mattel integrated its assembly line and hired a black foreman. "It was unheard of in those days to put a black production worker next to a white production worker and have them all share toilet facilities," Ruth Handler told me. And in recognition of its policies, Mattel was honored by the Urban League. But Mattel's most startling project, little known outside the toy world, began in 1968, when, as a response to the Watts riots, it helped set up Shindana Toys—the name means "competitor" in Swahili—a black-run, South Central Los Angeles–based company that manufactured multicultural playthings before they were trendy.

By 1969, Mattel shared its Toy Fair showrooms with the likes of Shindana's Baby Nancy, a doll with authentic black features and a kinky "natural," and later with Talking Tamu, who said eighteen different "now" things like "Cool it, baby," and "Can you dig it?" Mattel ceded toy store space to Shindana rag dolls Sis, Coochy, Wilky, and Natra. And it watched Shindana score its first million-dollar hit with a stuffed talking doll that featured Flip Wilson on one side and Geraldine Jones, his female alter ego, on the other. Pull the doll's cord and it squealed, "The devil made me buy this dress!"

The world of Shindana—of top Mattel brass working side by side with the founders of Operation Bootstrap, the Watts-based job training program under whose auspices the toy company was formed—was a far cry from the way the thirtieth-anniversary issue of *Barbie* magazine depicted Barbie's world in 1966. "Our inner cities burned but the pot roast couldn't," the caption says under a picture of Barbie at a Tupperware party. "Mom and Dad

When I was a kid I had this black Barbie.

I loved my Barbie but I got the feeling she was out of place in white suburbia.

My best friend thought my Barbie ought to be the maid.

My sister thought she should be a white person with a sun tan.

I like to think of that time as the start of a life of political activism:

My Barbie was the only Barbie, the rest a pale alternative.

©allmink 1/11/94

"PALE ALTERNATIVE," BY ABBE SMITH, A FEMINIST CARTOONIST AND THE DEPUTY DIRECTOR OF THE CRIMINAL JUSTICE INSTITUTE AT HARVARD LAW SCHOOL

and the leaders they elected tried to keep a lid on things." As I said in this book's opening chapter, studying Barbie sometimes requires the ability to hold contradictory ideas in one's head at the same time. When it comes to Mattel and representations of racial diversity, this is especially true.

Although the Handlers have not been part of Mattel for twenty years, the company can still be viewed as a cousin to the Hollywood studios. Mattel actually did get into the movie business in the seventies, when its Radnitz Productions produced the Academy Award–winning *Sounder,* another multicultural product that predated the multicultural vogue. Securities analysts consider toys part of the entertainment industry, and corporate toymakers, like corporate moviemakers, keep their eye on trends. Beginning in the seventies, when nonwhite Americans became more visible in movies and on television, they became more visible as dolls. In 1980, Mattel issued Black Barbie and Hispanic Barbie—which, however imperfect, were still the first mainstream leading ladies (as opposed to supporting actresses) of color. Corporations also keep their eye on their bottom line. By the mid-eighties, businesses woke up to the fact that there was an audience for multicultural merchandise. Between 1980 and 1990, gross income among African-American and Hispanic households had increased 155 percent. And according to data from the 1990 U.S. census, these groups combined had a gross income just under $500 billion.

Traditionally, the needs of ethnically diverse consumers had been met by smaller companies—the equivalent, in movie terms, of independent filmmakers. In the seventies, Shindana introduced two Barbie-like fashion dolls: Malaika, taller and stouter than Barbie; and Career Girl Wanda, about three-quarters as tall as Barbie and as proportionately svelte. But in 1991, when Mattel brought out its "Shani" line—three Barbie-sized African-American dolls available with mahogany, tawny, or beige complexions—there could be no doubt that "politically correct" was profitable.

"For six years, I had been preaching these demographics—showing pie

charts of black kids under ten representing eighteen percent of the under-
ten population and Hispanic kids representing sixteen percent—and nobody
was interested," said Yla Eason, an African-American graduate of Harvard
Business School who in 1985 founded Olmec Corporation, which makes
dolls and action figures of color. "But when Mattel came out with those same
demographics and said, 'Ethnically correct is the way,' it legitimatized our
business."

Some say that the toy industry's idea of "ethnically correct" doesn't go far
enough, however. Ann duCille, chairman of the African-American Studies
Program and an associate professor of English at Wesleyan University, is a
severe critic. After studying representations of race in fashion dolls for over
a year, she feels that the dolls reflect a sort of "easy pluralism." "I'm not
sure I'd go so far as to say I'd rather see no black dolls than see something
like Shani or Black Barbie," she told me, "but I would hope for something
more—which is not about to happen." Nor is she wholly enamored of Imani
and Melenik, Olmec's equivalent of Barbie and Ken. "Supposedly these are
dolls for black kids to play with that look like them, when in fact they don't
look like them. That's a problematic statement, of course, because there's
no 'generic black kid.' But those dolls look too like Barbie for me. They have
the same body type, the same long, straight hair—and I think it sends a
problematic message to kids. It's about marketing, about business—so don't
try to pass it off as being about the welfare of black children."

Lisa Jones, an African-American writer who chronicled the introduction
of Mattel's Shani dolls for the *Village Voice,* is less harsh. Too old to have
played with Christie—Barbie's black friend, born in 1968—Jones recalls as
a child having expressed annoyance with her white classmates by ripping
the heads and arms off her two white Barbie dolls. Any fashion doll of color,
she thinks, would have been better for her than those blondes. "Having been
a little girl who grew up without the images," she told me, "I realize that
however they fail to reach the utopian mark, they're still useful."

People who accuse Mattel of having lacked a multicultural vision may not know about its relationship to Shindana Toys—a failed yet prescient experiment. To appreciate why Shindana was a breakthrough, one has to look at the history of American toys, which since the nineteenth century have been used to caricature immigrants. One shoo-in for the Toymakers' Hall of Shame is a common late-nineteenth-century bank called the "reclining Chinaman." It depicted a Chinese man with playing cards sprawled against a log. At the log's base was a rat—alleged to be a staple in the Chinese diet—and a lever which, when pulled, caused a coin to fall from the man's hip into the bank while his hands moved to reveal that the cards were all aces. The toy promulgated the notion that Chinese people were shifty and—because they accepted jobs at lower wages than less-recent immigrants—stole money from "American" workers.

The 1924 "Chicken Snatcher" is another stunningly awful plaything. This wind-up toy, which, according its advertisement, "will delight the kiddies," featured a "scared Negro" who "shuffles along with a chicken dangling in his hand and a dog hanging on the seat of his pants." But even when toys weren't poking malicious fun at unassimilated foreigners or African Americans, they were erasing them through omission. Until the civil rights movement of the 1960s, dolls were predominantly white; black children couldn't play with little effigies of themselves. The effect of this invisibility was quantified in the late 1930s and early 1940s, when two African-American social scientists, Drs. Kenneth and Mamie Clark, did a study using dolls to investigate black children's self-esteem. Given a choice between a white doll or a black doll, 67 percent of the black children they surveyed preferred the white doll. They dismissed the black dolls as ugly and bad.

The Clarks' troubling findings were not without impact. In 1954, Thurgood Marshall, arguing for the plaintiff in the landmark case *Brown* v. *Board of Education of Topeka, Kansas,* used the Clarks' testimony to document the psychological damage that had been suffered by blacks because of segregation. Marshall won the case, which resulted in the Supreme Court decision to integrate public schools.

To set the scene for Shindana's launch, we must return to the 1965 Watts riots, which broke out in midsummer after a Los Angeles coroner's jury excused as "justifiable homicide" the police killing of an unarmed black teenager carrying a baby—a verdict eerily similar to the one in the 1992 trial of the officers accused of beating Rodney King. In August, when the embers were far from metaphorically cool, Lou Smith and Robert Hall formed Operation Bootstrap. They wanted to take the community's anger and channel it constructively. In reaction to "Burn, baby, burn," their motto was "Learn, baby, learn."

Elliot Handler hooked up with Bootstrap in March 1968. "I thought it would be a good idea to get something started in the black neighborhood to see if we could train some people and turn them into entrepreneurs," he told me. But he had no connections—until he met the late Paul Jacobs, a left-wing writer, former union organizer, and brother of Cliff Jacobs, Mattel vice president in charge of market planning.

A staff member at the Santa Barbara–based Center for the Study of Democratic Institutions, Paul Jacobs had become friendly with Lou Smith while researching his 1967 book, *Prelude to Riot: A View of Urban America from the Bottom. Prelude* is a bitter book; the cover of its paperback edition shows an American flag and some crumbling buildings sticking out of a battered garbage can. To understand what Michael Harrington had termed "The Other America," Jacobs immersed himself in it. He didn't just debrief a handful of black leaders, he interviewed dozens of families in their homes—often having to overcome their skittishness and distrust. He also probed abuses of authority in the Los Angeles Police Department, producing a document so damning that L.A. Mayor Sam Yorty said Jacobs "ought to be investigated" for having written it.

Jacobs concluded that the violence in Watts wasn't just a response to police mistreatment. It expressed the community's frustration at being excluded by poverty from the consumer culture. He writes: "To buy a house in the Valley, spend a weekend at Lake Arrowhead, have babies who grow up to become teenagers attending the senior prom, visit Hawaii . . . shop downtown before going to the PTA fashion show, learn to ski at Sun Valley, take scuba diving lessons . . . these, the life patterns of middle-class Los Angeles . . . are unknown to these generations of unemployed, underemployed and low-paid workers." He might as well have said "these, the life patterns of Barbie"—so close were his examples to the situations for which she had outfits. He also blamed television advertising—of the sort Mattel had pioneered—for heightening black frustration. The ads, he said, ensured that the economically disenfranchised were intimately familiar with all the products they could never afford. Jacobs's undisguised distaste for Barbie's "America" made him an unlikely mediator between Bootstrap and Mattel; yet he not only introduced them, he helped keep their marriage together.

By 1967, Bootstrap had opened a student-staffed car repair shop and a factory where apprentice seamstresses made clothes. It held classes in typing, keypunch, English, and business math. And it ran "Kiwanda," a pricey boutique in Pacific Palisades that sold student-made dashikis to upper-middle-class white people.

If Smith and Hall were intrigued by the idea of going into the toy business, they didn't initially show it. "We went down into some little ramshackle place that was being used as a training center," Handler told me. "And we sat down and I explained to these people—Lou and the guys around him—what I wanted to do. And they didn't believe me. They said, 'Are you serious?' 'Is this some kind of a deal?' 'What's going on?' So we had to talk for quite a while and through Paul's help we finally convinced them we wanted to do something."

"I think what Lou and Robert were feeling was not so much skepticism as: Are they really going to live up to what they are telling us?" said Marva

Smith, the widow of Lou Smith, who died in 1976. (Hall is also no longer alive.) "We need their assistance in every area. This is all new to us. Will they be there in the long run?"

A Philadelphia-born civil rights activist who came to L.A. to be the West Coast director for the Congress of Racial Equality (CORE), Smith's dream for Shindana was to make dolls that looked black, dressed black, and talked black—"Brother and Sister dolls made by brothers and sisters," as a 1971 Shindana promotional flyer put it. He wanted games that taught history from an African-American perspective. And he wanted to make enough money from the toys to support other Bootstrap projects, like its day-care arm, the Honeycomb Child Development Center.

Yet even with Mattel's help, this wasn't easy. Articulate, charismatic, and fiercely Afrocentric, Smith didn't change his style to court white investors. "He'd meet with presidents of banks, universities, or large corporations in his dashiki and his jeans," Marva Smith told me. And he was so distrustful of government agencies that he refused to apply for a Small Business Administration loan. Rather than change Smith's mind, Mattel donated $150,000 to set up a toy factory on Central Avenue.

The plant's opening ceremonies in October 1968 attracted national attention. Ironically, Mayor Sam Yorty, Paul Jacobs's avowed enemy, presided at the festivities, which Jacobs also attended. Hatchets were seemingly buried—or at least shelved. "I know you don't agree with a great many of the positions in which I believe and sometimes with the way in which I express them," Jacobs wrote to the Handlers in a letter dated shortly after the opening, "but in this case we seem to have a common understanding."

The optimism continued at Toy Fair, when buyers, introduced to Shindana by Mattel's sales force, responded positively to Baby Nancy, who, with her molasses complexion and kinky Afro, was very unlike the café-au-lait, Caucasian-featured "black" dolls that had been put forth by mainstream toymakers. Her appearance was so radical, in fact, that creating it posed a technical challenge. To make her Saran hair look "natural," James Edwards, Shindana's head designer, told me, "You'd sew it into the doll's head, then stick it into the oven and it would crinkle up."

Nor did Shindana produce only dolls. It licensed images of the Jackson Five for a card game, and issued "The Black Experience American History Game," in which players, to quote the catalogue, "begin their existence as slaves and work their way . . . to the present." Today, the Jackson Five cards are avidly sought by collectors because they feature a Michael who still looks black.

African-American celebrities seemed eager to hop on the Shindana bandwagon. Besides its Flip Wilson doll, Shindana made talking, stuffed versions of Redd Foxx and J. J. Evans, the lanky son from TV's *Good Times*. It issued a Marla Gibbs fashion doll and a football action figure based on O. J. Simpson, who, as he was married to Shindana designer James Edwards's cousin, found the offer hard to refuse. When supercool detective *Shaft* appeared in the movies, Shindana introduced Slade, a black crime-fighter with a nubby Vandyke, a canary leather pants suit, and a briefcase full of "ransom money." Intended as a role model, Slade had street smarts *and* a sheepskin. "He grew up in the ghetto where he learned to survive," the catalogue says. "He went to war and was taught to fight. Now, after college, he puts it all together as a tough secret agent."

Mattel had agreed to support Shindana for its first two years, after which, ideally, it would be self-sufficient. In an internal memo dated eleven months after the plant's opening, Mattel marketing director Cliff Jacobs expressed optimism, as well as concern that the trust, which had been hard to establish, not break down. "Black people were suspicious and did not want to be 'put down' by the 'con,' " he wrote. So it fell to Mattel to provide the "best trainers" possible—"not second-rate people who can be spared from their regular jobs," but people who " 'talk the language' and are in complete sympathy with the project."

The "best trainers" meant Jacobs himself, who led a weekly marketing seminar at Shindana. It also meant senior engineer Adolph "Dolph" Lee and Art Spear, vice president for manufacturing, who would later head Mattel. Spear never allowed Mattel's burgeoning financial problems to interfere with his commitment to Shindana. "Art was the kind of person who was at my disposal twenty-four hours a day," said Robert Bobo, who joined Shindana in 1974 as its president. "If I needed him for anything, he was a phone call away." And on one occasion, Spear did, in fact, save the day. Shindana had unexpectedly run out of the plastic it needed to make a certain doll, and Spear immediately found a source at Mattel. If a company the size of Mattel had been undersupplied, Spear reasoned, it would endure. But the shortage could have wiped out Shindana.

"I always thought about doing a sitcom on Shindana—called *Making It to the Top in the Dark,*" Edwards told me. "Playing on the idea of dark skin and also 'in the dark'—as in not knowing what you're doing." Listening to Edwards, whose comic timing is a cross between Eddie Murphy's and Jay Leno's, the idea sounded plausible. It might, however, have been too volatile for seventies television. Take the time Shindana had to come up with a name for its "Little Friends"—a rainbow of Hispanic, Asian-American, Native-American, African-American, and European-American toddlers. "A white person may buy a black doll for their kid, but they didn't want to buy a black *baby* doll," Edwards said. "Because a baby doll would give the kid the idea that they could have a black baby. And white parents did not want their kids with the idea of having a black baby. So we started playing with the idea of 'Little Friends'—like your kids would play with other ethnic groups in preschool. And tried to get that 'baby' thing out of their brains."

Then there was Shindana's outrageous cast of characters. Smith and Hall were militant, civil-rights types, Edwards said. "Other blacks were at the other end of the spectrum—where if you talked to them, you thought they were white. Then you'd have another guy with a 'street' kind of personality." And if this olla podrida weren't spicy enough, there were Shindana's assorted investors—not just Mattel, its initial backer, but "the president of Chase Manhattan bank, here in South Central, talking to all these personalities."

Ironically, the largest purchasers of Shindana products weren't African-American. December is the key sales month for toys, but because black parents tended to do their Christmas shopping later than white parents, Shindana's merchandise was often sold out by the time they went into the stores. Nor did toy buyers—almost entirely white and male at the time—take Shindana seriously enough to reorder. Because of its relationship to Mattel, Bobo said, "There was a lot of token buying." But no real commitment to the toys: "Nobody took them on as a real product that they could make money on," Edwards told me. "You'd go in there and they'd say, 'What do you jungle bunnies want? We gave last year.'"

By the mid-seventies, domestic production had become so expensive that Shindana was forced to move most of its manufacturing to the Orient. "We had little places called Shindanatown in Hong Kong and Taiwan," Edwards told me. But the move was not uncontested. "I can't even begin to tell you how much arguing there was against that," Shindana plant manager Ralph Riggins said. "One of the things Bootstrap wanted to do—and did—was put the unemployable to work," Bobo told me. But financial realities left Shindana no choice: either build overseas or go broke.

The deemphasis on Shindana's local factory depressed company morale, as did the death in 1976 of Smith and his school-age daughter in a car accident while they were on vacation. Shindana's optimism and hope began to be poisoned by cynicism and distrust, reflected in a board game that it brought out in 1980: "Manipulation: The Mammoth Corporation Game." A sort of "Monopoly" for minority businessmen, it details not only "the mechanics of borrowing money from a bank for business purposes," but also how to stay out of jail if you can't pay it back.

"Well, you know, they didn't have much use for the white man's 'manipulation,' " Cliff Jacobs told me. " 'Anybody can run a business; you guys are trying to keep it a big secret'—I can just hear them telling us. Of course when it came to planning for themselves, this was not one of their great strengths."

And so, in the early eighties, Shindana sputtered out. By 1979, Edwards, Bobo, and Riggins had left. Only Herman Thompson, who headed its sales force, and Earl Coss, who replaced Bobo, remained. Like Moses, who expired before entering the Promised Land, Shindana blazed the trail to the modern multicultural marketplace, only to perish on its outskirts. Over its dead form, the next generation of companies—Olmec Corporation, Golden Ribbon Merchants, Cultural Exchange Corporation—strode through the gates.

ROGER WILKINS, A CIVIL RIGHTS ACTIVIST AND ASSISTANT Attorney General under President Lyndon Johnson, is probably not the first person one thinks to contact when one is doing a book about Barbie. But I ran into him in the greenroom at Cable News Network in December 1993, and, because I tend to be single-minded about my research, our conversation turned to Barbie. Wilkins told me that his sister, who is in her early forties, had been opposed to Barbie dolls because they coded European standards of beauty. Moreover, to encourage her daughter to take pride in her heritage, she had given the girl a Swahili name. But when Mattel came out with its Shani line, his sister did an about-face. Shani, which means "marvelous" in Swahili, was, in fact, her daughter's name. And the child now has several of the dolls.

"We are living in a moment where 'the other' has a certain kind of commercial value," Ann duCille dryly observes. One reason is, of course, that racial and ethnic minorities have significant disposable income. But other forces had an influence, too.

In 1985, Dr. Darlene Powell Hopson and Dr. Derek S. Hopson, two married psychologists, duplicated Drs. Kenneth and Mamie Clark's experiments using dolls to explore black children's self-esteem. Their results were shocking: they suggested that in the forty years since the Clarks did their research—despite landmark legal decisions, acts of Congress, and the civil rights movement—little had changed. Sixty-five percent of the black children they interviewed preferred white dolls, and 76 percent said the black dolls "looked bad" to them. "It was so disheartening," Darlene Powell Hopson told me. "I remember sitting at McDonald's—of all places—in Harlem, crying, saying, 'I don't want to do this. I can change my topic. I can do something different.' " She had begun collecting the data for her dissertation in psychology at Hofstra University. But her husband, who had already earned his Ph.D., urged her to forge on, which she did.

When Powell Hopson and her husband presented their study at the American Psychological Association's annual meeting, it was greeted with "despair around the world." *The New York Times* published their findings on the front page of its science section, and they were picked up by periodicals ranging from *Essence* to *USA Today*. This led in 1990 to the publication of their book, *Different and Wonderful: Raising Black Children in a Race-Conscious Society*, which not only details their research, but suggests ways that parents of color can help their children develop a healthy sense of self.

Different and Wonderful caught the eye of Mattel, when it was beginning plans for a new line of African-American fashion dolls to be introduced in the fall of 1991. The key in-house players on the project were African-American: Mattel product manager Deborah Mitchell, who has since left the company, and designer Kitty Black Perkins, who clothed the original Black Barbie. Mattel also brought in an African-American publicist, Alberta Morgan Rhodes from Morgan Orchid Rhodes, a firm that specialized in target marketing. Intrigued by the people and the project, Darlene Powell Hopson accepted Mattel's invitation to be a consultant.

Not all of Powell Hopson's suggestions were implemented, but many were—the most significant of which was making not one but three dolls with varying pigmentation. The series includes Shani, the lead doll, who has a medium-brown complexion; Asha, who is very light; and Nichelle, who is very dark. In *The Color Complex: The Politics of Skin Color Among African Americans*, authors Midge Wilson, Kathy Russell, and Ronald Hall argue that skin color plays a part in the formation of social hierarchies within the African-American community. One of the many studies that the authors cite—mounted, in this case, by Wilson and two of her students at Chicago's DePaul University—shows how the self-image of black women is sometimes negatively affected by the darkness of their skin. In this study, eighty participants—black and white, male and female—were asked to examine photographs of twelve African-American women and describe them. "Regardless of the individual woman's attractiveness," Wilson, Russell, and Hall write, "the study participants nearly always rated the dark-skinned women as less successful, less happy in love, less popular, less physically attractive, less physically and emotionally healthy, and less intelligent than their light-skinned counterparts." They were, however, believed to have a good sense of humor—attributable to what the authors called "the Whoopi Goldberg effect."

Rather than deny the existence of color bias, Powell Hopson has found that by using dolls with different skin tones in play therapy, she can help undermine negative stereotypes—or at least determine how they took shape within a specific child's family. "A child might have the lighter-complexion doll—Asha—taking control or being the leader," Powell Hopson told me. "I'd see that and try to explore that with her. . . . And then I might see how that dynamic is reflected in her home environment—whether it's the lightest child feeling ostracized or more valued than her siblings because she's lighter in complexion."

Nor do all families give preference to lightness. "My grandmother, who was very light, used to say, 'You see this color? I'm not proud of this; this means my mother was raped by the white man,'" said Olmec founder Yla Eason.

Powell Hopson wanted at least one of the Shani series to have short hair—to reflect the way African-American women actually look. But because of little girls' fascination with "hairplay," the dolls have lengthy locks. Nor was Powell Hopson pleased that her guidelines for "Positive Play"—activities aimed at mothers to steer children toward greater self-esteem—were not packaged with the dolls. But otherwise, she was proud of the product and its launch.

"If you didn't know better, you'd think the Powell Hopsons designed it—to Mattel's credit," Yla Eason said. "If I were coming out into the ethnic market, I'd want to put a black face on my look, to say: 'I'm not exploiting you.' You never saw Jill Barad's face when they were talking about Shani; you only saw the Powell Hopsons." She added: "But all they really said was, 'Black dolls are good; they help black self-esteem. We've got a book and Mattel's got a black product.'"

Surprisingly, Mattel did not showcase designer Kitty Black Perkins, who, between her sincerity and up-from-Jim-Crow life story, is very hard not to admire. It has since rectified this by featuring her on a 1994 infomercial that highlights the work of individual Mattel designers. Black Perkins has come a long way from Spartanburg, South Carolina, where, during her childhood, segregation loomed. There were "a lot of things that when I look at now I cringe," she told me. "To this day, I don't think my mother will ever go to a restaurant in South Carolina because she had been discriminated against all this time."

Black Perkins took refuge from the unpleasantness in art class, where her talent, even then, stood out. "I must have been ten or eleven years old, and I always knew that I was going to do something with my hands, and something creative." Today Black Perkins has a cosmopolitan lifestyle; she jet-ted to Milan to work on the series of Benetton Barbies—multiracial dolls clothed not in Benetton miniatures but garments that evoked the company's "United Colors" feeling. "I give my daughter dolls of all colors," Black Perkins told me, "because she lives in a world that is a lot of different colors." This, too, is a far cry from the white dolls of her youth: "I played mostly with the dolls that my mother would bring home that her employers had given her."

Although even competitors applauded Shani's introduction, the line has not been without minor slipups—among them, in 1992, the design of Shani's boyfriend, Jamal. "They didn't make Jamal look sweet enough," Eason said. "Ken is just an arm-piece, an escort—he's not to look sexually threatening or even interested in sex." But with Jamal, "It was like uh-oh, don't come *near* my daughter; I know what you're interested in." Mattel has since shaved off Jamal's David Niven mustache and eliminated what Ann duCille referred to as his "terribly tacky yellow suit." He now looks more like Eason's Melenik doll and less, said duCille, "like a pimp."

I interviewed Powell Hopson in her Connecticut office just after the 1993 introduction at Toy Fair of "Soul Train" Shani, linked to the television dance program. With restraint and diplomacy, Powell Hopson confessed that she would have preferred a more scholarship-oriented line that year, and a wardrobe without "the hot pants and the high boots and fishnet stockings." And while both she and her husband thought the idea of using Kente cloth—a traditional African fabric—on the dolls was good, they felt it might have been done with greater decorum. "He didn't like the fact that it was being used for a brassiere," Powell Hopson said. "As a blouse, fine; but not as a brassiere."

The point of this chapter is not for scholars or rival toymakers to snipe at Shani, but to understand why, despite the best intentions, mainstream manufacturers sometimes produce objects that are less than ideal. Jacob Miles, whose recently established Cultural Exchange Corporation is best known for its "Hollywood Hounds," anthropomorphic stuffed animals with multiethnic personalities, thinks that minority-run companies are by definition more in touch with their audience. "I'm an African American," he told me. "An ethnic consumer making product for the ethnic consumer—making product for myself. Our products become the community's products—so they're essentially buying from themselves. It's not something coming *to* the community, but something coming *out of* the community."

Miles is no stranger to the toy business; he was an executive at both Kenner and Tonka before striking out on his own. He remembers a pattern behind the scenes at the big companies: toning down ethnic extremes to avoid alienating the white majority. "What we've learned as educated blacks is that you can't buy your way out of racism in this country," Eason told me. Even the late Reginald Lewis, the Harvard-educated chairman of TLC Beatrice and one of the nation's most successful African-American entrepreneurs, "with his billion-dollar company and his $400 million income and his $12 million penthouse, couldn't stand on the street in New York and catch a cab easily because he was black." This is why she feels consumers of color won't desert minority-run corporations; she and her audience are linked by a subtext of slights, often invisible to the white majority. (In case she's wrong, however, she has entered into a limited financial relationship with Hasbro.)

Regardless of its limitations, Mattel's Shani line is an attempt at inclusivity—at making consumers of color part of the company's imagined "America." Its Dolls of the World Collection, in which diverse cultures are also represented, seems to have the opposite goal—which brings us back to the Mattel pattern of contradictory messages. Far from authenticity, these dolls have the theme-park bogusness of the "foreign lands" at Disney's Epcot Center, where the world, a set of dangerous, polyglot, disease-ridden, poverty-stricken countries, has been sanitized into the "world," a set of safe, monoglot, hygienic, affluent simulacra. Without jet lag or lost luggage, "international" tourists can purchase souvenirs, sample ethniclike cuisine—even drink the water. (A human version of Barbie is, in fact, currently featured in a musical at the Orlando theme park. In it, she and her official friends travel through the "world"—that is, through a set of caricatures of foreign countries.)

To be sure, some of the Dolls of the World are less reductive than others. Malaysian Barbie, which the workers in Mattel's Malaysian factory helped design, gets high marks for authenticity and attractiveness. Ann duCille actually called it beautiful. But Jamaican Barbie is another story. "She looks like a mammy," Eason told me. "She's got the head rag and the apron, and I'm like, 'Why did they pick *that* slice of life?' When they did the Nigerian Barbie at least they made her a regal person." DuCille is blunter: "That's the one I call the anorexic Aunt Jemima."

The phrase book of "foreign" expressions on Jamaican Barbie's box seems almost calculated to patronize. It includes: "How-yu-du" (Hello), "A hope yu wi come-a Jamaica!" (I hope you will come to Jamaica!), and "Teck care a yusself, mi fren!" (Take care of yourself, my friend!). But to place this in perspective, even English Barbie—a blonde with whom American Barbie allegedly shares a common tongue—is cast in this series as "the other." Her box also features a glossary of *English* words.

There is a common thread in this, and it involves Mattel's coding of an "American" identity for Americans to emulate. Americans define themselves not just by what they are, but by what they are not: Jamaican, Malaysian, English, Scottish, Italian, Australian—to name but a few of the officially "alien" Barbies. To be "American" is to lose the *caricatured* ethnicity of the Dolls of the World; yet it is not to lose all ethnicity. In Mattel's "America," as in the one invented by other parts of the entertainment industry, racial diversity is recognized—even *authorized*—through its visibility. It may be an "easy pluralism," as duCille says, but it is a pluralism nonetheless.

I have to credit Susan Howard, an African-American journalist and Barbie-collector, with pointing this out to me—and with coining the term "designated friend" for Barbie's first pals of color. When we met for an interview, she showed me a Sun Lovin' Malibu Christie, Barbie's black friend from the seventies. Howard considers the doll, which has tan lines, to be educational. "You'd be surprised how many white people don't know that black people tan," she said.

Howard does not hide her hobby; Black Barbie sits like a mascot on her desk at *Newsday,* and she has others—including a 30th Anniversary Special Edition—at home. Far from remembering Barbie with rage, Howard, who grew up in Fort Wayne, Indiana, and now lives on Long Island, thinks of the doll as "an empowerment tool because she did so many things and she made me feel good about myself." She adds, "I'm sure that some feminists would balk at that idea."

The "empowerment" had to do with the visibility of blacks among Barbie's first friends. In 1968, Mattel's official "America" looked a lot like Howard's integrated neighborhood—and seeing even an imperfect reflection of her world gave her a sense of validation. Unlike Lisa Jones, Howard, in her early thirties, *was* young enough to have played with Christie, who, while far from her twin, resembled her more closely than did white Barbie. "When you're a kid who basically has no one to play with other than yourself and a few friends, this doll becomes your friend," she told me. "You don't know how much it meant to me that Barbie had a friend like Christie. Because that meant, well, Barbie likes black people. And it may sound silly, but it was important for me to know that Barbie liked someone like me. The proof was in her 'designated friend.' "

CHAPTER NINE

MY FAIR BARBIE

When writer Jill Ciment was working on *The Law of Falling Bodies*, a novel set twenty-five years ago in the lower-middle-class southern California suburb where she grew up, she had a hard time figuring out how her characters should dress. Searching through old issues of *Vogue* was fruitless; the clothes were too chic, representative of a class above the one she sought to depict. But while browsing through the Rizzoli bookstore in SoHo, where she now lives, she picked up Billy Boy's *Barbie: Her Life and Times* and experienced a breakthrough.

"I needed [the characters] to wear schlocko but hip clothes," she told me. And the illustrated book jogged her memory: there on its pages were herself and her friends—the "hood" or roughneck crowd, as she describes them. Barbie's pre-1967 face brought back her own grooming ritual—the heavy black liner and "blue stuff" around the eyes, the white lipstick—a look that was defiant in its knowing garishness. It was also democratic: "Anyone could get miniskirts and fishnet stockings and see-through plastic raincoats; they weren't like the high-class fashions of today, which really are impossible to afford. There was always a cheap ripoff at Zody's or White Front."

BARBIE AND KEN, COLLECTION OF

CORAZON YELLEN SYLVIA PLACHY

In *Taste: The Secret Meaning of Things*, Stephen Bayley tells us that "nothing is as crass and vulgar as instant classification according to hairstyle, clothing and footwear, yet it is . . . a cruelly accurate analytical form." Because Barbie is a construct of class—as well as a construct of gender—this crass, vulgar, and accurate investigation cannot be avoided. "When it comes to the meaning of things, there are no more powerful transmitters than clothes, those quasi-functional devices which, like an inverted fig, put the heart of the matter in front of the skin," Bayley writes. Yet powerful though the transmissions may be, many Americans deliberately ignore them.

If you want to make an American twitch nervously and avoid eye contact, raise the issue of social class. To do this is to invite being misunderstood. One is perceived as either a wild-eyed socialist, directing middle-class attention to the exploited classes beneath it, or an anxious snob, sneering at others to retain a hold on one's own tenuous position. When forced to acknowledge class differences, Americans often argue that this country has infinite class mobility, which is, of course, hyperbolic—for everyone except Barbie. Barbie can not only ascend the social ladder, she can occupy several classes at once.

In the early sixties, Barbie was positioned as a high school baton twirler and prom queen. Yet when Jacqueline Kennedy was in the White House—and the middle class briefly stopped denying the existence of a class above it—Barbie's trunk contained all she would need for a term at Mrs. Kennedy's former boarding school in Farmington, Connecticut. In the hierarchy of class, Barbie had duel citizenship, a status she made even murkier when she donned the flashy, synthetic clothes that inspired Ciment.

To chart Barbie's course as a social mountaineer, we will have to define her peaks and valleys. Sociologists usually carve society into five classes: upper, upper-middle, middle, lower-middle, and lower. In *Class*, his facetious investigation into social status, however, Paul Fussell advances a more nuanced palate. It has nine classes: top-out-of-sight (the *Forbes* four hundred), upper, upper-middle, middle, high-proletarian, mid-proletarian, low-proletarian, destitute, and bottom-out-of-sight (the homeless). While destitute and bottom-out-of-sight are virtually irrelevant to Barbie, her lifestyle is a sort of Chutes and Ladders game among the other seven.

According to Fussell's guidelines, Barbie began a downward trajectory in 1977. Her "SuperStar" face, with its vapid grin, sent her plummeting. "You'll notice prole women smile more, and smile wider, than those of the middle and upper classes," Fussell writes. "They're enmeshed in the 'have a nice day culture' and are busy effusing a defensive optimism." Likewise, when Barbie's miniature wool suits gave way to polyester dresses, she sank. "All synthetic fibers are prole," he writes, "partly because they're cheaper than natural ones, partly because they're not archaic, and partly because they're entirely uniform and hence boring."

Fussell's tone is one of bemused detachment, a defense against accusations that he may be taking class differences too seriously. On the rare occasions when the unspeakable is spoken, this tends to be how it is expressed. But particularly in the eighties, when middle- and upper-middle-class children had to confront the prospect of being worse off economically than their parents, class slippage became more than a facetious concern. Barbie as a class role model, far more than Barbie as a gender role model, may, in fact, be the linchpin of many mothers' continued misgivings about her.

After interviewing numerous upper-middle-class, Eastern Establishment women, I can say with certainty that most do not interpret the doll as an updated Neolithic fertility icon. They view her as a literal representation of a modern woman. Many object to her on feminist grounds—one hears the familiar "that body is not found in nature" refrain. Then the word *bimbo* arises. But let a woman talk longer—reassuring her that she's not speaking for attribution—and she'll express her deepest reservation: that "Barbie is cheap," where the whole idea of "cheap" is rooted in social hierarchies and economics.

On a recent HBO special, Roseanne Arnold, who, incidentally, collects Barbies, excoriated what she considered to be Barbie's middle-class-ness. Why didn't Mattel make, say, "trailer-park Barbie"? But to many upper-middle-class women, all post-1977 Barbies *are* Trailer Park Barbie.

Ironically, given the knee-jerk antagonism to Barbie's body, it is one of her few attributes that doesn't scream "prole." Her thinness—indicative of an expensive gym membership and possibly a personal trainer—definitely codes her as middle- or upper-middle-class. In *Distinction*, French sociologist Pierre Bourdieu notes that "working class women . . . are less aware of the 'market' value of beauty and less inclined to invest . . . sacrifices and money in cultivating their bodies." Likewise, Barbie's swanlike neck elevates her status. A stumpy neck is a lower-class attribute, Fussell says.

The 1961 Ken, with his lean body, subdued expression, and miniature Brooks Brothers wardrobe, was coded for upper- or upper-middle-class life. His first decline came in 1969, when Mattel gave him a beetle-browed, smiling face and discontinued his preppie clothes. Worse, his chest and thighs were beefed up, preventing him from wearing his original togs. No longer could he sport a plausible dinner jacket; he suffered the indignity of wearing a "Guruvy [sic] Formal" that lowered his class precipitously. True, the caved-in chest that leading man Jimmy Stewart revealed when he removed his shirt in Hitchcock's 1954 *Rear Window* became less dashing in 1977, when George Butler's *Pumping Iron* popularized muscles for men whose professions did not involve heavy lifting. But with his close-set eyes and heightened brawn Ken remained prole-coded through the 1980s.

Mattel made a decision to smarten him up in 1992—ironically by giving him a face it had originally designed for an updated version of Midge's fiancé, Allan. But even with California's casual sartorial code, Ken never regained his lost standing. Barbie's initial 1967 face change, by contrast, did not reduce her status. The Twist 'N Turn face did not simper; its expression, though perky, was still aloof.

In a recent issue of *Allure*, Joan Kron dared to lift the lid on "Secret Beauty Codes." She points a finger at types of "class stigma" that differentiate a female executive—or a female member of the upper or upper middle class—from, for instance, her secretary. In contrast to the female investment banker's flat heels, simple clothes, virtual absence of makeup, and classic bob, the "working girl" will have "high heels, too-short skirt . . . exaggerated makeup, and Big Hair"—characteristics that upper-middle-class mothers have with dismay observed in Barbie. These mothers have, in fact, singled out best-selling Totally Hair Barbie, with her ankle-length-tresses and tight, thigh-high minidress, as particularly horrifying; she looks, one observed, like "a professional fourth wife." The mother's joke veils this concern: While women of uncertain pedigree have since time immemorial married their way into the upper classes, "mastery of the self-presentation codes—being appropriately glamorous but not ostentatious—is," in Kron's words, "considered proof that one belongs."

Significantly, there is class differentiation within the Barbie doll line itself; Barbie still maintains the ability to exist in several classes simultaneously. In 1992, for example, "Madison Avenue" Barbie, dressed and coiffed in the style of Ivana Trump, was exclusively available for about sixty dollars at FAO Schwarz, Manhattan's tony Fifth Avenue toy emporium. In the Lionel Kiddie City in Union Square, however, a less prosperous neighborhood, the shelves were stocked with fifteen-dollar "Rappin' Rockin' Barbie—Yo!" dolls packaged with rhythm-generating boom boxes.

Although Madison Avenue Barbie does, in fact, look like Ivana, the doll seems to have been deliberately coded for parody. Her pink and green outfit is not made of natural fibers, nor is her flashy pink teddy. Likewise, Mattel designer Carol Spencer's "Benefit Ball" Barbie—in a splashy blue evening dress with mountains of orange hair—bears a strong resemblance to Georgette Mosbacher. But her coiffure is so huge and her dress is so flamboyant that she, too, seems to parody Mosbacher, which, as Mosbacher is not known for understated dressing, is no mean feat. Of the outfits Barbie might wear to lunch at Le Cirque, Janet Goldblatt's "City Style" Barbie, an off-white Chanel-inspired suit with a small quilted handbag, is the most plausible, particularly on a doll with shorter hair.

Just as the Native American Barbie does not copy the uniform of a specific tribe but reflects an outsider's interpretation of Native American identity, the upper-class Barbies reproduce not real upper-class clothing but an outsider's fantasy of it. They emulate the eighties' rich-person soap-opera look—the look of *Dynasty* and *Dallas*—not the pared-down landed-gentry lifestyle deciphered for the middle classes by, say, Martha Stewart.

Then there are the "Gold Sensation" Barbie and "Crystal" Barbie advertised in magazines such as *Parade*. Priced at $179 and $175 respectively, these "Limited Edition" Barbie dolls can be bought for four "convenient installments" of $44.75 or $43.75. From their red fingernails to their glittering clothes (the Gold Sensation comes with "a 22 karat, gold electroplated bracelet"), these dolls are a proletarian daydream of how a rich person would dress. Fussell would, of course, mock these objects ("Nothing is too ugly or valueless to be . . . 'collected' so long as it is priced high enough," he writes) but I find them vaguely poignant. In her *Allure* article, Kron observes that it has been many years since, for example, long, brightly painted talons connoted "lady of leisure"; they now imply its opposite, as does every other detail on the dolls.

Seeing them in their wildly excessive getups reminded me of an affecting scene in the movie *Mystic Pizza*. In it, Julia Roberts plays the beautiful daughter of a Portuguese fisherman who dates a patrician young man. When he invites her home to dinner, she chooses a bare, flashy dress (based perhaps on *Dynasty* notions of upper-class life) that painfully brands her as an outsider. (Class coding is also an issue in Roberts's later movie *Pretty Woman*, but unlike *Mystic Pizza*, in which Roberts's sister moves up the class ladder by earning a scholarship to Yale, *Pretty Woman* suggests that the sole way a woman can ascend socially is by hooking the right mogul—a distasteful message indeed.)

Although some toys reach across class boundaries, others are clearly targeted to a specific social echelon. Dolls in the Pleasant Company "American Girls Collection," for instance, are geared to please middle- and upper-middle-class moms. Seemingly dressed by Laura Ashley, educated by Jean Brodie, and nourished by Martha Stewart, these dolls are almost intimidatingly tasteful. Sold with historical novels (about them) and simulated antiques, they are intended to inculcate in their young owners a fondness for archaic things—the core, says Fussell, of upper-class taste. Felicity, a doll dressed as an American colonial girl, comes with a Windsor writing chair, a wooden tea caddy, and a china tea cup—"all she needs to learn the proper tea ceremony." She must unlearn her skill, however, when her father, in one of the novels, decides to boycott tea to protest George III's unfair tax on it.

Then there's Kirsten, a Swedish pioneer, whose accessories include a handmade rag doll, a school bench, a carpetbag, handknit winter woolens, and a wooden trestle table set with dainty stoneware dishes. Other dolls in the series include the dauntingly refined Samantha, a Victorian child who studies at "Miss Crampton's Academy, a private school for proper young ladies"; Molly, a bespectacled lass who pores over *Gaining Skill with Words* to take her mind off Dad, fighting overseas in World War II; and, the collection's newest member, Addy, a courageous African-American girl growing up during the Civil War. One is not likely to see Totally Hair Samantha or Rappin' Rockin' Kirsten—Yo! The Pleasant Company understands the class anxieties of its buyers, as well as their discretionary income: since 1986, over eleven million American Girls books have been sold.

To be sure, many Barbie dolls, particularly those directed at children and not adult collectors, are thoroughly rooted in fantasy and do not attempt to miniaturize real life. The "Twinkle Lights" Barbie—who has flashing fiberoptic strands emerging from her chest—and the "Bath Blast" Barbie—whom children "dress" in aerosol foam—are far from scale models of reality. A throbbing fringe of fur above her breasts would get a real woman inducted into Ripley's Believe It or Not, just as traipsing around in nothing but shaving cream might get her arrested. But Mattel's market research and my own observations have convinced me that three- to six-year-old girls really do possess a boundless appetite for anything colored fuchsia. Yet because "taste" is learned—that is to say, imposed—anxious middle- and upper-middle-class parents attempt to steer their children away from these natural desires.

In *The Hidden Persuaders,* a color researcher tells Vance Packard that "the poor and the relatively unschooled" favor brilliant colors; seemingly, they were never forced to unlearn their childhood preferences. "Scientific observation shows that cultural needs are the product of upbringing and education," Bourdieu writes in *Distinction.* "All cultural practices (museum visits, concert-going, reading, etc.), and preferences in literature, painting or music are closely linked to educational level . . . and secondarily to social origin."

To study how education perpetuates class differences in England—a process similar to what occurs in most of the industrialized West—one need merely screen Michael Apted's *28-Up* and its sequel, *35-Up.* Apted's video documentary charts the lives of fourteen male and female British subjects, representing the top and bottom of the social scale. In the first of serial interviews conducted every seven years, John, Andrew, and Charlie, three upper-class seven-year-olds, were studying Latin and trying to decide if they would go to university at Oxford or Cambridge. By age twenty-eight, having graduated from prestigious schools, they were pursuing upper-class careers; but because the film dramatized how their educations preserved class inequality, all but one refused to be interviewed as adults.

What is more, so striking were the boys' accents that one could identify

their class without paying attention to the content of their speech. Their elo-
cution was radically different from that of Talking Stacey, Barbie's English
friend whom Mattel issued in 1969. She sounded working-class, like the
Liverpudlian rock stars fawned over by American girls. Likewise Talking
Barbie has never been afflicted with Locust Valley Lockjaw. The infamous
1992 "Math Class Is Tough" Barbie had the voice of a Valley Girl, placing
her socially somewhere between lower middle class and high prole. But like
Eliza Doolittle, Barbie is, in matters of speech, a chameleon. In *Dance!
Workout with Barbie*, an animated exercise video also issued in 1992,
Barbie has an older, less overtly proletarian voice. "We're fulfilling what
we've always said—that she has many voices," Mattel vice president Meryl
Friedman, who supervised production of the video, told me. "She's open-
ended."

Unlike their upper-class counterparts, the three working-class boys in *35-
Up* did not, at age seven, speak of universities; they had no clear idea what
a "university" was. At thirty-five, one was a bricklayer, another a cab driver,
and the third a workman in a meat-packing plant. At seven, the working-
class girls had a vague notion of higher education, although they sensed that
it was beyond their financial grasp. Significantly, though, when they became mothers, they developed academic aspirations for their children. The
working-class men, however, were defensive about their lack of "opportunities"; they failed to see the distinction between class and money.

In the documentary, however, that distinction is hard to miss. Bruce, an
Oxford-educated patrician who teaches school in Bangladesh, is desperately poor—though he remains upper-class. And Nick, a farmer's son who
studied physics at Oxford, is no longer in his original class; but because of
the rigidity of the English system, neither is his new position clear. Not surprisingly, Nick fled to a less structured country—America—where he is a
professor at the University of Wisconsin at Madison.

Even within America itself, the West Coast is less structured than the

"CANNABIS NATION," AUTHENTIC BARBIE
DISCO OUTFIT, COLLECTION OF KAREN TINA
HARRISON, NEW YORK CITY GEOFF SPEAR

East Coast. Joan Didion's family may have been in California for six generations, but most people's haven't. Many nonnative Californians came to escape what they perceived to be suffocating social hierarchies at home; to them, the state's openness is a blessing. But transplants whose sense of self derived from their position within the Establishment may find its absence a threat. Under the cruel glare of the Pacific sun, shabby gentility just looks shabby.

In part, the extent to which Establishment women are uncomfortable with Barbie reflects the degree to which she embodies West Coast style, which, exported by the Hollywood-based entertainment industry, seems to have been snapped up without protest in the Midwest and Sunbelt. "Whatever the fashion, the California version will be more extreme, more various, and—possibly because of the influence of the large Spanish-American population—much more colorful," Alison Lurie explains in *The Language of Clothes*. "Clothes tend to fit more tightly than is considered proper elsewhere, and to expose more flesh . . . virtuous working-class housewives may wear outfits that in any other part of the country would identify them as medium-priced whores."

Even "the opposition between the classical sports and the Californian sports," Bourdieu says, expresses "two contrasting relations to the social world." The classical sports—those practiced by the French bourgeoisie—reflect "a concern for propriety and ritual" and "unashamed flaunting of wealth and luxury"; the Californian sports, by contrast, involve a "symbolic subversion of the rituals of bourgeois order by ostentatious poverty." To be sure, Barbie has engaged in her share of classical sports—skiing, tennis, riding—but she is more profoundly associated with democratic sports—surfing, snorkeling, Frisbee-throwing—that the middle classes can afford. Nor do these sports require expensive childhood lessons to be performed successfully by adults. Barbie's egalitarian sports, however, are usually "new" or "trendy"; in 1992, her whole tribe was equipped for rollerblading. Barbie has, however, never fully embraced a working-class identity, avoiding such traditional nonbourgeois sports as bowling.

Sometimes a parental struggle over Barbie is not a scrap over a toy at all. It is a clash of East versus West, intellectual culture versus physical culture, rootedness versus deracination. Consider Barbie's history of opulent bathrooms—unabashedly lower-class by Fussell's standards. "The prole bathroom is the place for enacting the fantasy 'what I'd do if I were really rich,' " Fussell writes. But on the West Coast, water truly is a luxury. In a land reclaimed from the desert, sprinklers *are* magical, as are irrigation canals. Like the Christian soul in baptism, the land, through water, achieves new life. The whole of southern California is as man-made as Barbie; in her hallowed hot tub, her sacred shower, her sacerdotal spa, she celebrates the miracle of manufactured existence.

Likewise, in the East, flashy cars are considered at best nouveau, at worst narcissistic. Top-out-of-sight classes drive beat-up station wagons, Fussell tells us. And he is correct: One would not have been likely to spot the late Jackie Onassis tooling around in a pink Corvette, pink Porsche, pink Jaguar, pink Mustang, or any of the other roseate conveyances in Barbie's garage. Yet cars have a different meaning in southern California, particularly for adolescents. They are like shoes. Transportation, autonomy, separation from parents—all these teenage "issues" are difficult without wheels. Regardless of social class, cars are a marker of puberty—as much as are female breasts or male beards. To display oneself in a fancy car seems as legitimate an adolescent impulse as to parade around in the absurd outfits one sees on MTV. True, perhaps to East Coast preppies, the cars and costumes are a tacky masquerade, a vulgar outdoor display. But having grown up in California, I can understand Barbie's pink Porsche; had my budget and my superego not had a say in the car I bought, I, as a teenager, might have driven one too.

In *Los Angeles: The Architecture of Four Ecologies,* Reyner Banham explains how he came to comprehend the centrality of the automobile in southern California culture, and the way that this influences a southern Californian's perception of space. "The first time I saw it happen nothing registered on my conscious mind," he writes, "because it seemed so natural—as the car in front turned down the off-ramp of the San Diego freeway, the girl beside the driver pulled down the sunvisor and used the mirror on the back of it to tidy her hair. Only when I had seen a couple more incidents of this kind did I catch their import: that coming off the freeway is coming in from outdoors. A domestic or sociable journey in Los Angeles does not end as much at the door of one's destination as at the off-ramp of the freeway."

To drive from, say, the Hotel Bel-Air to Mattel's headquarters in El Segundo is to experience Los Angeles County as a theme park. Crawling at breakfast with film-industry types—faces as familiar as Mickey's and Goofy's—the hotel, with its quasi-Spanish pretense, its swan pond, and its burbling fountains, reminds one of Disneyland's New Orleans Square. Then one pulls onto the San Diego Freeway, a speeded-up Disney autopia, and cruises past the Los Angeles International Airport, where landing airplanes, as if part of a heart-stopping ride, appear to descend within inches of the sunroofs on the cars ahead. On the left there is a vast memorial park with a sparkling faux-classical temple. As readers learned in Evelyn Waugh's *The Loved One,* even death can be themed.

Mattel Headquarters, too, rises above its clean, new industrial plaza like a theme-park corporation. It is gray, erect. Inside are Barbie dioramas and baby dolls; outside it is almost comically masculine—no postmodern whimsy, no coy touches of pink.

Traveling this path each day for a few weeks (though not throughout my entire stint in Los Angeles), I quickly unlearned eastern verticality. I did not unlearn archaism, but I grew tolerant and curious about the new. Even if Los Angeles, as some believe, has proved to be a failed evolutionary experiment, a basin of crime and drought and fouled air, I understood what its horizontality might have meant in the postwar world—a patch of green for every citizen; a romance with the earth; an urge to flee the aridity of sky-box living for the succulence of freshly sprinkled soil. To Banham, it represented "the dream of a good life outside the squalors of a European type of city . . . a dream that runs back not only into the Victorian railway suburbs of earlier cities but also the country-house culture of the fathers of the U.S. Constitution."

Seduced by California, to which I had not returned since I left for college, and sucked into Barbie's tiny world, I began to see a dignity in Barbie's houses. With a little imagination, one could discern the influence of the *Art & Architecture* Case Study Houses—bold, modernist designs from the likes of Pierre Koenig, Craig Ellwood, Charles and Ray Eames—that sprang up in California from 1945 until the early sixties. Barbie's original Dream House, although a jumble of colors, is clean and simple in design—pared down by virtue of its function, which involved folding up into a portable carrying case.

Barbie's 1964 Go-Together plastic furniture also had a sort of Danish modern, psychiatrist's-office look to it; but her revamped 1964 Dream House abandoned Case Study starkness in favor of Levittown rococo. When asked to decipher its confluence of styles, and, as Mattel's catalogue put it, "all the elegant accessories Barbie has chosen," West Coast architecture critic Aaron Betsky, author of *Violated Perfection,* was nonplussed. "Well, there's a brick wall that's right out of late Frank Lloyd Wright thirties school," he said, squinting at the Mattel catalogue. "Then there's this slightly Biedermeyer sofa and chair set, next to the television. And over there, next to the modern kitchen, these fake sort of Scandinavian arts and crafts chairs that have suddenly become bar stools."

The hodgepodge of styles in Barbie's house might be interpreted as a reflection of her class anxiety. "Having a period room or a correctly designed room at a certain point becomes very risky socially," Betsky explained. "Because it means that you're sort of snooty." To attract the maximum range of buyers, her furniture could convey neither hoity-toity nor hoi polloi. "If your room is eclectic, it means you've inherited things," he said. "It means that you have a family history and you're not just right off the boat. So it becomes very acceptable to have pieces that show that if you didn't inherit them from your grandmother who lived in West Essex, then at least you had enough money to go on a trip to West Essex and pick up a few pieces, even if they don't quite go with what you got downtown at Macy's."

Barbie also came on the scene at a time when labor-saving devices were liberating middle-class wives from the drudgery of household chores. As affordable mechanical servants replaced the costly human variety, class distinctions blurred. In 1963, New Jersey's Deluxe Reading Corporation issued a "Dream Kitchen" for Barbie-sized dolls that was a monument to the democratizing effects of technology. What its young owner got was no less than the control center of a suburban spaceship—with a deluxe maize-colored range, a chrome-plated turquoise refrigerator, a sand-colored dishwasher, and a magical garbage disposal tucked away in a salmon-colored sink.

One of Barbie's odder flirtations with archaism came on her 1971 Country Camper—a democratizing vehicle that made pastoral retreats, once restricted to country-house owners, available to anyone who could afford a car. In order to invest the camper with luxury, its plastic kitchen cabinets have ovoid Baroque moldings—the sort of thing one would see in their original incarnation at Versailles.

Not surprisingly, when Barbie achieved superstar status, her houses became more ostentatious. Yet even Barbie's three-story town house, with its Tara-like pillars and ersatz wrought-iron birdcage elevator, is an outsider's interpretation of upper-class life. Authentic valuables are to Barbie's possessions what a pungent slab of gorgonzola is to "cheese food"; her furniture and artwork would not look out of place in a Ramada Inn. For all her implicit disposable income, her tastes remain doggedly middle- to lower-middle-class. As pictured in the catalogue, the town house also reflects *Dynasty* thinking. Both Ken and Barbie are absurdly overdressed—he in a parodic "tuxedo," she in a flouncy confection that barely fits into the elevator.

If Barbie was supposed to be putting on airs, she was doing it ineptly. She bought a lot of things, but they were things whose selection required no connoisseurship. Barbie is a consumer, not a climber. Except for her body, which is slimmer than the average woman's, Barbie is the great American common denominator. She is rich, but not top-out-of-sight; smart but not cultivated; pretty but not beautiful. Far from embodying an impossible standard, she represents one that is wholly achievable. Even the destitute and bottom-out-of-sight can use her as a template for their daydreams.

OF COURSE WHEN I SAY BARBIE'S STATUS IS WITHIN THE grasp of most Americans, I mean North Americans. In Latin America, where blond Barbie outsells all other dolls, Barbie leads a life that few of her young owners will ever replicate. Like Mickey Mouse and Ronald McDonald, Barbie is a pop cultural colonist, a "global power brand," as Mattel vice president Astrid Autolitano puts it.

Because of import restrictions, Mattel has had only two affiliates in Latin America—Mexico and Chile—but the North American Free Trade Agreement will probably change that. Other countries—Brazil, Argentina, Peru, Venezuela, and Colombia—have been served by local licensees. Rather than hindering Barbie's market penetration, however, this simply led to a new dimension in her class mutability. In markets with limited buying power, Mattel or its licensees introduced dolls at lower prices. "Those lower-price dolls basically offer us an opportunity to reach the lower classes, which we call in our jargon, 'Class D'—so as not to say 'lower classes,' " Autolitano told me. On the positive side, this makes Barbie a less-exclusionary product; girls of negligible means can dip their toe in the chlorinated swimming pool of North American consumption. On the negative side . . . well, Ken Handler—after whom the male doll was named—has a few thoughts.

Now entering his sixth decade, Ken Handler is no stranger to South America. He spends half the year there, slogging through swamps, consulting with shamans, stalking indigenous herbs. While on the board of directors of Bronx AIDS services several years ago, he became interested in antioxidant drugs, which many believe can inhibit the cell mutagenesis that causes cancer. The strongest antioxidants, he says, are harvested near the Equator, where they have been toughened by exposure to intense ultraviolet light. When I spoke with him in the winter of 1993, he was raising $7 million to build a laboratory in Ecuador to refine these drugs, and working with a team of physicians to get FDA approval for them.

Handler does not look like his plastic namesake. He is soft-spoken and erudite, with a high forehead, shoulder-length gray hair, and a shaggy gray beard, resembling a mature self-portrait of Leonardo da Vinci. Perhaps as a reaction against his parents, he has embraced archaism with a vengeance. He restores eighteenth- and nineteenth-century town houses in Greenwich Village, and lives in one of them. He plays the harpsichord, specializing in music from the seventeenth century. He spent years on the board of New York's Metropolitan Opera. He admires his parents—"They provided a home with a lot of love," he insists—but he cannot bear the dolls they invented.

To his parents' bewilderment, Ken, as a child, had no interest in toys. He spent his free time reading, playing the piano, or listening to jazz or classical music, which led to his majoring in music at the University of California at Los Angeles. He remembers his youth as a long struggle with his sister, Barbara, who did not go to college. Even something as innocuous as a family drive frequently exploded into a battle for control of the car radio. Ken wanted to listen to opera; his sister Barbara demanded rock 'n' roll. "Every time I got my choice, which wasn't very often, she would have a fit," he said. "God, she knew how to pull the strings on Mom and Dad.

"My sister was a conform freak," he told me. "She loved Barbie. If you'd seen her at age sixteen to seventeen, she *was* Barbie. She went to the beach with her friends; they had the van; they did that life."

Barbara, a comely redhead now well into her fifties, has a policy of not giving interviews. The numerous snapshots of her in Ruth Handler's family album, however, suggest that she is less allergic to being photographed. "It's a shame she won't talk because she owes a lot to that little doll," Ken said. "She used to sell towels," he continued, referring to a bath shop she once ran in Beverly Hills. "And then she decided she wasn't going to sell them anymore. I think she likes to play golf. She used to like to play tennis, then she hurt her leg or something . . . she's had kind of an easy life."

Talking with Ken was a little like playing *Jeopardy!* His conversation leapt from virology to Verdi, from the frontiers of medicine to Met musical director James Levine. I found myself thinking of Nick in *35-Up*—the professor who claims to have close ties to his family, yet who, because of his education, is effectively living on another planet.

"I don't think we've ever had a Barbie in the house," Ken said with amusement. "Philosophically, I didn't want my children to play with it. My oldest [daughter] is so uniquely talented that I've always felt that any gesture toward looking a certain way or being a certain way was not a positive thing. If she had said, 'Dad, get me a Barbie,' I would have gotten it for her. But she knew about it; she'd seen it; she never asked—so I never got it." Samantha, his oldest, currently makes her living as a psychic; but his second daughter, Stacy, an art student, also expressed no interest in the doll. Nor did his son, Jeff, a high-school senior.

"I felt a lot of indignation about the effect the dolls had on impressionable children who are either overweight or couldn't make themselves into that image and felt inferior as a result," he told me. "This bimba—and I say 'bimba' because it's feminine—never has a serious thought. And she has a figure no young lady could ever achieve without a severe anorexic leaning or surgery."

When I suggested that these days Barbie has a fairly impressive résumé, he cut me off. "They're not really careers—they're putting on a costume and pretending. . . . It's no different than some sort of drag show."

Ken's parents don't understand his irritation. "They've never meant for this doll to have—they never see the negative side of it. They don't understand it; it's beyond their ken, to make a pun . . . to them it's just good play. And yet they're very vain people, my parents. They care if you're a little overweight. They care if—I had lost a few pounds because I got these little critters that I always pick up when I go to South America. And my parents said, 'Gee, you look terrific—you lost five, ten pounds or something.'"

Critters or no, Handler is rhapsodic about South America. The curative values of the virgin rain forest are not merely those of the plants he gathers; they are metaphorical. They have to do with the purity of the air, of a life unstriated by social class and uncluttered with material possessions. Never a beachgoer when he lived in Los Angeles, he loves the South American shore. "I like walking down the beach and watching the fishermen fish and the pigs run wild. It's nice going to the beach with a bunch of pigs.

"I'll tell you what I would like to do with Barbie and Ken if they were to suddenly come to life," he said, "provided they could learn enough Spanish because nobody speaks English down where I go—most of them speak Indian languages. I would like to take Barbie and Ken and train them as ethnobotanists, so that they would take the skills they learned at the university at Pepperdine or Malibu or wherever they go to school, and work with the indigenous people.

CAMBODIAN REFUGEES WITH BARBIE
SYLVIA PLACHY

Teach them how to tell time with a wristwatch. Motivate them in learning the skills of their antecedents, through the shamans, who are still alive."

He grew more animated. "I'd like Barbie and Ken to take their blond selves—*rubino* or *rubina* means blond down there—and tan themselves in the sweat of the equatorial jungle sun and give themselves to people that desperately need to learn from them. If Barbie and Ken would come down there with me, I would make sure they have enough work for the summer. But they couldn't drive their van down there, unless it was a four-by-four. And the banditos—if they saw that van, they might want it. So Barbie and Ken might end up having to thumb their way through Guatemala or someplace." He chuckled.

I didn't have the heart to remind him that Barbie and Ken were already there. With their van. And that they probably had taught something to the indigenous people. Just not ethnobotany.

CHAPTER TEN

GUYS AND DOLLS

If people subscribe to the theories of men's movement mythologizer Robert Bly—and the sales of his book *Iron John* would suggest that they do—gentlemen have preferred blondes since the dawn of history. A "Woman with the Golden Hair" dances through the male unconscious, not a "flesh and blood woman," but a "luminous eternal figure," Bly says. From her face emanates a whisper: "All those who love the Woman with the Golden Hair come to me." Men search for the perfect embodiment of this being, projecting their hunger onto models, centerfolds, flight attendants, and aerobics instructors. But such desire is not exactly sanguine for its objects: "Millions of American men gave their longing for the Golden-Haired Woman to Marilyn Monroe," Bly writes. "She offered to take it and she died from it."

Scion of a sex toy, Barbie, far more than any human, is equipped to withstand such toxic projections. Age cannot wither her nor custom stale her infinite plasticity. "I think if you look at the silhouette of the *Playboy* Bunny, it looks like a Barbie doll," retired Mattel designer Joe Cannizzaro told me. "So do men want to date a Barbie doll? Probably. But do men notice it? Only if shown. They wouldn't go looking for it."

BARBIE AND FRIEND SYLVIA PLACHY

Well, not at Toys "R" Us, anyway. But according to Dian Hanson, editor of *Juggs, Leg Show,* and *Bust Out!,* Barbie's body, even without detailed genitalia, is proportioned to inflame all the common permutations of heterosexual male desire.

Hanson, born in 1951, is one of America's preeminent female pornographers. Unlike that of Susie Bright, editor of *On Our Backs,* a magazine "for the Adventurous Lesbian," Hanson's audience is primarily straight men. She credits her success to market research: she asks her readers what they want and they tell her. Readers of *Leg Show,* her magazine for foot fetishists, "tend to be white-collar, educated people with computers," she told me. "They write me a lot. The letters pour in every day. I've asked them to explain: Do you know where your fetish came from? What are your earliest memories? And I've learned a great deal. A lot of what I know, I know from these guys directly."

Hanson does not have the tough look that one might expect from a sultana of smut. Lean, fit, and proportioned like a fashion doll, she wears little makeup and has long, healthy blond hair. Her features are as even as a cover girl's, and her smile is so wholesome she could sell toothpaste. Slightly tan, she radiates a sort of patrician outdoorsiness; one could imagine her teaching sailing or skiing at a tony resort. When I met with her at her SoHo office on a bone-chilling winter day, she was wearing blue jeans and L.L. Bean duck shoes—not what I'd anticipated. Her office, however, did not disappoint: nearly every flat surface was covered with brightly colored genital prostheses or stiletto-heeled pumps—marabou-trimmed mules, rhinestone-studded slippers—many of which, because of Hanson's large feet, were bought in transvestite boutiques.

"One of the reasons my magazines are very successful is because I realize you can't separate sex from love," she explained. "When a man has a breast obsession, he's looking for security and love and blissful, mindless protection." This led her to create *Bust Out!,* which features narrow-hipped professional sex stars with huge silicone breasts that, she says, appeal to men who grew up with Barbie. "When the mother holds the baby up where the breast is, it's just huge—as big as his head if not bigger—and it's filling his vision, filling his nose, filling his ears. Everything is blocked out by the breast, and the breast is comfort and safety. The desire to have a breast as big as your head is really taking yourself back to that infantile period and being able to lose yourself.

"I learned this really from doing *Leg Show*," she continued. "The breast thing was so common I didn't think about it. But I had to figure out why men were obsessed with feet and legs and groveling before them. I learned that men get security from legs, because when a little child is scared, he grips his mother's legs. They're always trying to get up under the skirt, holding on to the legs—and the legs represent safety. A loving mother may pick up the child and hold him, but a less loving, harsher mother may just leave the child down there, so the legs are all he gets. When a boy with a stern, withholding mother grows up, he often fastens on a harsher, more demanding woman as his love object."

Such men also fasten on Barbie's fetishistic shoes, which "raise the foot, contort it, and display it as if it's on a pedestal—which is precisely what most foot fetishists want. Foot fetishists think of the foot like the breast; and a man who likes the breast wants to see it lifted up and displayed. He wants a big push-up bra. Men who are into breasts don't want to see the breast just lying there. They really love those low-cut fifties dresses where they see cleavage really *displayed*. A shoe like Barbie wears does the same thing: It draws attention to the foot, much more than, say, a bare foot walking down the street. You're taking the foot and you're elevating it. You're serving it on a platter."

But far from being symbols of female passivity—or devices that impede movement—spike heels can be interpreted as symbols of strength. They make the wearer taller, so that she or he (the shoes are *de rigueur* with drag queens) towers over the nonwearer the way that Mom towered over her little boy. Nor do they mimic feminine curves; they are sharp, pointy, masculine.

"Submissive men" who buy *Leg Show* are into "the highest, most dangerous, most hobbling heels because they see them as a symbol of feminine power," Hanson explained. "Because they could be hurt by those shoes. They could be pierced. And they like being walked on with them."

You don't have to be a psychoanalyst to see how childhood experiences shaped Hanson's readers. She can even pinpoint the decade a man grew up in by the type of hosiery that excites him. Men who were toddlers in the seventies (when their mothers wore pantyhose) are turned on by pantyhose; older men prefer garter belts.

Nor are boys alone influenced by the earliest bonds with Mom. Children of both sexes are originally matrisexual, Nancy Chodorow writes in *The Reproduction of Mothering,* and remain so for most of their preoedipal period, or until they are about four or five. Freud, in fact, found that a girl's infantile attachment to her mother has a major impact on both her succeeding oedipal attachment to Dad and her eventual connection to men in general.

Hanson doesn't just grill her readers about the origins of their sexual desires; she has also probed her own. Brought up in Seattle by parents who were part of a secret fundamentalist religion, she remembers Barbie as her beacon. Just as aspiring doctors send their Barbies to medical school or aspiring models pose her on runways, aspiring pornographers—well, the doll, Hanson says, made Hanson what she is today.

Hanson was nine when Barbie first appeared, and her parents, members of the Constitution party, a right-wing group similar to the John Birch Society, refused to let her have one. They considered the doll—along with rock 'n' roll and *Mad* magazine—to be part of a conspiracy to sexualize "American youth and thereby weaken it, by making it promiscuous," she recalled. "With my parents, it was always hard to tell whether it was the

'Communist Conspiracy' or the 'Jewish Conspiracy'—they sort of melded together in my mind." But its pomps, her parents felt, would "enflame our sexual organs and ruin our white morality, which was of course the basis of everything that made America great.

"My father said, 'The purpose of dolls in the life of girls is to train them to be good wives and mothers,' " she continued. "And girls should play only with baby dolls so they can learn to care for real-life families. He felt—and his religion feels—that women have no creative abilities, women have no place in the world except to support their husbands and raise their children. I think Barbie probably turned my dad on. My dad is a very sexual person . . . and he saw Barbie's sexuality. But once Barbie was proclaimed to be this sexual conspiracy object, she became much more provocative to me."

At first, Hanson would sneak off to friends' houses to play with their Barbies. But after about a year or so, when owning the dolls didn't appear to have any ill effects on her cousins, her mother caved in and gave her one.

TOMI UNGERER, EROTIC DOLL SCULPTURE, COLLECTION OF LES MUSÉES DE LA VILLE DE STRASBOURG

"When I got Barbie, it was like my parents had given me heroin," Hanson said. "The first thing I did was strip all her clothes off and marvel at her breasts and feel her breasts and look at her body and those tiny arched feet and the whorishly arched eyebrows and the solid thick eyelashes and the earrings that stuck straight into her head." She paused. "They were pins. It was very exciting to me to pull the earrings in and out. I did it to the point that they just fell out after a while."

Hanson usually played with Barbie in the company of her younger brother, who became a cross-dresser and committed suicide in his twenties. "I was supposed to play with my sister but we didn't get along. My brother was more appreciative of Barbie's sexuality . . . I had Barbie and Midge, and we used to parade them around naked in their high heels. We painted nipples on them one day to make them more realistic. And we were mortified that we couldn't get the paint off. So my parents were going to know that we had sexualized the dolls."

Nevertheless, because of the rituals of their religion, her parents' idea of "sexual repression" was not what everyone would consider repressive. Her father, a chiropractor and "naturopath," practiced nudism, and her mother gave birth to the children at home. "It was a sexually charged household," Hanson said.

"I lived out my own emerging sexual fantasies with Barbie," she continued. "I only wanted the sexy clothes, and my mother wouldn't give them to me. She bought me childish clothes—a blue corduroy jumper. We'd put Barbie in it without the blouse and the breasts would show. The two outfits that I coveted—and saved up money for, and had to fight with my mother over—were both strapless: the pink satin evening gown that fit real tight. It could barely go over her legs it was so tight. And you could pull her top down. The other one was the gold lamé strapless sheath dress with a zipper up the back.

"I didn't like Midge because she didn't have a sexy face," Hanson said. "The old Barbie looked dominant: sharp nose, sharp eyelashes—she was a dangerous-looking woman. And of course she had those symbols of power on her feet. . . . I don't consider Barbie sexual anymore. I looked at new Barbies a year or so ago, and their faces were infantile—more rounded and childlike."

Hanson used Barbie to imagine her idealized future self, which in her case meant an object of male desire. "Barbie was an adult woman whom I could examine," she said. "And I wanted very much to be Barbie." Nor was Hanson the only budding sex maven to fixate on the dolls. "I definitely lived out my fantasies with them," Madonna told an interviewer. "I rubbed her and Ken together a lot. And man, Barbie was *mean.*" Likewise, Sharon Stone's thoughts in *Vanity Fair* suggested an autobiographical episode: "If you look at any little girl's Barbie, she's taken a ballpoint pen and she's drawn pubic hair on it."

Hanson left home at seventeen and became a respiratory therapist. After a bad first marriage, she found herself divorced in Allentown, Pennsylvania, where she met a man who was starting a sex magazine called *Puritan.* "I started working on that magazine and it was like a dream come true, to get to be a pornographer," she effused. "I wanted to be appreciated in that way. I used to be a provocative dresser. I was very promiscuous. I'd wear hot pants and see-through blouses and things like that. But as I've gotten older and more successful in my career, looking a certain way doesn't worry me anymore. And I'm grateful—because there's nothing worse than being forty-one years old and still needing that kind of attention."

What Hanson learned in her odyssey through the porn world was "traditional sexual power"; she internalized the visual coding of the early Barbies—a way of presenting herself so that, as she saw it, she was sexually in control. "I could make men love me—I could make men want to see me and be with me and stay with me because I was a great lay," she said. "Men really will stay with a woman and love a woman if she's very sexy. It's exactly the opposite of what my parents told me." Hanson has, in a way, realized the Barbie fantasy, the girl-version of the American Dream. She has a steady boyfriend, a place in the city, a getaway in the country, and a lucrative job that she loves.

Significantly, Hanson scorns the face of the current Barbie. Much of the original doll's "traditional sexual power" emanated from its heavy-lidded, almost vampiric gaze—the "aggressive eye of the gorgon," as Camille Paglia has put it, "that turns men into stone."

"That is the most powerful eye," Paglia told me. "It is far more powerful than the 'male gaze,' which, as defined by feminism, is simply a tool by which men maintain their power in society. A woman lying on a bed with her legs open is not in a subordinate position. She is in a position of total luxury, like an empress: 'Serve me and die'—essentially that. . . . That very sultry and seductive woman seems half asleep, but what is awake is her eye." And it is the eye that implicitly draws the male observer to the woman—at his peril. The eye "hypnotizes you; it paralyzes you; it puts you under a spell."

Some, however, feel that the characterization of women as vampires in art and myths has less to do with women's real nature and more to do with how the men who created the art and myths perceived them. Even when they are well into adulthood, boys still fear and dread Mom for the power that she once held over them—and they extend that fear to all women, demonizing them into a lethal army of femmes fatales. Men "create folk legends, beliefs and poems that ward off the dread by externalizing and objectifying women," Chodorow writes. Yet regardless of whether the vampiric female gaze is an objective fact or a metaphorical construct, it is a recurring theme in the history of male heterosexual desire. And it is as crucial as Barbie's breasts in understanding why straight men slaver over flesh-and-blood versions of the doll.

Male heterosexual desire, however, is not shaped by boyhood experiences alone. It is influenced by what the culture designates as "erotic"—not merely pornographic nudes, but artistic ones. A nude, by definition, should arouse in the viewer "some vestige of erotic feeling," Kenneth Clark writes.

Historically, society has eroticized particular female body types at particular times. In *Seeing Through Clothes*, Anne Hollander shows how from ancient statues to modern photographs, the look of the unclothed figure has been influenced by the fashions of its day. Today, artists sexualize the female breasts and buttocks, but from medieval times until the seventeenth century, bellies were all the rage: whether a painting's subject was a virgin or a courtesan, she could not have too big a tummy. Likewise, the mega-mammaries that men pant over in *Bust Out!* were in the 1500s considered abhorrent, and usually featured on witches and hags. It wasn't until the mid-nineteenth century, when women cinched in their waists with corsets, that commodious breasts became alluring, in, for instance, paintings by Gustave Courbet and Eugène Delacroix.

Barbie's large breasts make sense as a function of her time—postwar America. Breasts are emblematic of the home; they produce milk and provide security and comfort. Some of the strangest market research in Vance Packard's *The Hidden Persuaders* dealt with what milk meant to soldiers in World War II. Just as G.I.'s pined over chesty pinups, they also thirsted for milk—and those on the front lines craved it more than those stationed near home. If one makes a link between the meanings of milk and its infantile source, the top-heavy, hourglass shape of postwar fashion that Dior introduced with his "New Look" wasn't solely about hobbling women so that they would retreat from the workplace. It was about meeting the returning troops' profound psychological needs.

Barbie's absent nipples also comment on the extent to which those body parts have been eroticized in American culture. As a clothes mannequin, Barbie has no functional need of nipples; yet their omission is critical to establishing her sexual "innocence" and suitability for children. "So long as only the upper parts of the breasts are exposed, and the balance hidden, no sexual excitement is produced and no shock is administered to modern morality," Lawrence Langer observes in *The Importance of Wearing Clothes.* "But let the nipples fall out and panic ensues!"

Barbie's combination of voluptuous body and wholesome image was precisely what Hugh Hefner sought in models for *Playboy,* which he founded in 1953. Although such classic pinups as Jayne Mansfield and Bettie Page appeared in the magazine's earliest issues, Hefner's ideal Playmate was the girl next door—a member of a sorority house, not a house of ill repute. She was a girl who looked, as David Halberstam put it in *The Fifties,* as if she'd "stopped off to do a *Playboy* shoot on her way to cheerleading practice." But although Hef's paradigm was a "good girl," she was—like Barbie—not on the prowl for a husband. Before his recent reconversion to marriage, Hef's longtime girlfriend was *Barbie* Benton.

"Something I've thought about with *Playboy* and the Playmates is that they're women who are not really procreative females," Hanson observed. "They have very narrow hips, very boyish figures, big false breasts and they're Playmates, not wives. So a man can escape the reality of his child-bearing wife. There's no possibility of her getting pregnant." The large breasts also encourage men to recall the scale of breasts in infancy. Hence, too, the look of infertility: Men dread fathering a rival.

Mattel claims Barbie's hair is long because of children's fascination with "hairplay." But ever since Milton's portrait of Eve in *Paradise Lost,* with her "golden tresses" falling "in wanton ringlets" to her waist, long hair has been part of the arsenal of seduction. Marian the Librarian must shake loose her spinsterish bun before she can be seen as enticing. "Long-haired models and messy-haired models are always more popular," Hanson explained. "If men want submissive women, they prefer them to be blond. If they want dominant women, they want them to be dark-haired. But in general they want lots and lots of hair.

"Sometimes I'll use women with very short hair in *Leg Show* because a lot of my readers feel so inferior and believe so much in female superiority that they don't think there should be any women who have sex with men," she continued. "They want them all to be lesbians." She handed me some photos. "Here's 'The Secret Sex Lives of Real Dykes'—a real lesbian couple in France who are posing. One of the women is older, non-made-up, rough-looking. And men can fantasize that they're lesbians, which a lot of them wish they were."

Body hair, however, is perceived as repellent, Hanson said, "except by the small groups of men who want them furry like apes." Like the nude female statues of ancient Greece, Barbie has no pubic fleece; but that's not, as in the case of the statues, a reflection of women's actual appearance. The average contemporary woman, unlike her archaic counterpart, does not depilate herself. Until recently, a nude rendered without pubic hair was considered arty, its opposite raunchy and obscene. But *Playboy*'s love affair with the airbrush ended that. Its models may not be fully defoliated, but they are certainly pruned.

Because of the historical association of hair with sexual power and passion, John Berger thinks that the absence of body hair, particularly in pornographic female subjects, is a way of making the male viewer more comfortable. The viewer doesn't want to satisfy a symbolically voracious woman; he wants a woman to satisfy *him*. It's hard not to pity John Ruskin for having been born too soon. Had he come of age when women aped Barbie and, by extension, Greek sculptures, he might have managed to consummate his marriage, instead of being revolted by the sight of his wife's pubic hair.

Although the original Barbie's scarlet talons no longer connote wealth, they still mean power. "Nails are very erotic," Hanson said. "There are men who like ragged nails because that indicates a rough nature—a woman who might drag them off to her lair and devour them. Others prefer short nails because they represent youth."

Barbie's firm, showgirl bottom was perhaps underappreciated when she first appeared. In the 1990s, however, with breast implants criticized as both life-threatening and fake-looking—attributes oddly cast as equal in their undesirability—"buns of steel" have been anointed by such arbiters as *Allure* and *W* as today's status symbol. As with the postwar breast boom, it was not ever thus. In the 1730s, the idealized female body curved at its sides but not at its front or back. "The figure was almost like roadkill, it was so flat," Richard Martin, director of the Costume Institute at New York's Metropolitan Museum of Art, told *Allure*. Next derrieres were veiled by layers of clothes. It wasn't until the advent of the miniskirt in the 1960s that the female hindquarters became an official object of desire. To achieve what *Allure* terms a "thumpable melon butt," a woman must not only firm her gluteus maximus, but (à la Barbie) wear high heels, which tilt the rear end as much as 20 percent. This tilt arouses a man's inner ape. When female chimpanzees are in heat, their genitals swell, and, as a seductive gesture, they angle their behinds in the direction of their mates.

"Older men and men who are looking for mates and for love relationships want bottom-heavy women," Hanson agreed. But Barbie-generation men prefer that effect to be achieved bionically. "Lip jobs, butt jobs, tummy tucks, and boob jobs" are no longer sufficient to qualify for a job in porn; the latest trend is "customized" genitalia. "I understand in L.A. it's fashionable among the young porn models to get collagen injections in their labia to make them look more swollen and excited," she said.

The fashion for exaggerated depictions of sex, however, is not confined to pornography. In mainstream movies, soulful lovemaking has given way to strenuous gymnastics—"übersex," Walter Kirn calls it—the erotic act interpreted as a cartoon car chase. Übersex is what occurs between human-Barbie Sharon Stone and Michael Douglas in *Basic Instinct*. It is rigorous, yet tidy—a mating of mannequins, "taking the basic Ken-and-Barbie poses familiar to naughty ten-year-olds and heaping on *Playboy*-approved perversions," Kirn writes in *Mirabella*. It is also utterly humorless.

Watching Stone and the other dolls in *Basic Instinct*, I thought of Jack Ryan and his R&D team in the 1960s, who eased some of their creative tension by playing pranks and shooting one another with water pistols. They also did what engineer Derek Gable and others have characterized as "a lot of racy stuff" with Barbie and Ken—modifying their anatomy and staging X-rated puppet shows. It's not surprising that imaginative grown men with senses of humor joked that way with the dolls. What is extraordinary, though, is that thirty years later their ribald gags would wind up in the movies, presented as everyday lovemaking.

DAVID LEVINTHAL, BARBIE AND G.I. JOSÉ I, 1972

One does not have to be female to affect Barbie's exaggerated "feminine" look, which may be part of its appeal. Before *The Crying Game*, a movie whose most beguiling "female" character isn't biologically female, one might have been hard pressed to argue that drag queens have a more profound understanding of "femininity" than do biological women. But merely possessing an XX chromosome does not guarantee a mastery of (or a desire to master) the stylized conventions of "femininity." The "feminine" signals that say come hither to heterosexual men can be affected by persons of any gender; they have also been in large part invented for women by gay men. "Cults of beauty have been persistently homosexual from antiquity to today's hair salons and house of couture," Camille Paglia writes in *Sexual Personae*. "Professional beautification of women by homosexual men is a systematic reconceptualization of the brute facts of female nature."

Barbie—who doesn't bleed, kvetch, or demand to choose her own outfits—may be, for some gay arbiters, the apotheosis of female beauty. The doll is built like a transvestite, with broad shoulders, narrow hips, and huge breasts. Significantly, in the late eighties and early nineties—when Barbie sales rocketed—the fashion industry worked hard to make the idealized female body that of a drag queen. Designers like Jean-Paul Gaultier (whom we have to thank for the torpedo brassiere Madonna wore *outside* her clothes on her Blonde Ambition tour) and Stephen Sprouse were among the first to use male transvestites, such as Terri Toye, a Barbie-esque blonde, to model women's clothes. Other designers followed: Todd Oldham employed Billy Erb, Kalinka engaged Zaldy Soco, and Thierry Mugler brought out Connie Girl—a striking black "woman" who is also a Barbie collector. Race is no impediment to copying Barbie: between his platinum wig and steep heels, black transvestite recording artist Ru-Paul—who, as a child, excised the breasts from his Barbie dolls and, more recently, reported on the introduction of Mattel's Shani doll for the BBC—does a good imitiation.

So does the Lady Bunny, the drag queen who organized "Wigstock," an annual transgender Woodstock-type festival that takes place in New York's East Village. She feels that the look of the early Barbies—the ones she knew as a little boy in Chattanooga, Tennessee—had a significant impact on her style. "I loved the shiny hair," she told me, "which is a kind of cheap wig hair. It's not meant to look natural, it's meant to look brassy and showbizzy. Which is a look I try to get—I love the wigs with the big bumps in the back." Size-twelve, Barbie-style mules also assist her trompe l'oeil; they lengthen her legs and curve their calves, making them appear more "feminine." If the shoes are a little small and the heel hangs over, that's okay, she explained. The overhang is called a "biscuit."

When she was a child, her parents were reluctant to buy her a Barbie; they feared it might affect her gender identification. When they eventually relented, she used the doll to puzzle out the components of "femininity," or "the tricks of the trade," as she calls them. She is still envious of the effortlessness with which the doll pulls off certain hard-to-achieve effects. "It's so easy for *her* to work those evening capes with the crinkled taffeta," she said. Had I only spoken to her while she was in drag, I might not have appreciated the extent to which her "look" was "worked," or been viscerally struck by how artificial the cues that telegraphed "feminine" were. When we made a date for tea, I had expected to interview her stage persona—a Barbie doll with a sweet southern drawl. But she met me as her offstage persona—a clean-cut young man wearing blue jeans and a hooded sweatshirt, the image of Ron Howard in *American Graffiti.*

Vaginal Davis, a poet, drag queen, and self-described "Blacktress," with the bearing of Norma Desmond and the seeming height (in heels) of Michael Jordan, also acknowledges a debt to the doll. As a child, Davis used Barbie and her friends to project herself beyond boundaries of gender and class, to invent the "woman" she is today. "Growing up in the inner city I wasn't a part of what you might call 'society,' " she told me. "And I always thought that I was born in the wrong social sphere—the wrong social class. I should have been a debutante. I should have been going to a Seven Sisters school. I should have been jet-setting to Milan and dining with heads of state and living a very Audrey Hepburn sort of life—far from my life in the projects, in Watts." Although she couldn't afford authentic Mattel outfits, she made clothes out of found objects and scrap materials—ball gowns and coronation dresses—inspired by her other childhood fascination: English royalty.

Some say drag queens perpetuate demeaning stereotypes of women; others argue that by caricaturing stereotypes of gender, they subvert them. What's interesting about both positions is the assumption that "femininity" is something quite different from actually being a woman, just as "masculinity" has little to do with actually being a man.

These days, for human beings, gender identity can be something of a morass. Nearly two decades ago, in an essay on "Primary Femininity," psychiatrist Robert Stoller used the term "core gender identity" to refer to a child's concrete sense of his or her sex. Stoller took into consideration the fact that the biological sex of a child and its gender were not always the same. Developmental geneticists had discovered that without some exposure to fetal androgens, anatomical maleness could not occur—even in a child with XY chromosomes. Likewise, with the wrong sort of exposure to fetal androgens, a fetus with XX chromosomes would develop as an anatomical male. Then there were the hermaphrodites for whom sex assignment at birth was completely arbitrary. For those of you who are counting, we are up to *five* sexes now. But because society only recognizes two, children who were not clearly boys or girls were nonetheless placed in one of those categories. And, ideally, their "core gender identity" developed in accordance with the decision that the attending physician made in the delivery room.

Today, the trendier gender theorists argue that the assignment of gender is by definition imprecise. Because of the limitations of the binary system, all gendering is "drag." "Drag constitutes the mundane way in which genders are appropriated, theatricalized, worn, done," Judith Butler writes in "Imitation and Gender Insubordination." "Gender is a kind of imitation for which there is no original," she argues. What the so-called genders imitate is a "phantasmic ideal of heterosexual identity."

Regardless of whether this "ideal of heterosexual identity" is "phantasmic" in people, however, it seems pretty real in Barbie and Ken—or maybe Barbie and G.I. Joe, since Ken, in response to research showing that pronounced male secondary sex characteristics scare little girls, has lost his macho edge. Barbie is a space-age fertility archetype, Joe a space-age warrior. They are idealized opposites, templates of "femininity" and "masculinity" imposed on sexless effigies—which underscores the irrelevance of actual genitalia to perceptions of gender. What nature can only approximate, plastic makes perfect.

Heterosexual men use pornographic renderings of the Barbie archetype for sexual fantasies, just as children use the actual doll for make-believe. Although Barbie looks like an adult, children wield power over her—in much the same way that a male viewer, through projected fantasy, wields power over the female object in a pornographic image. In her short story "A Real Doll," A. M. Homes picks the scab off this relationship and probes it through the musings of her narrator, a boy who is "dating" his sister's Barbie. This involves making the doll complicit in his autoerotic escapades—"the secret habits that seem normal enough to us, but which we know better than to mention out loud." Rape her, fondle her, feed her Valium. Masturbate into the hollow body of her boyfriend. Barbie will never squeal.

In writing the story, Homes was interested not only in the doll, but in "what it means to be a 'good girl' or 'good boy' at that really odd moment

DAVID LEVINTHAL, BARBIE AND G.I. JOSÉ II, 1972

when no matter how hard you try, you can't," she told me. "Because you're coming into a sort of sexual life and it seems inescapably perverse—no matter what you do."

Although Homes was aware of the doll as a child in Chevy Chase, Maryland, it was not central to her life. "I grew up in one of those families where we didn't have guns or dolls or anything," she said. "My parents' idea of a good gift would be a blank piece of paper. If it could have been Marxist Barbie, it probably would have been fine. But Barbie symbolized all the wrong things."

Homes bought her first Barbie while a graduate student at the University of Iowa. When she displayed it above her fireplace, she found visitors could not resist undressing it. "These were adult people coming into my home, immediately going to my mantel and taking off the doll's clothing," she said. "Men, women, *whatever* came in the door. And I thought: Why are they doing this? And they would proceed to then tell me all the horrible things that they had done to Barbie as a child—sort of abusing her in my presence. People were telling me how they chewed her feet off, they took her head off. And I told them: You're maniacs."

But the anecdotes stayed with her, as did Barbie's powerlessness. In "A Real Doll," she contrasts the difference between a boy's perception of the doll and a girl's. The boy is comfortable with Barbie's foreignness and objectification; the girl, who compares Barbie unfavorably with herself, is not—and she retaliates by mutilating the doll. Not all little girls gravitate as naturally to Barbie's "feminine" affectations and "traditional sexual power" as did Dian Hanson or the Lady Bunny. "We live in a world where it's hard to be a person and a girl," Homes told me. "When I put on high heels—number one, I've actually broken my leg just trying to walk in the things. But I become a very different person. Because I can't even cross a room as Amy Homes. All of a sudden, I'm crossing as Amy Homes, Girl.

"Men think they would like a real-life Barbie, but if they met her, they wouldn't want to go near her," Homes elaborated. "She'd be seven feet tall and she'd be too scary." *Playboy*'s 1991 photo spread on the "Barbi Twins," however, suggests otherwise. Photographed wallowing in wet sand on Maui, the pair—who call themselves Shane and Sia—are a bizarre assemblage of anatomical components, notably four gargantuan breasts that, proportionately, are even larger than the doll's. Former belly dancers with slim hips that would look right at home on a fourteen-year-old boy, the two actually described themselves to *Newsday* as "truckdrivers in drag." Although *Playboy* presents them with its characteristic earnestness, there is something almost laugh-aloud funny about their mismatched body parts. And, to their credit, they seem both to have understood and exploited the fact that they are walking errors in scale. First they named themselves after an eleven-and-a-half-inch doll; then, in 1989, posted giant photos of themselves on a billboard over Sunset Boulevard. It was as if Barbie, the ultimate controllable object, got her revenge by starring in *Attack of the Fifty-Foot Woman.* Or perhaps I should say "Barbi"—their *e* disappeared after objections from Mattel.

Evidence suggests that the doll themes that excite heterosexual men are not of equal interest to lesbians. In 1989, when *On Our Backs* published photos of a Barbie-like doll used as a dildo, readers protested. "Is this what you call erotic?" one less-than-euphemistic reader began. "Barbie is the ugliest piece of shit to come out of Amerikan factories." Fantasies involving scale, power, and, well, brand penetration would appear to be principally male.

Grown men amusing themselves with adult female dolls is not new in the history of fetishism, which, as Louise J. Kaplan has explained, "involves using deadened and dehumanized objects as a substitute for living, excited persons." The German Lilli doll is part of an international tradition of pornographic miniatures. Mascot Models, an English firm, currently markets six-inch replicas of naked women with detailed genitalia in the sort of hobby shops that sell model trains, boats, and airplanes. The "girls," which often come with boots or whips, can be assembled with "thick superglue or five-minute epoxy" and (oral fetishists beware!) are made of metal parts containing lead. Far safer to gnaw upon are the Japanese-made miniatures of Caucasian women in bondage that artist David Levinthal used in his 1991 series of photographs called *Desire.* Available by mail order only, they come in chains, ropes, and leather gags; their legs splayed or trussed up like a dead deer's. One even hangs on a cross. Like their English counterparts, the dolls must be glued together and painted.

There is even a historical interface between soft pornographic miniatures and the toy industry. When Louis Marx ran Marx Toys, he produced several limited editions of "American Beauties"—six-inch plastic nude or seminude female figures that he handed out as gag gifts to his friends. Only Ruth Handler dared blur the line between fetish and toy, taking an object familiar to readers of Krafft-Ebing and recasting it for readers of Mother Goose.

For subscribers to Dian Hanson's *Leg Show,* however, Barbie has lost none of the Lilli doll's fetishistic appeal. When Hanson invited her readers to comment on Barbie, many replied—the most eloquent of which was a rural New England foot fetishist who wished to be identified only as "Resident." Part Russ Meyer, part Jonathan Swift, his fantasy, if filmed, might be titled *Barbie Does Brobdingnag.*

"Barbie's legs are the most noteworthy feature of her whole body," his letter begins. "I've spent hours caressing them and examining them, kissing them and sucking them. I've found that their form and shape closely resemble real women's legs. They are warm to the touch and bend in much the same manner as the human leg does, with the curvature of the calf becoming more round when the knee is bent." Barbie, he feels "lacks only three human features: 1) leg and foot scent, 2) a rounded heel and 3) digits for toes.

"I have an incredibly strong sex drive and realized long ago that most women either don't understand or take seriously my love of their legs and feet," he explains. "I ended up being left out in the cold all the time— lonely, depressed and frustrated. Thus the Barbie doll is important to me. I can play out my sexual fantasies with the kind of woman I want in real life. I can dress her and undress her any way I want. Her elegant legs can be posed in a variety of positions. My favorite is with her back leaning against a pillow, legs bent slightly at the knee with her two hands holding onto her thigh, which may be raised up as if she were massaging it. . . .

"If they made a life-size, realistic, fully functional Barbie doll I would probably marry it," he goes on. "I have grown to love Barbie as if she were a real woman and I envy 'Ken' with a passion. Why Mattel hooked her up with such a John Doe is beyond me. Hooking sweet and beautiful Barbie up with a guy ruins the magic.

"I don't buy any of the bad press that's attributed to the Barbie doll and her image," he concludes. "Jealous people always make false accusations about things that they feel inferior to."

While I would not have expressed it in a sentence ending in a preposition, I can understand "Resident's" indignation. It must be burdensome, when you have an intense emotional relationship to a thing, to endure the callous, uncomprehending remarks of people. Or to yearn, as Bly puts it, for a "Woman with the Golden Hair," and end up stuck with . . . a woman.

CHAPTER ELEVEN

OUR BARBIES, OUR SELVES

Midway through my interview with Jan, a thirty-three-year-old business writer who lives in New York City, she asked me not to use her real name. For her, to talk about Barbie was to talk about her mother. It was to recall her disquietude on the eve of puberty. Jan had learned firsthand how a young woman's feelings about her changing body and awakening sexuality can be poisoned by a parent. And she had learned this wordlessly—through a doll.

In *The Second Sex*, Simone de Beauvoir notes that in both French and English, a "doll" is a female adult, and "to doll up" means to don fussy, feminine clothes. This, she feels, is more than a linguistic coincidence. Not only men but also women objectify women, and they begin by objectifying themselves. A woman "is taught that to please she must try to please," Beauvoir writes. "She must make herself object; she should therefore renounce her autonomy. She is treated like a live doll and refused liberty. Thus a vicious circle is formed; for the less she exercises her freedom . . . the less she will dare to affirm herself as a subject." Clearly, this objectification existed long before Barbie, but it may have fresh meaning in the post-Barbie world.

BARBIE WITH PHOTO OF CORAZON YELLEN

SYLVIA PLACHY

It certainly does for Jan, an Asian American who was born in South Korea and adopted by a German-American mother and an Italian-American father. Jan spent her childhood in Orange County, California, and graduated from high school and college in Indiana, where she managed to be both "popular" and smart—a pom-pom girl who was an honor student and the editor of the school newspaper.

Jan's first encounter with "the whole Barbie phenomenon" took place in California in 1965. "I must have been five or six," she told me. "That year, for Christmas, I got a Skipper doll and a little forty-five of Gary Lewis and the Playboys' 'She's My Girl,' and all day I had Skipper bouncing around to this song. She was a dark-haired Skipper, and she very much had that sixties look—eyeliner and little bangs and long hair. I thought Skipper was the end-all and be-all of the earth, until I phoned one of my friends to compare gifts. She started talking about how she had gotten this Barbie, which was a much different kind of doll. And I immediately felt rooked—why had I gotten the little sister? Why hadn't I gotten the star of the show?"

Jan's adoptive mother argued that the younger doll was closer in age to Jan. But, Jan recalled, "It made me feel in playing with other girls that I didn't have what it took. Because all I had was a Skipper, I could never really get into the whole dating thing. I could never have this rich fantasy life—meet a man, have romantic love. I was always relegated to being the little sister."

Nor did Jan's identification with Skipper end when she outgrew dolls. "I have never felt particularly pretty or attractive or sexually interesting. I have always thought that I was more like, not a little sister, but an androgynous person."

This was not the revelation I had expected from Jan—chic, downtown Jan in her stylish black suits and crimson lipstick—who had competed in beauty contests as a teenager. I had expected her to talk about racial identification: how it felt for an Asian American to play with a doll that coded Caucasian standards of beauty. But all Jan wanted to discuss was Barbie's voluptuousness.

"Barbie always looms," Jan said. "That sort of ideal looms—and other women have it. Other women possessed these dolls; other women learned the secret. Maybe this is taking this Barbie thing too far, but I feel like other women had a certain kind of girl experience that I didn't—that they understood something about being sort of seductive and perky that I didn't get. I was always kind of a gal-along-for-the-ride, never feeling I could identify with the Marilyn–Jayne Mansfield–Barbie character."

By withholding Barbie, Jan believes, her mother deliberately tried to stunt her sexual development. And it nearly worked: Despite her cheerleader looks, she projected so much standoffishness that she scared boys away. It wasn't until she was eighteen that she had her first date. Fortunately, her father, an engineer who wore Vargas Girl cuff links and joked about "va-va-va-voom actresses," projected a different message. "My mother was a very threatened person," Jan said. "Because she was very unattractive. And my father was quite handsome. I think she felt threatened by me sexually—by any woman who was attractive.

"You know what dolls my mother did give me?" Jan suddenly blurted. "Trolls! I never had a Barbie house but I had a troll house. I was thinking: Is this what she wants me to identify with—these horrible things with purple hair?"

Today, no one observing Jan and her handsome husband—"a cross between Jeff Bridges and Jeff Daniels," she says—would suspect that she had a Skipper Complex. Yet just as I will never quite shake the legacy of Midge, Jan has been forever burdened with Skipper. Jan, however, doesn't scapegoat the doll; in therapy, she learned to distinguish between the message and its messenger.

That distinction, however, has increasingly begun to blur. The Barbie doll has become so synonymous with female sexuality that at Sierra Tucson, a trendy Arizona substance abuse clinic, women in treatment for "sex addiction" are required to carry one with them at all times. Lugging around Barbie, Alethea Savile explained in London's *Daily Mail*, forces them to reflect constantly on their objectified sexual selves.

Nor is it news that people connect Barbie's oddly proportioned body to adolescent eating disorders. According to a group of researchers at University Central Hospital in Helsinki, Finland, if Barbie were a real woman she'd be so lean she wouldn't be able to menstruate. Her narrow hips and concave stomach would lack the 17 to 22 percent body fat required for a woman to have regular periods—and a failure to menstruate is one of the symptoms of anorexia nervosa, a condition of self-starvation that principally afflicts young women. Significantly, though, Barbie isn't alone in her emaciation. The same researchers found that beginning in the fifties, when Barbie was introduced, life-size department-store clothes mannequins began to be made with the appearance of 10 percent body fat. Mannequins from the 1920s, by contrast, were stouter: Were they suddenly made flesh, they would have no trouble getting their periods.

This thinning down might be of greater alarm if it were without precedent, which it isn't. In the history of art, representations of the figure have often been distorted so that their drapery would fall in a pleasing fashion—and Barbie, like a clothing-store dummy, is a sculpture that exists to display garments. "The body of the *Ceres* in the Vatican Sala Rotunda is visibly distorted in some dimensions for the sake of displaying the clothes to advantage, rather than the other way around," Anne Hollander notes in *Seeing Through Clothes*, and she doesn't exaggerate. The statue's giant breasts seem to sprout from its shoulders, and there is room for a breast and a half between them. Nor was such distortion unusual in classical sculpture. "The identical body without the dress would look somewhat awkward, whereas a perfectly proportioned body could not wear such a fully draped costume without looking swamped and bunchy," Hollander says of the *Ceres*. The same could be said of Barbie.

The controversy over Barbie's thinness heated up in 1991, when High Self Esteem Toys of Woodbury, Minnesota, introduced "Happy To Be Me," a doll whose measurements were alleged to be more "realistic" than you-know-who's. Abetted by a tenacious PR firm, Cathy Meredig, Happy's developer, took her crusade to the press. Two percent of girls in the United States become anorexic at some point in their lives, she explained to *The New York Times*, 15 percent become bulimic, and 70 percent view themselves as fat. "I honestly believe if we have enough children playing with a responsibly proportioned doll that we can raise a generation of girls that feels comfortable with the way they look," she told *The Washington Post*.

And the press embraced her. From *Allure* to *People*, pro-Happy pieces sprang up like dandelions in a summer lawn. The vice president of the National Association of Anorexia Nervosa and Associated Disorders in Highland Park, Illinois, called Happy "a much-needed development." Yet by 1994, Happy was virtually history. Mothers may have told reporters, "Wow! A doll with hips and a waist," but they bought Barbie.

Meredig blames Happy's poor showing on Mattel's "stranglehold on distribution channels," which, given the way it snuffed out competitors like Hasbro's Jem, may have some truth. But it strikes me that Meredig is fighting something far larger than a toy company—even one big enough to be listed among the *Fortune* 500. One of the clippings in Meredig's own press kit confirms that Barbie doesn't instigate but merely reflects society's notions of beauty. Photocopied alongside a Minneapolis–St. Paul *Star Tribune* article on Happy is the giant ad printed next to it—for "Southlake Hypnosis," a weight-loss clinic in Edina, Minnesota. "I just lost 30 pounds and I feel terrific," the ad says in type larger than Happy's headline. "Now I can wear a two-piece swimsuit!"

Meredig claims to have based Happy on the Venus de Milo, but her classical allusion masks an ignorance of the historical relationship between the sculpted figure and its drapery. The Venus, as Hollander points out, may have ended up armless by chance, but she was "legless by design"—and without the heavy folds obscuring her stumpy legs, even her contemporaries would have thought her dowdy. By contrast, Charlotte Johnson, Barbie's first dress designer, understood the historical interdependence between the figure and its drapery. She also understood scale: When you put human-scale fabric on an object that is one-sixth human size, a multilayered cloth waistband is going to protrude like a truck tire around a human tummy. The effect would be the same as draping a human model in fabric made of threads that were the thickness of the model's fingers.

Because fabric of a proportionally diminished gauge could not be woven on existing looms, something else had to be pared down—and that something was Barbie's figure. One wonders how Meredig could have failed to notice the glaring incongruity between the scale of human-sized cloth and that of its miniature wearer. Or did Meredig so obsess on the naked doll that she forgot that girls were supposed to dress it?

Even in the raw, however, Happy leaves much to be desired. She is so cheaply manufactured that she makes Barbie look like an heirloom. When I handled an actual Happy doll, the first thing I noticed were not its measurements ("36-27-38" to a fashion doll's "36-18-33," Meredig's press materials said), but its receding hairline. Its hair sprang out of its head in widely scattered clumps, as if its balding pate, like that of a desperate middle-aged man, had been reforested with plugs. Then there was the hair's creepy texture. Whatever else one may say about Barbie, her hair feels like hair. It is made out of Kanekalon, a fiber used for human wigs, which Mattel designer Joe Cannizzaro arranged to have extruded in lengths long enough to meet the requirements of the sewing machines used on doll heads.

In appealing to educated, aesthetically minded parents concerned about body image, Meredig seemingly forgot how snobbish such parents can be about cheesy toys. Even Roland Barthes, who rhapsodized about plastic's versatility, turned up his nose at plastic playthings. Such toys, he said, lack "the pleasure, the sweetness, the humanity of touch" that their wooden counterparts possess—fancy words to express a plain old "prejudice" against them, suggests psychologist and *Toys as Culture* author Brian Sutton-Smith.

Nor is it as if Happy had no impact on Barbie. Ever watchful of its competitors, Mattel has included some very Happy-esque modifications on the dolls in its 1994 line. These include Gymnast Barbie, a doll with flat feet (like Happy's) that can stand without support, and Bedtime Barbie, a stuffed doll with a plastic head that I predict will be a favorite with mothers. Far from being a sexpot with a wardrobe from Victoria's Secret, Bedtime Barbie wears a frowzy flannel housecoat and fuzzy slippers. She is Slattern Barbie, Cellulite Barbie—a doll with thick ankles, sagging breasts, and squishy thighs—as unthreatening to Mom as Roseanne Arnold before her surgery.

But even if Meredig had produced an aesthetically pleasing doll—one that didn't wear chalk-colored, Dusty Springfield lipstick or require Rogaine—she still probably wouldn't have dethroned Barbie. For a kid, being stuck by Mom with a Happy is a lot like being stuck with a Skipper—or perhaps worse, since while Skipper may not be sexually mature, she at least conforms to societal norms of attractiveness. And those norms are, of course, at the center of this fuss: In a world where women's bodies are objectified and commodified, is it better for a girl to aspire to an arbitrary standard of "perfection" or to avoid disappointment by keeping her standards low?

This is not, however, to let Barbie off the hook. In the doll's early years, before women spoke openly about anorexia, Barbie's props encouraged girls to obsess on their weight. In addition to pink plastic hair curlers, Barbie's 1965 "Slumber Party" outfit featured a bathroom scale *permanently set at 110.* Mattel also gave her bedtime reading—a book called *How to Lose*

Weight that offered this advice: "Don't Eat." Ken, by contrast, was not urged to starve. His pajamas came with a sweet roll and a glass of milk.

THERE IS NO WAY TO AVOID PLUNGING INTO THE EATING disorder wars here, because for some, Barbie is a symbol of them. I say "wars" because experts disagree on why many women succumb to destructive, diet-related behaviors and others don't. I should say up front that I never had an eating disorder. As a teen, I was neither fat nor thin. I saw skinny models in *Vogue* and *Mademoiselle,* but never once thought of missing a meal. This doesn't mean I can't empathize with the many women for whom eating involves more than the mere slaking of hunger. But in high school, I was too preoccupied with homework, swim-team practice, and the domestic responsibilities that fell to me after my mother's death to evolve rituals around food.

To puzzle out why I had escaped the dietary scourges that afflicted many of my contemporaries—and to determine whether Barbie might have had a small manicured hand in inducing such blights—I interviewed therapists who treat anorexics, bulimics, and compulsive eaters. I read Kim Chernin, Susie Orbach, Louise J. Kaplan, and Naomi Wolf. And what I found were contradictions. In *Female Perversions,* Kaplan interprets anorexia not as a movement toward an idealized Barbie body, but as a flight from it. The anorexic transforms herself through emaciation into a sort of "third sex," liberated from menstruation and covered with a downy, masculine fuzz. "Behind [the anorexic's] caricature of an obedient, virtuous, clean, submissive, good little girl is a most defiant, ambitious, driven, dominating, controlling virile caricature of masculinity," Kaplan writes.

There is no universal consensus on why women become obsessed with dieting. One group of theorists views the problem as the result of a conspiracy. Now more than ever, the evil media have enshrined freakishly thin models who make normal-sized women feel like hippopotami. Another camp says, "So what?" As long as people have lived in communities, there have been community "standards of beauty" which, by definition, have been both arbitrary and hard to meet. Yet another group says it isn't the standards of beauty, but the importance a young girl places on them, which is a reflection of how her family feels about them and the degree to which her family encourages nonconformity. If Mom is so threatened by her daughter's chubbiness that she ships the girl off to a kiddie fat farm, the daughter may develop a lifelong neurosis about food. Likewise, if Dad makes clear that only slender women are sexually desirable, his daughter may obsess on appearing slender.

One theme, however, recurs in much of the diet-disorder literature: Mothers are involved in how daughters view their bodies. "While it might be hard to imagine the subtle transactions that occur around feeding in infancy, they are obvious during adolescence when the young woman's body changes precipitate a whole range of reactions around the family dinner table," Susie Orbach explains in *Hunger Strike: The Anorectic's Struggle as a Metaphor for Our Age*. Mothers frequently encourage their teenage daughters to eat differently, as a way of losing baby fat or clearing up their complexions. Thus food restraint "becomes the domain of the two females who may either cooperate or squabble over it."

Reading Orbach, I had a chilling thought about my own adolescence. I had owned Barbie dolls, studied fashion layouts, and done all the girl-things that were supposed to have made me a slave to the bathroom scale. Yet I couldn't have cared less. What was missing from my picture? Bluntly: Mom.

This is not to blame all mothers for infecting their daughters with an urge to compare their bodies unfavorably with the cultural ideal. But historically, through words and actions, mothers have interpreted and taught the looks and behaviors associated with "femininity" to their daughters. To place this in perspective, Chinese foot binding, a stunning cruelty in the service of "beauty," was not literally imposed by men upon women. Rather, it came about through "the shared complicity of mother and daughter," Susan Brownmiller explains in *Femininity*. "The anxious mother was the agent of will who crushed her suffering daughter's foot as she calmed her rebellion by holding up the promise of the dainty shoe, teaching her child at an early age that the feminine mission in life, at the cost of tears and pain, was to alter her body and amend her ways in the supreme effort to attract and please a man."

Nor is it as if mothers impart damage consciously. Given mothers' biological capacity to nourish their young, it is hardly surprising that tensions between them and their daughters might be played out through food. "Women are traditionally the primary feeders," explained psychotherapist Laura Kogel, a faculty member of the Women's Therapy Center Institute in Manhattan (founded by Susie Orbach, Luise Eichenbaum, and Carol Bloom) and a coauthor of *Eating Problems: A Feminist Psychoanalytic Treatment Model*. "So whether the woman is breast- or bottle-feeding, food and mother tend to be one."

Abby, a thirty-two-year-old Vassar graduate and recovering anorexic, feels very strongly that family dynamics rather than idealized images of women contributed to her eating disorder. "I grew up in Greenwich Village," she explained. "I was the child of a single mother who was a devout feminist. I wasn't allowed to watch TV until I was thirteen because my mother believed that its patriarchal stereotypes would have a bad influence on the way I identified myself as a woman. Instead, I was given *Sisterhood Is Powerful* and *Ms.* magazine. My mother hated Barbie and what she represented. I wasn't allowed to have a Barbie, much less a Skipper or a Midge. And the irony is that I was severely anorexic as a teenager. When I was fifteen, I stopped eating. I'm five foot nine and at my lowest weight, I was just under a hundred pounds. I lost my period for three years. Today, I have come to realize that my anorexia was a reaction to a very controlled and crazy family situation. I

JULIA BARNES MANDLE PERFORMING
"CHRISTMAS CONSUMPTION" DECEMBER
1992 WEBSTER/YAO PHOTOGRAPHY STUDIO

became obsessed with being thin because it wasn't something my mother valued. I think overreacting to Barbie—setting her up as the ultimate negative example—can be just as damaging as positing her as an ideal."

"My eating disorder had nothing to do with my Barbie dolls," said a forty-year-old novelist who prefers that her name not be used. "The year my mother took me out of boarding school, I was totally miserable. She was really punishing me for getting ahead of her—for going to this fancy school. She was horrible to me when I got home—really cold and cruel. And I decided to stop eating, but I was so afraid of her that I felt I had to disguise it. The one meal we all had together was dinner, and I became the family cook. I cooked these beautiful meals that I barely ate. It was my hunger strike to make her acknowledge what she'd done. I was going to starve myself until she was nice to me. It's amazing that I eat today." She laughed. "All my friends' mothers noticed that I was losing weight, but my mother said nothing—until the following year when I was on birth control pills and I gained a few pounds. Then she said I was getting fat."

"When I deal with a family and with mothers," Kogel told me, "because I don't like mother-blaming and because I am a mother, I try to see the fullness of the mother—as a three-dimensional person with her own insecurities, anxieties, and strengths." Yet to understand is not always to exculpate. For one of Kogel's clients' mothers, "appearance was everything. She just shamed her daughter at every moment. She said, 'You're fat; you're ugly.' The daughter has recently looked at pictures of herself as a child and she was actually adorable. There were no gross deformities. But the mother took all the badness inside herself and projected it onto her daughter."

Because of my own experience, I have a hard time attributing eating disorders to a cultural conspiracy—an idea that is easy to discredit through caricature, as Elizabeth Kaye did in *Esquire*. Kaye quotes Naomi Wolf's description of the alleged fashion cabal in *The Beauty Myth:* "It has grown stronger to take over the work of social coercion. . . . It is seeking right now

to undo . . . all the good things that feminism did for women." Then Kaye
adds, "This is the language of a science-fiction writer describing the Blob."

Yet because there are profits to be made off women with negative body
images, people do fan the members of negativity. In 1992, columnist Ann
Landers, a citadel of nonparanoid thinking, published some words of cau-
tion for "those who are borderline nutty on the subject of weight loss." They
included statistics showing that the diet industry had expanded to $33 bil-
lion a year and that women spent $300 million each year on plastic surgery.
By age thirteen, 53 percent of American high-school girls were unhappy
with their bodies. And even I began to half-believe the conspiracy theorists
in January 1993, when Columbia Pictures announced that it had winnowed
about thirty pounds off the woman in its logo, transforming her into a torch-
bearing skeleton.

Sadly, in the eating disorder wars, the conspiracy camp is about as likely
to shake hands with the family pathology crowd as Queen Elizabeth is to
host a fund-raiser for the IRA. Which is too bad, because the "cause" of an
eating disorder seems to vary between individuals, and involves some combination of cultural and familial issues.

One of the most sensitive dramatizations of an eating disorder and its conflicting causes is Todd Haynes's 1987 movie *Superstar*, a forty-three-minute
documentary written with Cynthia Schneider that uses mutilated fashion
dolls to enact the death of seventies pop singer Karen Carpenter from
anorexia nervosa. Although the concept sounds like a campy bad joke, the
movie is profoundly affecting. "In *Superstar*, Haynes vindicates Karen from
the junkyard of popular culture, forcing us to rethink her achievements,"
Joel Siegel wrote in Washington's *City Paper* when the film came out. "I had
ignorantly dismissed anorexia as a uniquely capitalistic affliction, a self-
induced neurosis that ironically compels the over-privileged to mimic the
physical deprivations of the starving poor. Haynes and Schneider convinc-
ingly argue that anorexia is a manifestation of a specifically *female* oppres-

SUSAN EVANS GROVE, "BATTERED BARBIE
(BUT KEN'S SORRY)," 1991

sion, a terrifyingly logical response to the demands imposed upon women by a sexist culture."

In *Art Forum,* artist Barbara Kruger observed: "It is this small film's triumph that it can so economically sketch, with both laughter and chilling acuity, the conflation of patriotism, familial control and bodily self-revulsion that drove Karen Carpenter and so many like her to strive for perfection and end up simply doing away with themselves." The only people, it seems, who didn't like *Superstar* were Karen's family and executives at A&M Records. They denied Haynes permission to use her songs and sent cease-and-desist letters so threatening that Haynes withdrew the film from circulation.

By dramatizing the story with Barbie-like dolls, Haynes recalls Beauvoir's thoughts on how society pressures women to be "live dolls," who slowly lose a sense of themselves as people. But society is not the only culprit. Anorexia, the film explains, "is often the result of highly controlled familial environments." And the parent dolls in Haynes's movie are nothing if not controlling.

The film opens with the voice of the doll portraying Mrs. Carpenter. "Nearly quarter-after and Saks is jammed by eleven," she chirps. When Karen doesn't respond, she walks to Karen's bedroom and finds Karen in a closet, sprawled dead—a victim, we later learn, of an overdose of ipecac, a drug that induces vomiting.

The Mom doll's face, modified by Haynes, is almost as scary as the Mom doll's behavior. Mom makes Karen wear hip-huggers that Karen believes make her look fat. Mom won't let Karen or her brother Richard move out.

"No matter how famous you all get," Mom says ominously, "you're going to keep living at *home.*"

Home is Downey, California—a grid of houses that resemble the Barbie doll's fold-up dwellings. As poignantly tacky as Karen's songs, Downey's matchbox mansions are an emblem of the postwar prosperity that changed the relationship of middle-class consumers to their food. After Haynes's camera has panned down a suburban block, it sweeps down a supermarket aisle—visually equating prefab houses with packaged foods—while a voice-over explains how, after World War II, food became more convenient, varied, and plentiful. But in defiance of this bounty, teenage girls began, in increasing numbers, to starve themselves.

Haynes makes an ironic connection between anorexia's symptoms and the content of the Carpenters' lyrics. After explaining the "high" that some anorexics get from constant hunger, Haynes cuts to the voice of Karen singing, "I'm on the top of the world looking down on creation . . ." And during Karen's short-lived marriage, the soundtrack plays "Lost in the Masquerade."

Yet even when Haynes uses the Carpenters for social commentary—they crooned their escapist lyrics at the White House the year Richard Nixon ordered the Christmas bombing of Cambodia—he never lets the political overwhelm the personal. *Superstar* contains many frightening images: shots of bombs falling and a red, white, and blue Ex-Lax box that flashes across the screen like a malignant American flag. But by far the scariest shot is filmed from the Karen doll's point of view. It shows her family hovering over her as she wakes up after fainting from malnutrition. "You're going to be under Mom's constant care," the Richard doll says, his face whittled into a malevolent grimace. "She's going to fatten you up."

Like puppets in a performance piece, *Superstar*'s dolls are never intended to be seen as anything other than dolls. The film is innocent of slick special effects. "This work is part of a tradition of independent, antimainstream, anticommercial filmmaking," explained John G. Hanhardt, curator of film

and video at the Whitney Museum of American Art. "It's made by an individual with a limited budget. And rather than that becoming a problem, it's the aesthetic of the piece.

"These dolls are sold as representing a way of looking, a way of appearing, a way of dressing, and a way of living," Hanhardt continued. And what Haynes does is rupture the seamlessness of that appearance. "He shows the complexity of the Carpenters as people," Hanhardt said, "and how they had to remake themselves into these popular icons—these things to sell."

Psychotherapist Laura Kogel remembers that the movie gave her chills. "They had to do with Karen not being seen as a person," she said. "And consequently she didn't see herself that way. You come to see yourself as a person through the eyes of those who raise you."

But the endorsement of critics and therapists was not enough to keep *Superstar* in circulation. "When the film came out, we had many rentals to clinics and classes that dealt with eating disorders," said Christine Vachon, a producer at Apparatus, the film company Haynes founded. "Everybody felt the subject was treated respectfully. It moved many people to tears." Because Haynes hoped the Carpenter family would allow clinics to show the film, he offered to donate all its profits to the Karen Carpenter memorial fund for anorexia research. "And they said no," Haynes said. "That really disappointed me."

IF PROFESSIONAL MODELS WERE FORCE-FED *SUPERSTAR*,

fashion magazines might look very different. In a 1993 *People* cover story, top models Kim Alexis, Beverly Johnson, and Carol Alt discussed the prevalence of eating disorders among models and how they had starved

JAUNE QUICK-TO-SEE SMITH, "PAPER DOLLS FOR A POST-COLUMBIAN WORLD WITH ENSEMBLES CONTRIBUTED BY U.S. GOVERNMENT," 1991 COURTESY STEINBAUM KRAUSS GALLERY, N.Y.C.

themselves to stay thin. Not to be outdone by her sister, Christine Alt, now a five-foot-ten-and-a-half-inch, 155-pound, "large-size" model, revealed that she had pared herself down to 110 pounds and developed an ulcer. "When Karen Carpenter died of anorexia," Christine said, "I remember seeing her picture in *People* and thinking, 'God, how lucky she was because she died thin.' "

Christine's remarks make one wonder about the Alt family. Sibling rivalry takes many forms, but sisters don't usually compete to see who can lose the most weight without dying. As near as I could tell, the problem with

"MATURE BARBIE," 1994: AGED BY RUSSELL PRESTON BROWN, SENIOR ART DIRECTOR, ADOBE SYSTEMS GEOFF SPEAR

these models was that they only saw themselves as objects. True, by definition, a model commodifies her body, but that commodification doesn't have to erase the person inside.

Still gorgeous at fifty, Lauren Hutton is proof that models can retain a sense of themselves as subjects—which, for older models, may make the difference between working or fading away. In an industry where "live dolls" used to be discarded when they showed signs of age, Hutton has made the transition from beautiful "girl" to beautiful "woman." She seems more visible as a model now than she was twenty-five years ago.

"When I first started modeling, I mostly worked for bad stylists in bad catalogue houses trying to get a break," Hutton told me. "And it was amazing. People would treat you like this sort of anonymous doll. They would touch you and be talking to each other—and I wasn't used to people touching me. I have dimples in my earlobes and I had a stylist try to smack a pair of pierced earrings through my dimples. She had her head turned talking. And I just went straight into the air because there were no holes there.

"The reason you become a successful model is because you learn how to make people see you as a person," she continued. "Not anonymous. You find a way of making contact. Of course, once I became famous, people were terrified of touching me in any way. But that's a whole other category."

Throughout her career, Hutton has defied the doll-like uniformity traditionally associated with models. On the advice of *Vogue* arbitrix Diana Vreeland, she refused to "correct" the now legendary gap between her front teeth. And in 1988, when she became the centerpiece of a Barneys New York ad campaign, she shattered the rule that live dolls don't age. "I thought it would be cool to show that someone who had been around awhile could be atrractive," Glenn O'Brien, creative director of Barneys, told me. "In a way, Hutton looks better now. Her character has kind of jelled. She isn't just a mannequin."

Significantly, Hutton has refused offers from toy companies to make a doll in her image. The first request came at the beginning of her career; the second in the late eighties, about the time Matchbox Toys issued its "Real Model Collection" with likenesses of Christie Brinkley, Cheryl Tiegs, and Beverly ("I ate nothing. I mean nothing") Johnson. "I had this instant repulsion at the idea," Hutton said. "And it was a weird feeling because I was flattered and repulsed at the same time."

In part, this had to do with her childhood distaste for baby dolls. "They looked larval," she told me. "What I really liked to do was to take their heads off and try to figure out how their eyes opened and shut. I never found out, because once you have the head off, you can't ever get the eyeballs back in. But with each doll, I convinced myself that this time, I would find out their secrets. So I decapitated many."

After some reflection, however, she discerned what really bothered her. "Giving little girls anything that makes them want to emulate a totem or an individual—rather than a generic idea of girlhood or womanhood—seems to be very unhealthy," she said. "It's like bad karma. If the greatest destiny is to find your own unique path, then one of the worst things you can do is suggest that people follow your way. I am not a totem. I have three younger sisters that I helped to raise, and when I started modeling, I wouldn't let my mother put my pictures up anywhere in the house."

Hutton was sixteen when Mattel brought out Barbie, a doll that didn't exactly win her heart. "I thought it was even creepier than the larvae I had beheaded," she said. "But when Brigitte Bardot came out, I remember thinking that she and the doll were sort of similar. You could say the first great international icon was Bardot. She was always pictured in a bouffant gingham skirt—spaghetti straps, big bouffant, and a tiny, tiny waist. She had that long fine neck and these long, long bones. And she'd be up on real high heels. And we were all trying to look like that."

Except that unlike most of her peers, Hutton was successful at it—which galled other women. "I would have women be incredibly rude to me right to my face. Rude and feline and mean—when I was as innocent as a lamb, just standing there. I've always liked women, so when they were rude, I would assume I'd misheard them." But as Hutton's celebrity grew, she had to acknowledge that her ears worked fine: "You'd go to dinner and the wife would shake your hand and her opening words would not be, 'Hello, how are you?' They would be, 'Oh, I hate you. When my husband said you were going to dinner, I said, Oh, my God, not *her*.'"

Yet when Hutton herself matured, she understood the resentment. "It took me about seven years to turn forty," she said. "I went from thirty-eight to forty-five and it was so horrible and so painful. I had been a celebrated 'girl,' and suddenly I was a woman and there was no place for women in our society—unless they had made some incredible mark, usually by imitating a man, in a business way. When I was turning forty, sometimes I would see a beautiful young girl and I would get so confused I'd want to hide. I suddenly understood what a lot of the feelings toward me had been about. And I had real sympathy. I would feel jealousy deep inside—and I would be very ashamed of myself because I've always loathed that in me, at any time about anything. I was seeing someone young and beautiful and I didn't feel that I was young and beautiful. And in fact, I wasn't: I was no longer a girl."

"But you were still beautiful," I couldn't help blurting.

"The beauty of women was not accepted or celebrated," Hutton explained. "It had no credentials, was not certified, was not allowed, did not exist in our society. It's a brand-new idea and it's just happening now in America."

If Hutton is right, this could mean a new challenge for Mattel: Mature Barbie. Not Crone Barbie or Decrepit Barbie, but a Barbie who's been around the block, and looks better for the wear.

CHAPTER TWELVE

THE WOMAN WHO WOULD BE BARBIE

Cindy Jackson, the Fremont, Ohio–born founder of the London-based Cosmetic Surgery Network, may be the ultimate Barbie performance artist. She has had more than twenty operations and spent $55,000 to turn herself into a living doll. She has had chemical peels, tummy tucks, face-lifts, eye-lifts, breast implants, and liposuction. She has even had two nose jobs.

"I'm registered with the British Internal Revenue as the Bionic Woman," she explained. "I run my cosmetic surgery bureau as a firsthand experience, so all my operations are tax-deductible. . . . The BBC even paid for my boob job." But no longer is she satisfied merely remaking herself. Her mission, which evolved while assisting other women through Barbie-izations, is to create "a bionic army."

In Barbie's early years, Mattel struggled to make its doll look like a real-life movie star. Today, however, real-life celebrities—as well as common folk—are emulating her. The postsurgical Dolly Parton looks like the post-surgical Ivana Trump looks like the postsurgical Michael Jackson looks like the postsurgical Joan Rivers looks like . . . Barbie. This chapter will not deal

CINDY JACKSON, AT HER HIGH SCHOOL
GRADUATION, 1973

CINDY JACKSON, NINETEEN OPERATIONS
LATER, 1993

with body image, ethnic identification, or self-esteem. It is about nuts and bolts—Mary Shelley—scalpels, silicone, and sutures. Cindy has earned a section of her own.

When we met at Sfuzzi, a restaurant on Manhattan's Upper West Side, for dinner in 1993, Cindy's lower lip was the only part of her body that had not been modified—and she had spent the afternoon talking to a Park Avenue doctor about enlarging it. She also wanted a fat transplant in her cheeks. "I have dents here which need filling in," she explained. "See my cheek here is flat—but I have dents underneath."

"I can't see them," I said.

"But they're there," she assured, craning forward so I could get a better view. Then she scrutinized me. "You don't need your eyes done," she said. I had discussed my drooping lids—and fear of pain—in a phone conversation months earlier. "Everybody's eyes will sag after a certain point." My jawline, however, was another story. "You might do a little liposuction there. But I wouldn't say it's an emergency case. Work on keeping your chin up a little."

As I involuntarily thrust my jaw upward, Cindy pulled out a hefty album of her "before," "after," and "during" photos. "This is what you look like when your eyes need doing," she explained, pointing to a snapshot of herself at twenty-seven, about ten years ago. She did indeed have slits for eyes and a posture reminiscent of Ruth Buzzi's character on *Laugh-In*. Blond, slender, and almost nondescript in her "prettiness," Cindy today is not Barbie's twin, but she does look more like the doll than she did when she started. She also favors Mattel fantasy clothes: glittery earrings, sleek, short skirts. We ordered dinner—a vegetarian pizza. Like the 1989 Animal Lovin' Barbie, Cindy is an ardent antivivisectionist. She has "adopted" a whale, belongs to "Cheetah Watch," and doesn't eat meat.

As we studied a picture of her post-op face, bruised and looking troublingly like the eggplant appetizer on an adjacent table, she told me, "I want patients to understand that it's major surgery. It's not like going to the beauty shop. There are real dangers—complications that happen, rarely, but they do happen."

Then she moved on to her philosophy. "Men are really drawn to women for their looks," she said. "They can't stand a sick woman, much less a sick, ugly, swollen woman. Besides, I think men worry that you're going to die on the operating table and there'll be nobody there to make their dinner."

As if on cue, our dinner arrived. Avoiding animal products is the extent of Cindy's health regimen; she keeps "fit" through surgery. "It's not me to go to a gym and exercise . . . I don't know that it's really good for you. You go to the gym and you have to keep going. I'm careful who I sweat with, too. I don't like to go in those places and do all those things. Especially now— people expect me to be perfect." She told me about her plans to have the loose flesh removed from her upper arms, an operation in which the scarring itself causes the muscles to appear taut. Thinking of the hours I had logged on the Gravitron to vanquish my own vexatious jiggle, the operation seemed almost a good idea. Then my eyes returned to Cindy's "in-between" photo. Cowardice, I concluded, was the better part of valor.

Cindy believes her appearance in the *National Enquirer* in January 1993 may have been responsible for Roseanne Arnold's decision to have a total surgical overhaul: that, in a sense, she recruited Arnold into her "bionic army." "ROSEANNE'S HUBBY IN PLOT TO ROB BANK: TOM ARNOLD'S OWN AMAZ-ING CONFESSION" appeared on the newspaper's front page, along with "AMY FISHER: I SHOULD HAVE SHOT MY LOVER" and "WYNONNA JUDD FIGHTS BACK: I'M NO LESBIAN." Cindy and her transformation were prominently featured on page three—hard for Arnold, had she seen the issue, to have missed. And Arnold these days is certainly a fascinating surgical confection: a zaftig woman with the cheekbones of Audrey Hepburn. Having once been applauded by feminists for her defiant refusal to look like a model, Arnold is now defensive about her makeover. "Well, we're not in a perfect feminist world," she told Liz Logan in *The Ladies' Home Journal.* "And we never will be. And even if we were, I would still have plastic surgery. It makes you feel really good about yourself. I mean, you have flaws that bother you and to erase them is great." A paraphrase, it struck me, of Cindy's surgery-is-power philosophy.

Before I met Cindy, I watched her on *Maury Povich,* stoically enduring the taunts of audience members who suggested that her money might have been better spent on psychotherapy. She was quick with snappy rejoinders—a skill essential for tabloid television. "*Jenny Jones* was my worst experience," she recalled. "They put me on with Queer Donna, who's a 360-pound gay man who parodies Madonna and worships her. Also with Frank Marino, a guy who had surgery to look like Joan Rivers, and a Cher look-alike who was also a man." Then a "plant" in the audience commented, "Everybody knows Barbie doesn't wear any underwear. Are you wearing underwear?" "Yes," Cindy snarled, "are you?"

She scowled. "I didn't grow up to be Barbie to be victimized like that. When I do the shows, I get to go home—I get a free trip, that's why I do it." "Home" now for Cindy is outside Chicago, where her sister lives. She is deliberately vague about the location because her sister, a married executive, frowns on her surgical way of life; she won't even have her ears pierced. "She has the perfect life and I have the perfect face and body," Cindy said.

Cindy does not have fond memories of her childhood in Fremont, where, as a teenager, she worked in a ketchup factory. There was the indignity of catalogue-shopping—tracing the outline of her feet to order shoes that pinched, like the pennies that were expended to buy them. But even amid the meanness, hope effervesced: in the form of a stylish doll with a bubble cut and curvilinear shoes that hugged its curvilinear insteps. Barbie didn't have a husband or babies; Barbie had careers . . . and options.

"I watched my mother give her life to be overrun by a man—my father," Cindy told me. "And not to fulfill her potential because of men and children. If I didn't have that freedom, I wouldn't have that husband or part-ner." Cindy's boyfriend, an audio engineer she met while performing in a rock band, is, she told me, very Ken-like—and to her, male good looks are as important as female ones. Like Barbie, however, she seems to prefer free-dom to marriage.

Even though they have no financial relationship—Cindy considers surgery consultants in the pay of physicians to be unethical—one compa-triot on her surgical crusade is Dr. Edward Latimer-Sayer, an English plas-tic surgeon. "Although Cindy has always talked about this Barbie-doll image, in England at any rate, the Barbie doll is associated with stupidity—a sort of nice body, vacant brain sort of thing," Latimer-Sayer told me. "And Cindy is anything but that." Although she dropped out of art school before moving to London to work as a photographer, she is well spoken and well read. She is also a member of Mensa.

Latimer-Sayer urged Jackson to get greater firsthand knowledge of surgi-cal procedures. "He kept inviting me to operations and I finally went," she said. "I can see I'm going to be a regular fixture in the operating room."

Most of Latimer-Sayer's patients are not like Cindy—who, because of her consumer watchdog organization, gets celebrity treatment. "I think I'd starve to death waiting for the models and actresses to show up," he told me. "The majority of my patients are housewives, nurses, hairdressers, secretaries. Ordinary people. They don't want to be out of the ordinary, but they just feel that one particular part lets them down. An attractive young girl with a big hooky nose doesn't feel normal."

Significantly, Latimer-Sayer's patients don't choose their doctor; he chooses them. A satisfied patient, he believes, is one with realistic expec-tations. When, for instance, I told him about my fear of pain, he suggested I might be a poor candidate for surgery. Some procedures require greater screening than others. "Liposuction is an operation where you really have to choose your patients well," he said. "You get a bulky patient and you try and get the fat off them, it simply doesn't work. You end up with lumpy, irregular areas and the skin hanging in folds.

"I identify with the patient what the aims of each particular operation are," he told me. "I mean, I don't mind patients having lots of operations. After all, I've got children to send through university." Latimer-Sayer also believes in using his time efficiently—especially with things like breast implants. "Some people fiddle about for hours—one wonders what they're doing. . . . But once you've done a few hundred, you ought to know where to cut the pocket and what size fits the pocket. In the main, operations take less time this side of the Atlantic than they do in America. Because American surgeons are looking over their shoulder for the lawyers all the time."

In talking with Latimer-Sayer, I got the sense that the hows of surgery were more important than the whys. Decisions to, say, westernize Asian eyelids should rest with the patient, not the surgeon. "If you have the double fold—what they call the European eyelid—you are considered more trustworthy, higher class, and you're more likely to do well in life," he told me. "If you have the Oriental eyelid with the thick upper lid with no fold, it's like being a second-class citizen. . . . Now if there's a little simple cosmetic operation to make somebody go from a second-class citizen on appearance to a first-class citizen on appearance, no wonder it's popular.

"If for instance, someone had developed a technique to make black people white . . . they would have been swamped, wouldn't they? Not because there's anything wrong with being black, but it's nicer to be white in a white society."

There is, however, one process he wouldn't touch with a ten-foot pole: penis enlargement. "A lot of men seem to want it," he said. "You take a bit of fat from somewhere where there's a bit to spare and put it in the penis and it's fatter. But the trouble is that fat doesn't stay there; it tends to absorb, and sometimes you can get all sorts of other troubles with it. It can generally turn into a horrible mess."

Cindy concurred: "As far as I'm concerned, with men who aren't very well endowed, it's cheaper to buy a Porsche and probably more safe."

Latimer-Sayer did not install Cindy's breast implants; they were put in as part of a BBC documentary on the process. And they have begun to cause trouble. They were supposed to have been placed behind the chest muscle, but one migrated; it has also hardened, a process known as capsular contracture. "I'm not happy with the encapsulation of my own implants," she told me. "I'm having them out." And yet, she said, pausing, "it's better to have had them and liked them than never to have had them at all."

In her role as watchdog, Cindy is also following the class-action suits filed by unhappy implant owners against Dow Corning, a maker of silicone implants. In April 1994, about a year after she and I had dinner, *The New York Times* reported that the lawyers representing the patients had unearthed a 1975 study by company researchers that showed that the silicone in the implants harmed the immune system in mice. Whether this fresh detail will slow recruitment for her bionic army remains to be seen.

One thing, however, is certain: there are already a lot of bionic women out there. "I don't even think I want to walk down the street in California," Cindy told me. "They've all done what I've done. Over there I'm just another Barbie doll."

CHAPTER THIRTEEN

BARBIE OUT OF CONTROL

In December 1993, a platoon of bellicose Barbies mysteriously appeared on toy-store shelves in forty-three states. Their fluffy skirts and lace-trimmed leggings were identical to those of their sister Talking Barbies, from whose microchips the nettlesome "Math class is tough" had been newly purged. But their voices were different. "Eat lead, Cobra," they bellowed. "Vengeance is mine!" Meanwhile, in the boy-toy ghetto of the same stores, a few "Talking Duke" characters in Hasbro's G.I. Joe line began to exhibit acute testosterone deficiencies. "Let's go shopping," they chirped. "Will we ever have enough clothes?"

This outbreak of gender trouble was no accident. A group calling itself the Barbie Liberation Organization revealed that it had surgically swapped hundreds of Barbie talk mechanisms with those of G.I. Joe. Loosely organized by a graduate student at the University of California at San Diego, the BLO claimed to be made up of artists, professionals, and concerned parents across the country. "One of our members is eighty-seven years old," a BLO spokesperson told me. "And she helped when we were brainstorming the switch. She didn't have that much of a problem with the Barbies. But she is

DEAN BROWN, "LIBERTY LEADING THE PEOPLE," 1985

a Hungarian Jew who had nearly all her family killed in World War Two. So she had a very strong reaction against the war toys."

Befuddled consumers brought the doctored dolls to the attention of the press, which, in the boring week between Christmas and New Year's, lavished attention. Not enough to justify the BLO's $9,000 out-of-pocket expenses perhaps, but quite a bit. Enough to make Mattel cross, particularly two weeks later when its big winter media event—the presentation by Jill Barad of a $500,000 donation to the South Bronx Children's Health Center, founded by singer Paul Simon—was upstaged by natural disasters. Part of Mattel's plan to contribute $1 million to various children's health clinics in 1994, the philanthropic photo opportunity had been scheduled for January 18—the day after Los Angeles was hit by a major earthquake and New York City paralyzed by a winter storm.

The BLO calls its surgery "political art," a critique of gender stereotypes in toys. Mattel calls it "product tampering," which, in fact, it is. The disparity between these perspectives is why the use of Barbie by artists will never be a simple affair.

There are many doors through which one could enter a discussion of Barbie in visual art. One could begin by dropping names—mentioning Andy Warhol's 1986 portrait of the doll or photorealist Charles Bell's wall-sized *Judgement of Paris,* also from 1986, which featured Barbie, Ken, and G.I. Joe. One might talk about how in the early eighties, photographer Ellen Brooks used fashion dolls to comment on gender roles, and that three of those photos were included in the Whitney Museum of American Art's 1983 Biennial. Or one could cite Scottish sculptor David Mach, who used hundreds of Barbies to critique consumer capitalism in a piece called *Off the Beaten Track.* Installed in 1988 at the University of California at Los Angeles's Wight Art Gallery, it involved a horde of blond, plastic caryatids propping up a giant shipping container—literally "supporting" the consumer economy.

Another door would lead one through the history of doll images in art. Freud's essay on the uncanny would, of course, reappear; one would talk about the creepiness of lifelike dolls and automata. One would mention, among others, German Surrealist Hans Bellmer, who in the 1930s photographed parts of female mannequins assembled in impossible configurations—legs sprouting where arms should be—as well as nude females wrapped with string to create the effect of misassembled joints. One would move the story to the present with one of Bellmer's aesthetic heirs—Cindy Sherman—whose deliberately nauseating photos of genital prostheses in the

CHARLES BELL WITH "THE JUDGMENT OF
PARIS," 1986 SYLVIA PLACHY

1993 Whitney Biennial were appropriately placed near an installation by another artist that featured a "puddle" of rubber throw-up.

These are not, however, the doors that interest me. Unlike icons such as Elvis and Marilyn, Barbie is a corporate property. And what distinguishes much of the best art using Barbie is that it has had to be produced almost surreptitiously. Mattel wishes to impose its authorized vision on the public, but the public has other plans. Barbie colonized people's imaginations in childhood, and they are impelled to bear witness. Some distort and pillory the doll; others place it on a pedestal. But always, the unauthorized witness-bearers take a risk. The corporation cannot have any old Tom, Dick, or Jane promulgating his or her personalization of a corporate-owned icon.

Such a personalization could "damage" the icon's image, or, worse, divert money away from the corporation. So the corporation has three choices: It must co-opt the artist's work, as, in a sense, was done with the Warhol image; Mattel's permission—not simply that of the Warhol estate—is required to reproduce it. It must commission art and impose "guidelines." Or it must do its best to squash it.

What further complicates the relationship of Mattel to the contemporary art scene is that many of Mattel's early corporate products (as well as the doll itself) are themselves works of art—exquisite miniatures that are, with aesthetic justification, preserved by collectors. Then there's the fact that art these days involves borrowing images. From Barbara Kruger's political collages to Richard Prince's manipulations of commercial photographs, "art" is about appropriation. Among its tenets, postmodernism suggests that no work of art or text is anything other than a reassembly of citations; thus, if all art is citations, all art is fair game to be cited.

What does it mean to cite Barbie? For baby boomers, Barbie has probably the same iconic resonance as certain female saints—though not the same religious significance. But how different the art of the Renaissance would have been if the Roman Catholic Church had required painters to place a trademark symbol on frescoes interpreting God and the saints. This is not, however, to imply that the Church would have disapproved of such an arrangement.

"I don't think the College of Cardinals used terms like 'copyright' or 'registered trademark,' but let's face it, the scripture was registered in essence and highly controlled by the Church," said Robert Sobieszek, curator of photography at the Los Angeles County Museum of Art and author of *The Art of Persuasion: A History of Advertising Photography.* "Somebody like Raphael was perhaps one of the greatest commercial artists who ever lived. He had a great client called the Church; he had a great set of art directors called the College of Cardinals; and he had a great product—salvation. He was doing commercial illustration to sell a philosophy—the history of Christianity or Catholicism. The fact that in the twentieth century, we see genius in that, artistry in that, or invention in that is really beside the point."

Renaissance artists also had a strong inducement to stick close to scripture; those who deviated were dragged before the Inquisition. Substitute law courts for Inquisition and you could be talking about today's corporate icons. Walt Disney's executors, for instance, wouldn't permit his mice or ducks to be reproduced in *The Disney Version,* Richard Schickel's trenchant 1968 analysis of the aesthetic underpinnings of the "Magic Kingdom." The Disney organization is notoriously vigilant about where and how its characters appear—appropriately, perhaps, licensing Mattel to produce doll versions of figures from *Aladdin, Snow White,* and *Beauty and the Beast.* Yet certain emblems and symbols—Frigidaire, Xerox, Jell-O—crop up so often that it would be impossible for a corporation to prosecute every unlicensed use.

What constitutes "fair use" for independent artists is now particularly relevant to Barbie, because Mattel has gone into the Medici business—commissioning artists to use its icon in an authorized context: a picture book, the proceeds from which will be given to an AIDS charity. The project resembles the advertising campaign for Absolut vodka, in which independent artists were commissioned to cannibalize their styles in the service of a product. This is not to say that commercial art—work commissioned for advertising or editorial use—cannot be "art"; photographers like Richard Avedon, Annie Leibovitz, and Sylvia Plachy, a major contributor to this book, all work on commission. But, as was the case with the Renaissance painters and the College of Cardinals, artists-for-hire frequently tailor their work to suit their clients.

Money also plays a part in "fair use." If an artist issues a series of images using a corporate icon exclusively to make a buck, a corporation may have grounds for a case. But when an artist cites an icon in a one-of-a-kind work

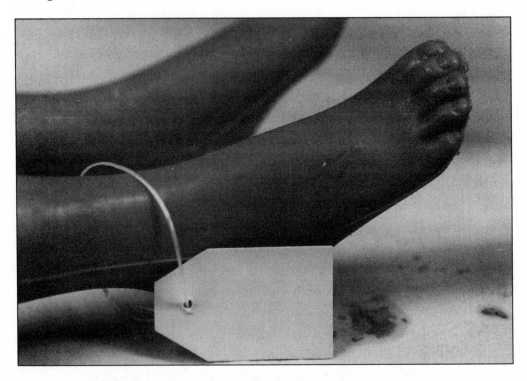

FELICIA ROSSHANDLER, "TWILIGHT OF THE GODS"—AND, NO, IT'S NOT A BARBIE FOOT.

from which he or she will realize scant profit, it may not be in the company's interest to take the artist to court. Copyright law, however, encourages corporations to fire off cease-and-desist letters at the slightest provocation. "If a company doesn't go after people that it feels are missing its icon, it's to the company's disadvantage," said Deirdre Evans-Prichard, curator of the Language of Objects project at the Los Angeles Craft and Folk Art Museum, who has written on art and copyright issues. "In a major court case, it would need to produce a file to show that it's been actively protecting its image."

No one could accuse Mattel of laxity in guarding its icons. Not wishing its trademarked dolls associated with *Superstar,* it joined A & M Records in sending threatening letters to Todd Haynes. More recently, it silenced Barbara Bell, an editor of the New Age magazine *Common Ground,* who claimed to channel Barbie, "the polyethylene essence who is 700 million teaching entities." She now channels "a generic eleven-and-a-half-inch plastic essence." Yet Mattel's behavior toward artists can also be baffling and unpredictable. It contributed the dolls for David Mach's *Off the Beaten Track,* a scorching piece that exposed it and its icons to ridicule.

Barbie has interested artists virtually since her inception. Second-generation abstract expressionist Grace Hartigan was perhaps the first significant painter to incorporate Barbie imagery in her work. Her 1964 painting *Barbie* was inspired by a *Life* magazine article on the doll and its $136 wardrobe. "When I was a little girl, I had 'Patsy Ann,' a doll that was about my age," Hartigan told me. "But here you had this doll with boobs and this castrated man and a wedding gown, and I just thought: 'That's our society.' I try to declaw the terribleness of popular culture and turn it into beauty or meaning. And I feel that I have won—I've triumphed over it. It's witchcraft in a way. The triumph of this is that it's a terrific painting. I've used the image, which I think is debasing to women, and I've turned it against itself and made it powerful."

With Hartigan's guidance—and the illustrated *Life* article in front of me—

I managed to locate the representational elements in her painting: a pink face in the upper-right-hand corner; a floor-length evening dress in the left foreground; a lone eye in the upper-left-hand corner; and in the center, a single disembodied breast. "The final painting comes from the original imagery," she explained. "It's just highly abstracted."

ROGER BRAIMON, KEN DOLLS, 1993

Tomi Ungerer, who is perhaps best known for his whimsical children's book illustrations, also gravitated toward the doll in the early sixties—not, however, producing objects for kids. Ungerer decapitated and dismembered the dolls, reassembling them—à la Hans Bellmer—in constructions with sadomasochistic and coprophiliac themes. Perhaps inspired by Freud's Little Hans and his investigations of doll "genitalia," one sculpture features a female torso hacked between its legs with a saw. Some constructions consist only of the doll's legs in spike-heeled shoes; in others, tubes link the doll's genital orifices with its mouth. Ungerer's "erotic doll sculptures" are now housed in the permanent collection of his work in the Musée de la Ville in Strasbourg, France.

By the late seventies and early eighties, when the first generation of Barbie owners had grown up, unauthorized Barbie art began to proliferate. Independent artists have taken essentially two tacks when it comes to representing Barbie. There are the reverential ones, who idealize the doll, and the angry ones, who use the doll for social commentary. Warhol was perhaps the first of the reverentials—the sardonic self-censorers—who managed to convey even greater vapidity in his portrait than exists in the doll's actual face. He was not happy with the image. "The portrait looks so bad, I don't like it," he recorded in his diary on the day of its unveiling. "The Mattel president said he couldn't wait to see it and I just cringed." Once an illustrator himself, Warhol and his scions are rooted in the tradition of commercial art; they include Mel Odom, whose pastel renderings of Barbie are as sleek as the design of a corporate annual report. But to Odom, the seductive surface is ironic. "I want to capture the soul of plastic," he told me.

Seattle photographer Barry Sturgill, whose work appears frequently in *Barbie Bazaar,* is also part of the reverential school. Widely regarded as the Irving Penn of Barbiedom, his photographs, characterized by dramatic, high-fashion lighting, are about female glamour. He makes the doll look like a top model from the 1950s. "I like the oldest face—the shelf-eyelash face," he explained. "She has a real 'don't mess with me, I'm Barbie' attitude. She was supposed to be a teenager and she looks like she's thirty-five."

The angry artwork is usually not so polished; nor does it critique the same things. Some artists use Barbie to comment on gender roles; some on colonialism and race; some on the consumer culture. Others, like Dean Brown and Charles Bell, use Barbie to comment on art history.

Maggie Robbins, a 1984 graduate of Yale University, is one of the angry artists. By day, she answers the telephone and edits copy at *McCall's* magazine. By night, she hammers hundreds of nails into Barbie dolls. The effect of her hammering has been to transform the dolls into unsettling pieces of sculpture. How the dolls are displayed dramatically affects how the viewer interprets them. Mounted on a wall, they are images of female strength, curvaceous suns emitting potent metallic rays. On their backs, however, they suggest other things: victimization, vulnerability, impalement by what Virginia Woolf termed "the arid scimitar of the male."

It's hard not to view Robbins's work without asking: Is it art or therapy? But after seeing her *Rotating Barbie* in a group show at Richard Anderson, a SoHo gallery, in 1993, I had to vote for "art." The piece, which she made as a birthday present for her ex-husband, is a kinetic sculpture involving reassembled Barbie parts; when activated, the figure lurches about as if it had been battered and is trying to crawl from its assailant. I couldn't take my eyes off it; nor could anybody else. People talked about it outside the gallery—sighing with relief because the artist was a woman. Had it been executed by a man, it might have been read as an exhortation toward violence, instead of a critique. "It's about being angry about everybody wanting to look like a Barbie," Robbins told me. "It's definitely much more anti-the-society-that-brought-you-Barbie than it is antiwoman. Because Barbies aren't women."

Yet to observe Robbins's work is to be curious about the gender of the artist. Christopher Ashley, who directed Paul Rudnick's *Jeffrey* off

Broadway, owns one of Robbins's *Barbie Fetish* series—the dolls impaled with hundreds of rusty nails. As Robbins tells it, his visitors become visibly less tense when they learn it is the product of female hands. But even Robbins isn't entirely at ease with the ferocity in her work. "Putting the nails into Barbie's face, into her eyes, was really, really hard to do," she said. "And the weird thing was: She didn't stop smiling."

When I visited Robbins in her Brooklyn studio, I found some of her Barbie mutilations so brutal I could scarcely look at them. In one, titled *Berlin Barbie*, Robbins has used carpet tacks to pin a blond doll to a pre–World War II German map. The glossy black tacks encrust the doll like a fungus; they suggest the eruption of rot from within. Robbins began the piece in the summer of 1991, while she was going through a divorce. She had spent time in Berlin with her husband in May and went back alone in August. She wanted the piece to address not only her personal upheaval but also the doll's Teutonic roots. (Mattel will no doubt be pleased to learn that Robbins has temporarily shelved her Barbies to work with another iconic female. She wrote the libretto for *Hearing Voices*, an opera about Joan of Arc, with music by composer Robert Maggio, which premiered at the University of West Chester in West Chester, Pennsylvania, in December 1993.)

Robbins is one of a number of young female artists who use the doll to critique women's societal roles. Susan Evans Grove, a photographer and a 1987 graduate of the New York School of Visual Arts, is another. In her Barbie work, shown at Manhattan's Fourth Street Photo Gallery in 1992, Grove takes Barbie out of the sanitized "America" that Mattel invented. She succumbs to the blights that afflict real women: homelessness, drug addiction, rape, domestic violence, sexual harassment, menstruation, skin cancer—a glossary of female misfortunes. "It was definitely cathartic for me to make all these bad things happen to her," Grove told me. "The one that got 'skin cancer' actually was *my* Malibu Barbie. She developed mold, poor thing." Grove's anger stemmed from the fact that she herself was dismissed as a Barbie. "Because I was short and light and fair, people assumed I couldn't do anything," she said.

Julia Mandle, a performance artist and 1992 graduate of Williams College, understands Grove's irritation. Although she now sports a Susan Powter haircut, she was once very Barbie-esque, which provoked incidents that caused her to revise her look. The first occurred when she was a high-school senior visiting colleges and a male upperclassman helped her gain admission to a campus pub. " 'Do you have any female friends who look like me so I can borrow their I.D.?' " she asked him. "And he said, 'Oh, there are probably a thousand girls here who look like you.' "

With her long blond hair and perfect figure—she had been bulimic since adolescence—Mandle admitted that there probably were. But the remark "stuck with her," and contributed to her anger, which erupted in a 1992 performance piece called *Christmas Consumption.*

Mandle, a Washington, D.C., resident, mounted the piece at the height of the December shopping season on a Georgetown sidewalk. To set the stage, she filled a shopping cart with diet literature and encrusted it with Barbies and Barbie-like dolls. She chalked eating-disorder statistics on the pavement. Then she transformed herself into a grotesque parody of Barbie—donned a lime-green bikini, platinum wig, and flesh-tone body stocking—and performed calisthenics to "Go You Chicken Fat Go," an exercise anthem. "The top kept slipping down," she recalled, "and guys would sort of come across and look, because from across the street it looked like I was wearing nothing." Fox News filmed her and shoppers, seeing the wire cart and assuming she was homeless, gave her money. "One reaction I had was a boyfriend pulling his girlfriend over and saying, 'I'm trying to get her to exercise, too; what should I do?' He was completely oblivious," she said.

Over a decade earlier, SoHo-based photographer Ellen Brooks, who received her M.F.A. from UCLA in 1971, critiqued the glorification of

women's helpmeet status with fashion dolls. Three of her pieces—*Balancers,
Guarded Future,* and *Silk Hat*—appeared in the 1983 Whitney Biennial. "I
wanted the doll to symbolize this kind of glamorous but secondary position,"
Brooks told me. In *Guarded Future,* a sinister-looking magician and his
female assistant hover over a malignant, spherical egg. *Revolvers,* which was
not included in the Whitney show, explores a similar power relationship: a

seated male orders his female assis-
tants—festooned with showgirl feath-
ers—to balance, like seals, on
spinning balls.

Brooks did not, in fact, work with
Barbie, but with Kenner's Darci—
applauded by doll expert A. Glenn
Mandeville as "the outstanding fashion doll of the late 1970s." As far as
Brooks was concerned, however, a
Darci was a Barbie was a problem,
and she didn't want her preschool
daughter going near any of them. "But
I couldn't very well say to her, you
can't play with these," Brooks
recalled. "Because she's watching me
play with them—creating these
worlds." Brooks hasn't worked with
dolls since 1984, but she has had
oblique contact with Barbie: Ken
Handler's daughter frequently baby-
sat for her.

THE <u>BIZARRO</u> CARTOON BY DAN PIRARO IS
REPRINTED WITH PERMISSION OF CHRONICLE
FEATURES SYNDICATE, SAN FRANCISCO,
CALIFORNIA.

Gender is also a concern of Bolinas, California, photographer Ken Botto,
whose photographs of toys were included in the 1992 "Pleasures and Terrors

of Domestic Comfort" show at New York's Museum of Modern Art. But unlike Brooks and her aesthetic successors, he doesn't see the early Barbies as constrained by their femininity. To him, they are powerful, dominatrix figures, sexually linked to Nazis and robots, looming portentously over impotent Kens. "The early Barbie had an attitude on her face; it wasn't blank," he told me. And his compositions, described by writer Alice Kahn as "Barbie Noir," were derived from the Helmut Newton S&M aesthetic that cropped up in late-seventies fashion photography. His current work focuses on ancient matriarchal power. Influenced by the writings of Camille Paglia, he has linked Neolithic goddess imagery to modern pornography to Barbie.

For Native American artist Jaune Quick-to-See Smith, Hollywood's invented "America"—the "America" of cowboy heroes vanquishing Indian villains—is a myth to be exploded and mocked. She does this in her 1991 piece, *Paper Dolls for a Post-Columbian World with Ensembles Contributed by U.S. Government.* The work features "Barbie Plenty Horses" and "Ken Plenty Horses"—Mattel archetypes customized with names from the Flathead tribe to which she belongs. The doll's outfits tell the story of what happened to her tribe over a century ago, when the U.S. government forced it to move from its traditional home to a reservation several hundred miles away. Smith's humor is mordant: her doll accessories include "small pox suits," a by-product of infected blankets issued by the government, and one of several tribal headdresses "sold at Sotheby's today for thousands of dollars to white collectors seeking Romance in their lives."

Produced to coincide with the quincentennial of Columbus's arrival in America, or as Smith puts it, "five hundred years of tourism in this country," *Paper Dolls* sprang out of the "trickster" or "coyote" component in her personality. "I always think that you can get your message across to people with humor better than you can in politicizing it in a dour sort of way," she told me. She also felt that "telling a true story about the reality of my family" would be more affecting than compiling a "laundry list" of complaints.

Some artists have used the dolls to make personal rather than political statements. Roger Braimon, who received an M.F.A. in painting from the University of Pennsylvania in 1992, used Ken and Ken-like dolls for a series of representational paintings stylistically evocative of the work of Édouard Manet. Although the dolls are fully dressed and their poses not sexually explicit, the paintings have a powerful homoerotic charge—in part because of a narrative element he repeated in the images, what he terms the "glossy decapitated portrait of a hunky male" that is packaged with Calvin Klein underwear.

"Coming out in my second year of graduate school was a big thing for me," Braimon told me. "I was comfortable with it—but not in my painting. So these Ken dolls were a perfect tool for me to express how I felt about male relationships. And sort of distance myself—by not actually painting a real person."

Photographer Dean Brown also makes a personal statement with Barbie, but it is about art history. He began using her as a model in 1980, while he was stationed with the United States Information Agency in Pakistan. Americans were not popular there at the time, and Barbie was less likely to smash his camera in a rage than were the people he photographed on the street. The result of his efforts was *A Capricious History of Western Art,* a portfolio that begins with a pastiche of the Lascaux cave paintings and ends with a variation on Marcel Duchamp's *Nude Descending a Staircase.* Brown also includes a gallery scene in which contemporary Barbies and Kens gaze at miniatures of his pictures.

In addition to Brown's wit, the first thing that strikes the viewer is how far the 1950s ideal of female beauty, which Barbie embodies, deviates from the classical ideal—not to mention from Vitruvian mathematical standards of human proportion. No way is that doll's foot one-sixth of her height; at just under an inch, it is closer to one-twelfth. The second is the extent to which Barbie is a natural model for works that derive their erotic energy from the display of breasts: Delacroix's *Liberty Leading the People,* Manet's *Olympia,* and the *Venus de Milo.*

Painted by Eugène Delacroix, whom Anne Hollander termed "the greatest Romantic expositor of complex passion through mammary exposure," the original Liberty's fascination owes much to "her gloriously lighted bare breasts." Brown's Liberty does not thrust her flag forward as Liberty does in the Delacroix version. She demurely picks her way over a sprawled G.I. Joe. She is above the battle, not within it; the vacuity of her expression precludes passionate engagement. She is a distant Liberty for a distant video-game war—and, significantly, the photograph is now in the collection of a female reporter to whom some Iraqi soldiers had surrendered during the ultimate video skirmish, the Persian Gulf War.

The *Venus de Milo* is another sculpture in which breasts are strongly eroticized, though Brown's version is more unnerving than voluptuous. Barbie is way too skinny to pass muster as a Greek goddess; she looks as if she has been placed on a rack and stretched. Nor does Barbie's legginess work for her. Draped female legs, like those of the original Venus, were considered beautiful in classical art; exposed ones, by contrast, connoted not beauty but strength, and were found on depictions of Artemis, a hunter and warrior.

Brown worked hard to transform Barbie into Venus; he chopped off her hair, wrenched off her arms, and bundled her legs in "a man's big white handkerchief" slathered with Elmer's glue. From clay he fashioned arm shards, nipples, and a navel; then he covered his handiwork with white paint. None of these affectations, however, diminished the perkiness of her expression or, for that matter, of her breasts.

In terms of body type, Barbie was far more suited as a stand-in for Manet's *Olympia.* Manet had painted a contemporary courtesan; in Brown's version, Barbie has never looked tartier—every bit a descendant of the sleazy *Bild* Lilli. By shrewdly posing his Olympia with crossed legs, Manet managed to avoid the issue of depicting pubic hair, eliminating what would have been a dramatic contrast between a human model and Barbie. And of course because Brown has used a current edition of the doll, his Olympia fixes the observer with the dead-on stare that so flustered viewers of Manet's original.

Now retired and living in suburban Maryland, Brown is currently working on "the original women's lib thing," Judith with the head of Holofernes, for which he bought a detached Ken head at a Barbie convention in 1987. Far from wishing to extirpate her eleven-and-a-half-inch rival, Brown's wife is trying to dissuade Brown from his latest venture: Barbie's funeral. "I've got a casket all made, and my wife doesn't want me to do it," he complained. "She doesn't like the idea of Barbie dying." But having given Barbie a navel—and, by implication, mortality—Brown has made the macabre scene logically inevitable.

(Photographer Felicia Rosshandler, by contrast, has had no inhibitions about killing Barbie and her kind; her chilling *Twilight of the Gods* features a close-up of an arched fashion-doll

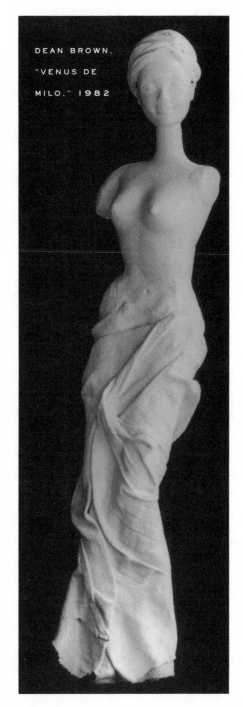

DEAN BROWN,
"VENUS DE
MILO," 1982

foot, tagged as if it were on a slab in a morgue. "To me, Barbie dies when she puts on her wedding dress," Rosshandler said. "She never ages; she never becomes a mother.")

Charles Bell's mural *The Judgement of Paris* also deals with death—and love. The famous scene, rendered by dozens of painters, depicts the first beauty contest, in which Paris, portrayed by a Ken doll, is forced to choose between Minerva, portrayed by a Barbie doll; Juno, portrayed by a Miss America doll; and Venus, portrayed by a Marilyn Monroe doll. Paris, of course, selects Venus—that is to say, love—and his choice leads to a megadisaster, the Trojan War.

The painting is different from Bell's other work—huge, photorealistic canvases of metal toys and pinball machines. And it is bittersweet; the myth he dramatizes is about opting for passion, even when it is fatal. "In the era of AIDS, I'm overwhelmed by the temporariness of life," Bell told me. "In the context of discovering our own mortality, things that had seemed important become less important. Eventually human kindness—and love—are the only things that really endure."

If Mattel has its way, however, corporate control of its icon will endure. A mere note from the toy company squelched *The Barbie Project,* an unauthorized theater piece that dramatized Mattel's corporate history and how children play with the doll, which was produced in 1980 at the Theater for the New City on Manhattan's Lower East Side. The show's director, Lauren Versel, who had initially petitioned Mattel for permission to film a documentary, didn't think her vision would ever be compatible with the company's.

Mattel has frozen other projects—Robin Swicord's musical comes to mind—but with visual art, its current tack seems to involve sponsoring authorized shows. In 1994, Mattel Germany opened a display of corporate-approved Barbie art in Berlin. Exhibited at the Werkbund-Archiv in the Martin-Gropius Bau (a gallery with a history of interest in commercial design), the pieces tended to be flashy but empty. Most involved clothing Barbie in exotic outfits. Yet there were a handful of images that made one look twice, and that might have raised Jesse Helms's blood pressure. These included depictions of lesbianism (after commenting in the exhibition catalogue that Barbie, at thirty-five, was "at last grown-up," artist Elke Martensen showed her in a leather helmet caressing the bare breast of another Barbie), fetishism (artist Holger Scheibe constructed an image of a sweaty, bare-shouldered adult male directing his puckered lips toward a Barbie clutched in his fist), and bestiality (artist Peter Engelhart placed Barbie in a "lovematch" with King Kong). And for crude sexual puns and sick-making imagery, Frank Lindow's *Barbie, ich hab dich zum Fressen gern!* (*Barbie, I would like to eat you!*) stood out: It featured blond Barbie and Asian brunette Kira "pickled" like fetuses in mason jars. But with these exceptions, the overall effect was bland.

American photographer David Levinthal was not included in the German show, but he is among the artists participating in Mattel's upcoming official coffee-table book—and the difference between the images he produced for that project and the ones he did for himself says much about the problems of working with corporate-controlled icons.

Levinthal is perhaps best known for *Hitler Moves East,* a book collaboration with Garry Trudeau that he began while at Yale Art School, from which he received an M.F.A. in 1972. In it, he photographs toy soldiers so that they look like real ones, ominously charting the course of the Second World War. His subsequent work has also pushed boundaries. In 1991, he executed a series called *Desire,* made up of enlarged Polaroids of miniature Japanese dolls that depicted Caucasian women in bondage. In soft focus, their surface was beguiling and seductive, but their content was disturbing—particularly to women. "I wanted people to look at these images, which I thought were very beautiful, and sort of halfway think, 'Wait a minute, I'm looking at an image of a woman tied in a chair, there's something wrong.'"

In graduate school, Levinthal began investigating sensitive sexual themes with Barbie and G.I. Joe. "I did a sort of narrative where Barbie had this straight preppie boyfriend. But she's attracted to this rough Vietnam vet," he explained. "The 'seventy-two ones just hit you because it's right there. . . . The race thing was very much in evidence in the late sixties, early seventies—the idea of Barbie as the Aryan virgin, and this character breaking through that. I called him G.I. José—that was at the height of my political incorrectness."

Yet his work for the authorized project, while it has an abstract beauty, lacks bite. "There was in the contract that there would be some editorial review, and I think anyone could use their own good sense and realize that you would try and make the work more accessible and less confrontational," he told me. "I wasn't going with the idea of saying, 'Let's really challenge with what we've got here.' " And he didn't.

GRACE HARTIGAN, "BARBIE," 1964

MAGGIE ROBBINS, "BARBIE FETISH," 1989

CHAPTER FOURTEEN

SLAVES OF
BARBIE

iona Auld credits Elizabeth Taylor with introducing her to Barbie. In 1990, after correctly identifying Taylor's favorite color (purple), her first film (*There's One Born Every Minute*), her most famous jewel (the Krupp diamond, given to her by Richard Burton), Auld, from Paisley, Scotland, won first prize in a contest sponsored by Taylor's Passion Perfume.

Soon she and her husband, a computer programmer, were on an all-expenses-paid trip to Las Vegas, San Diego, Los Angeles, and Hollywood. "I stayed at the Beverly Hilton; I had champagne; I had caviar; I was driven around in a limousine," she told me. But it was in Anaheim, California, that Auld's life changed. She visited a doll museum and became an almost instant convert to Barbie-collecting.

Auld began to amass dozens of dolls, virtually turning over her dining room to Mattel. Her five-year-old daughter was warned to steer clear of the treasures: "She has her own Barbies; she knows that she can look at but not touch mine." And when Auld placed an ad in *Barbie Bazaar*, requesting "BARBIE LOVING PENPALS FROM THE U.S.A.," there was no turning back. Thirty-five people responded, six of whom she met for the first time at the 1992

MEL ODOM, "MISS BARBIE"

Barbie-doll collector's convention in Niagara Falls.

Auld did not conceal her heritage at the conference. Sporting a tartan and a tam-o'-shanter with a red pom-pom, she appeared in the life-size doll-clothing fashion show as Barbie in Scotland. Like the Native American Barbie, which doesn't replicate the costume of a particular tribe, Mattel's Scottish Barbie doesn't wear the tartan of a specific clan. Auld, however, personalized her costume by wearing the pattern of her own—MacLennen—clan.

Nor was Fiona the only non–American-born collector on the runway. Ex–beauty queen Corazon Ugalde Yellen, daughter of a Philippines air force general under Ferdinand Marcos, executed a few theatrical turns as Barbie in the Philippines. Unlike the other participants, for whom the show appeared to be a goof, Yellen strutted crisply and imperiously—hips tucked forward, shoulders thrust back—as if she were vamping down a Paris runway. Before moving to Beverly Hills, she was a professional model, having posed for Macy's and Western Airlines.

Next came Rebecca Taylor, a wispy young woman from Tyler, Texas, dressed as Casey, the Mod waif with a single earring whom Barbie befriended in 1968. With one ear tinted kelly green, Taylor elicited first a groan, then applause from the crowd. The earrings on most vintage dolls stain their lobes with an unsightly emerald-colored eczema that, because it

SYLVIA, COPYRIGHT © BY NICOLE HOLLANDER, 1992

cannot easily be scrubbed off, is the bane of many a collector's existence. Taylor was followed by Judy Roberts of Spokane, Washington, who persuaded her husband Gary to model "Business Appointment," an outfit from the days when Ken still shopped at Brooks Brothers.

No two collectors are identical. Some women started amassing the dolls when they were children; some women began when they *had* children; and others aren't women at all—roughly a third of the delegates in Niagara were men.

Nor can one generalize by disposition or demographics. Some are misers, who puff up when describing the financial worth of their collections; some are innocents, who do not see the dolls as constructs of class or gender but as awe-inspiring miniatures; and some are sophisticates, who see the doll and her paraphernalia as campy artifacts of middle-class life—or "life," since camp sensibility requires a certain sardonic detachment. There are celebrity collectors like Danielle Steele, Roseanne Arnold, Demi Moore, and Norris Church. Many, however, seem to be like Auld—for whom Barbie is not an end in herself, but a pretext for making friends around the globe.

At the 1992 convention, I felt as if I were on a theme-park ride. I ate lunch the first day at a table hosted by an African-American collector, who lured me to her room for a peek at a prized possession—an issue of *Hustler* from July 1976 that featured a photo spread entitled "Vulva of the Dolls." I do not recall the images clearly, but in my notebook I jotted: "Bugs Bunny violates Francie with plastic carrot." Also at my table were Bob Young and Richard Nathans from Tempe, Arizona. Long before Mattel issued *Dance! Workout with Barbie,* Young had been animating the doll, frame by frame, manipulating Barbie in an aerobics routine with his grammar-school-age niece.

The convention food seemed straight out of childhood: red Jell-O with fruit and, at the Saturday night banquet, pineapple-glazed ham. Mattel's presentations also had a grade-school quality, like filmstrips for social studies class. The most surreal was a slide show, narrated by designer Carol Spencer, that traced the evolution of her Classique Collection from its inception (she designed the outfits while watching *Murder She Wrote*) to its production in Mattel's two plants in China. "The bicycle is the most common transportation means in China," Spencer recited as slides of Chinese peasants and bicycle racks appeared on the screen. "It's my understanding that they're not allowed to own automobiles." Next came shots inside the factory: Asians peering at tiny objects in front of large machines. "This is the heat setting of the rhinestones on the tights of Hollywood Premiere Fashion," Spencer said. "They're placing the rhinestones with tweezers onto a special fixture, and positioning the fabric over the rhinestones, and then the press goes down and heat actually sets the rhinestones onto the garments."

Other processes included face-painting and eyelash-rooting ("an extremely difficult operation . . . the operator was trained for two months"). The crowd applauded wildly when Spencer's Benefit Ball Barbie—the Georgette Mosbacher look-alike—had her eyelashes installed and clipped.

The convention had one redemptive moment. Doll authority Sarah Sink Eames had been rumored to have information about a prototype for "Colored Skipper"—Barbie's African-American sister, who antedated Black Barbie by several years. Eames not only confirmed that such an object existed, but that it was in her collection.

Many collectors told me that the 1993 convention in Baltimore, hosted by doll artist, illustrator, and former window-dresser Mark Ouellette, was a splashier production than the one in Niagara. It had six hundred participants and a waiting list of three thousand. But such extravaganzas are a recent phenomenon. The first Barbie conclave, held in October 1980, attracted under two hundred people. It took place in Queens, New York, at the Travelodge International Hotel, not far from Kennedy Airport.

Sybil de Wein, who, with Joan Ashabraner, published *The Collector's*

Encyclopedia of Barbie Dolls and Collectibles in 1977, was another key figure in the first wave of collectors. Referred to by Cronk as "our Barbie Dean," De Wein floated through the 1992 convention like a sort of dowager empress. Even with a broken elbow, the doughty widow from Clarksville, Tennessee, managed to comport herself with the dignity one expects from a Southern Lady. She graciously signed copies of her book when new collectors came to pay court.

Although doll aficionados had probably been stockpiling Barbies since 1959, they didn't get organized until the seventies. Back then, camaraderie took precedence over commerce. Collector Ann Nawricki "got us started on the right foot by reminding us that no matter how we love dolls they are still inanimate objects and are never as important as people (and friendship)," Cronk, editor of the Barbie collectors' bimonthly newsletter, wrote to its six hundred subscribers in September 1979.

By January 1980, Cronk's bulletin, *The Noname Newsletter,* had a fancy new title—*The International Barbie Doll Collectors Gazette*—and a stylish logo with drawings by artist/collector Candy Barr. Cronk, however, maintained an unprepossessing tone, often telling stories in an Erma Bombeck voice about her own Barbie-related mishaps. At one point, a network TV crew asked her to demonstrate her dolls, including the 1979 Kissing Barbie. "They had me holding her at a very difficult angle," Cronk wrote, "and in the process of struggling to hold her still and press the plate, I pulled her bodice down, leaving her topless on CBS's film." Then there was the time she tried to conserve money for Barbieana by making her children purchase the family's shampoo. "Before leaving for Girl Scout camp, I found myself shampooing with something called strawberry Earth Born Shampoo," she writes. "The following day I was pursued by about 1,000 bees, all trying to pollinate me! The next time Scott's turn rolls around to buy shampoo I just pray it doesn't turn out to be Banana or I will make sure I avoid the zoo!"

Cronk also offered her opinions on new products. "The thing that really

rings my chimes," she wrote in February 1980, "is the new commode. . . .
We can truthfully say Barbie has everything now as her pink commode has
real 'flushing' action! It is pink and there is no mistaking who it belongs to
as her name is on the tank! Part of the dream furniture grouping, it comes
with a small chest with towels (what, no toilet paper?). Another new item is
a round bathtub with continental shower. . . . Where does the water go?
Hmm, come to think of it, where does the water go in the toilet?"

But for Cronk, the highlight of 1980 was meeting Charlotte Johnson at
Barbie's twenty-first birthday party during Toy Fair on February 11.
Johnson, who had just retired, regaled *Gazette* editors with war stories,
including the trials of designing a Barbie-sized mink coat for Sears. The
Gazette ran her photo in front of a revolving display of historical Barbies. It
was among her last public appearances; felled by Alzheimer's disease,
Johnson is currently in a nursing home.

Collecting has changed a lot in the fourteen years since that first convention, however. "There used to be a preponderance of older women whose
children had Barbie and they wanted it," said doll dealer Joe Blitman. "Now
it's different. There's a new guard of people in their late twenties to early
forties—probably two to one, female to male. And it's a more urban group."

Whether they amass Barbies or bric-a-brac, Kens or incunabula, Francies
or Fabergé eggs, collectors frequently share certain personality traits—
acquisitiveness, obsession, and an intense connection to objects, sometimes
at the expense of people. In *Collecting: An Unruly Passion,* psychoanalyst
Werner Muensterberger locates the beginning of the collecting impulse in
early childhood—"in the objects that are always there when the child's need
for comfort . . . is not immediately met; when the child does not have a mother's breast, or a loving pair of arms to allay frustration." For many grown-up
collectors, to pile up treasures is to stave off childhood feelings of aban-
donment, to erect a tangible (yet frangible) hedge against ancient anxiety.
The urge begins with a child's first "not-me" objects—Winnicott's transi-

tional objects—a category into which, as we have seen earlier, Barbie sometimes falls. But even when objects are not intended as playthings they often
function that way within their collector's psyche. "What else are collectibles
but toys grown-ups take seriously?" Muensterberger asks.

Sometimes the lust to amass new and snazzier objects can dominate a collector's life, just as betting dominates the life of a gambler. It can even
supersede work and family, Muensterberger says. "It's an addiction,"
explained Jan Fennick of J'aime Collectibles, an antique-doll dealership on
Long Island. "There are a lot of layaways. They'd sooner buy Barbie clothes
than buy clothes for themselves. They see something they want at the prices
they want, they figure they won't be able to find it again. The shoes can wait;
or the house can wait; or the car can wait. . . . Nobody's starving or homeless because of Barbie, but people joke about it."

"There are tens of thousands of collectors—everything from casual to passionate to obsessive," Blitman said. "Some people . . . have their job, whatever they do, and the rest of their life is Barbie."

"Ownership is the most intimate relationship that one can have to
objects," Walter Benjamin writes in "Unpacking My Library," his essay on
book-collecting. The relationship reflects not merely a nostalgia attached to
the things, but to their period, their workmanship, and their previous owners. "A lot of people are drawn to the hobby because they like to sew for the
dolls," said Blitman. Other Barbie aficionados customize the doll's look.
"They paint the face; they reroot the hair; they spend hours and weeks and
months, sometimes," doll expert and *Barbie Bazaar* contributing editor A.
Glenn Mandeville told me. "People today are taking Barbie and really making it a mannequin that they drape their own dreams on."

To collect artifacts from the past is to own the past—and sometimes, to
imagine a better past than the one that actually existed. The baby boomers'
fascination with the sitcoms of their childhood—what nostalgia network
Nickelodeon terms "classic television"—has a lot to do with a longing for

an idealized past. Many of the male Barbie collectors did not fit seamlessly into their heterosexist nuclear families. As a child, one male collector, who now has several hundred dolls, took an after-school job to buy Barbies and hid them under a loose board in the basement, until his mother discovered them. "I've given those dolls to an orphanage," she told him. "And we're not going to tell your father."

By manipulating early Barbies and Kens, collectors can both control and fit into that lost world—or, through parody, deflect the sting of its rejection. Barbie and her props lend themselves to the playing out of revised scenarios. With their fold-away walls and sketchy details, her houses resemble a TV soundstage.

Because Barbie is an emblem of female glamour, acquiring her can mean something different to a female collector from what it does to a male. "A lot of women are buying Barbie because they can't be Barbie, and they live out this dream of being slender and pretty and popular and all that through the doll," Mandeville said.

Historically, Mandeville added, doll-collecting has not been the unique domain of women; "a lot of so-called manly men have been interested in dolls." John Wayne's collection of kachina figures, for example, is currently on display at the National Cowboy Hall of Fame in Oklahoma City. But it takes a tough man to challenge a gender convention, which is what buying Barbie involves. "There are a lot of men that I sell to who have P.O. boxes—who whisper on the phone," Blitman told me. "Some collect with their wives, although you get the feeling that the husband is more the collector than the wife. They start out collecting Ken, then they get one Barbie because it will look good next to the tuxedo. And suddenly they're into the first seven years—if not more—of Barbie."

"A lot of gay men are into Barbie," said Jan Fennick. "She's as much of an icon as Madonna or Marilyn or Judy Garland. . . . To me, the ultimate male bonding is when you know forty-year-old men who play with Barbie dolls on the kitchen table together. And I have friends who do this—they play with the Color Magic—sticking the heads under water to see whether the colors change." In fact, so substantial is Barbie's gay following that *The Advocate* devoted an extensive article to the phenomenon, alleging that the prose in *Barbie Bazaar,* the bimonthly collector's bible that debuted in 1988, "seems to swish off the page."

A glossy, four-color, ninety-page magazine, *Barbie Bazaar* bears little resemblance to Cronk's black-and-white, ten-page *Gazette.* Between its sophisticated design and professional artwork, doll expert and former *Details* editor Beauregard Houston Montgomery calls it "the only fashion magazine I can bear to read." Although its founders, Karen Caviale and Marlene Mura, are at the vanguard of collecting's second wave, they have tried not to abandon first-wave values, including the relationships formed over dolls. "We're not totally object-oriented because the collectors have their own network of people that they become very good friends with," Mura told me.

Caviale added: "Some Barbie collectors are very competitive. If they know of something good, they won't share that information. But the majority of collectors are very helpful."

Although Caviale, a first-generation Barbie owner, has been collecting since 1980, *Barbie Bazaar* seems to have sprung mostly from its founders' longing to go into business for themselves. Mura, an insurance agent, met Caviale through Caviale's boss at the Girl Scouts, where Caviale was a public relations director, and in 1986, they began investigating the feasibility of a collector's newsletter. "Because of desktop publishing, the cost of producing a magazine was a little less out of our reach," Caviale told me, but that didn't mean it was without risk. To borrow money for start-up costs, they had to put up their own property as collateral.

Barbie Bazaar's first year was rough; it began as a monthly with only about five hundred subscribers. Collectors responded cautiously to its ads in *Dolls* and *Doll Reader;* they weren't sure Mura and Caviale could deliver what they promised. But after the first few issues, circulation grew. Mura and Caviale also cut costs in 1989 by bringing out the magazine every other month. Today, *Barbie Bazaar* has a circulation of twenty thousand and an 85 percent renewal rate.

The magazine was conceived during the doll's "We Girls Can Do Anything" years—which had, for Mura, particular resonance. Unlike Caviale, who came of age in the seventies, Mura went to college in the fifties, when, in order to be allowed to study business administration, she had to major in "secretarial science." "I'm a feminist," Mura told me, "and I have to say that the fifties made me support women and appreciate women. It was a battle to be who you wanted to be. You couldn't accomplish it in the fifties. In the nineties, you can." Or Mura and Caviale can, anyway. By 1992, the magazine was sufficiently profitable for them to kiss their day jobs good-bye.

The collectors are such a diverse group that it would take an entire book to do justice to them. But I did spend time with a few—and *all* they seemed to have in common was Barbie. At the Niagara convention, Corazon Yellen invited me to come see her four thousand dolls, a thousand of which are Barbies. So a few months later, when I was in Beverly Hills, I took her up on her offer. She buzzed me through the fortified gateway of her Benedict Canyon house and greeted me in a low-cut minidress and cowboy boots. Even without a Stetson, she could have passed for Western Stampin' Barbie.

The wife of a Los Angeles building contractor, Yellen is a collector of many things: antique furniture, bibelots, nineteenth-century porcelain dolls, French fashion dolls, Madame Alexander dolls, and, with her husband, classic cars. She is also the author of *Total Beauty and Life*, a how-to book dealing with a broad range of topics, from buying furs to building pectoral muscles. Before escorting me through her Barbie trove, she encouraged me to have a seat in her living room and peruse the book. I learned about "exotic-vertical" and "sultry-horizontal" eyeshadow techniques, and

how to use "deep blue, blazing amethysts" to create "Spellbinding Eyes"—
the sort of tips Barbie herself might impart.

Yellen's collection also suggests a strong psychic affinity with the doll. In
one display case, nearly all of Barbie's first fashions—called the "900
series" because of its stock number—were displayed on vintage dolls, next
to which were snapshots of Yellen, identically clad. She created dioramas
with Hispanic Barbie sprawled provocatively in lingerie, while Ken, with a
chilled bottle of champagne, looked on. Again, nearby, were matching photos of her. "I belonged to an Asian-
American theater group here," she
told me, explaining that the doll's
clothes were replicas of costumes she
had actually worn. One doll even held
a miniature copy of Yellen's book.

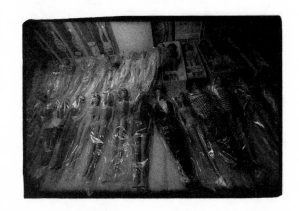

Like Beverly Hills itself, Yellen's
doll room teems with famous figures:
James Dean, Marilyn Monroe, Sonny
Bono, the Man from U.N.C.L.E., and
the Six Million Dollar Man. She even
has a platoon of soldiers clustered
around an austere photo of her father,
the Filipino general. But perhaps her

BARBIE COLLECTORS' CONVENTION, 1992

SYLVIA PLACHY

most startling mannequin is the life-size statue of herself, bedecked with
rhinestone earrings, a tiara, and "exotic-vertical" eyeshadow. She owns two
such effigies, one fashioned by a sculptor and one cast from life.

"Even though public collections may be less objectionable socially and
more useful academically than private collections, the objects get their due
only in the latter," Walter Benjamin wrote. But Evelyn Burkhalter's Barbie
Hall of Fame in Palo Alto, California, seems to be the best of both worlds.
She owns all seventeen thousand of its dolls—worth about two million dol-

lars—but she lets the public look at them. And she has permitted TV crews from three continents to film them.

A fount of Mattel lore, Burkhalter begins her tour by showing museumgoers the Lilli doll and concludes with Mattel's newest products. In July 1992, I made the mistake of visiting her on a Saturday. And the gallery, about the size of a two-car garage, was packed: not with collectors but with children, who were transfixed—pressing their palms and noses against dozens of glass cases. Oblivious to the summer heat—Burkhalter feared that blasting the air conditioner would overload a circuit—the children squealed and gaped and jostled for better views, when they weren't tugging at Burkhalter, who, as a mother of four and grandmother of seven, appeared miraculously calm.

Founded in 1985, Burkhalter's museum is located above the office of her husband, a Stanford-educated audiologist. About twenty-five years ago, she said, her husband founded a school for hearing-impaired children between three and six years of age. Burkhalter's first contact with Barbie involved sewing doll clothes for school fund-raising events.

In the mid-eighties, fifteen years after Ruth Handler had had a mastectomy, Burkhalter also battled breast cancer. Assuming she and Handler would have much in common, she sought her out at a department-store promotion for Nearly Me. But to Burkhalter's disappointment, Handler took no interest in Burkhalter's museum. "She came out and said, 'Can I help you?'" Burkhalter told me. "I introduced myself and she said, 'I don't want to discuss Barbie with you or with anybody else. But if you want to talk to me about bras, I'd be happy to give you my time.' And I just turned around and walked out."

Nor did Burkhalter have the patience to deal with Billy Boy, a collector and jewelry-designer-turned-Mattel-consultant who appeared at her museum shortly after it opened. Boy, a New Yorker who now lives in Paris, was working on "The New Theater of Fashion," a collection of Barbie clothing by name designers loosely based on "Le Petit Théâtre de la Mode," a post–World War II exhibition of real-life fashions displayed, for economic reasons, on dolls. He has since parted company with Mattel and Barbie, describing the doll on a recent BBC documentary as an "insulting image of women." Boy now manufactures his own doll, Mdvanii, named, some say, for the fortune hunter who married Barbara Hutton. It has greater detailing than Barbie—nipples and pubic hair—and a price well into the hundreds of dollars.

"The minute he downed Barbie, he killed his own business," Burkhalter told me. "I refused to buy one and I was telling everybody, 'Don't buy one; it's the only way you can stop the offensive things he's saying about something that you're collecting.' "

(Barbie is not the only figure whose relationship with Boy went sour. In his diaries, Andy Warhol reveals an initial fascination with the young man, which, by July 1986, had degenerated into contempt. He accuses Boy of "social climbing," and observes: "Billy Boy had a fight with the paparazzi . . . because he wanted to be *in* the pictures.")

Between her candor, knowledge, and willingness to display her rarities, Burkhalter is something of a rarity herself. Other major collectors are less generous. Glen Offield, whose five thousand dolls, including about two hundred one-of-a-kind prototypes, are valued at over a million dollars, is far from forthcoming (he refused me an interview), although he did allow *Smithsonian* magazine to photograph them for its cover in December 1989. He also permitted Mattel to shoot them for trading cards of Barbie's wardrobe through the years.

To be fair, however, Offield has recently received the kind of publicity that would make anyone want to avoid the press. On October 9, 1992, Offield's dolls were stolen from his San Diego house, and two fires were set to conceal the missing Barbies. "They meant everything to me," Offield told the *Los Angeles Times*. "I could do without eating. I don't know if I can live without them." He did not, however, have to try. Within two weeks, the dolls turned up, jammed into a rented storage closet under a freeway overpass. They had been shanghaied, the Associated Press reported, by Bruce Scott Sloggett, a male video pornographer for whom Offield once worked, and who died October 24, 1992, of a drug overdose.

Although he owns a vast, valuable hoard, New York–based collector Gene Foote has managed to maintain a sense of self-irony about his hobby. Foote's principal occupation is musical theater. He directed European productions of such shows as *Sweet Charity, Annie Get Your Gun, Pal Joey, Little Shop of Horrors,* and *A Chorus Line.* With his Barbies, he also stages production numbers—elaborate dioramas that he has been photographing for a book-in-progress called *For the Love of a Doll.* "It's literally the story of Barbie," he told me, "but I don't treat her as a product. I treat her as a human being. She's just a girl named Barbie; yet I give all of the Mattel facts."

Foote grew up in Washington County, Tennessee, in a house without electricity or running water. He still has a trace of a southern accent and a warm, courtly, old-fashioned manner—which includes referring to Barbie owners of my generation as "Barbie girls." As a boy, to entertain his younger female cousins, he made paper dolls from figures in the Sears Roebuck catalogue. "I'd cut out one of the women who had on the girdles or the underwear and glue her on cardboard. Then I would draw clothes for her and color them and cut them out," he explained. His cousins told him: "You made us Barbies before there were Barbies."

By far the strangest Barbie "collector" that I met was, in fact, an object in Foote's collection. As part of a 1965 ensemble called "Me 'N' My Doll," Mattel's Skipper doll was issued her own tiny Barbie—barely over an inch in height, with a painted red swimsuit and yellow hair. And I was struck by the total containment of Barbie's world. It wasn't enough for Skipper to receive Barbie's sisterly counsel; she, like every other girl, needed a Barbie totem—a thing onto which she could project her idealized future self—to internalize the Barbie ethos.

For Beauregard Houston Montgomery, a New York City partygoer and wit-at-large in the style of Quentin Crisp, collecting Barbie isn't about closed universes or looking inward. It is about looking outward and upward to the heavens. Amassing the dolls, he said quite seriously, is a "way of dealing with alien abduction."

"People who have been kidnapped start collecting," he continued. "They have collecting manias. Some people collect dirt, like specimens. Other people collect plants." Or dolls that resemble their captors. To demonstrate this, he showed me his Barbie Fashion Queen, which, with its bulging eyes, nose defined by two dots, and insectoid face, did seem strikingly similar to the "aliens" described by alleged abductees. "I was about two, and I was visiting my grandmother on a farm in Missouri," he said. "And I remember waking up in the night and seeing this thing looking in the window, this creature—looking in at me with huge eyes. It seemed to float—like, hover—and it kind of glowed. And I remember screaming and yelling for my parents until it finally disappeared."

Was he actually abducted? Did he plan a hypnotic session with Harvard psychologist John Mach to find out?

"What do I need to remember being on a spaceship for?" he snapped. "People already think I'm insane; that would only verify it."

To convince me of his sanity, Montgomery telephoned his friend, illustrator Mel Odom. On a three-way conference call late one night, Odom told me that his painting of the 1964 Miss Barbie had a distinct otherworldly quality. "It's the most E.T. image ever made for children," he told me. "I had friends looking at it, asking, 'Who's the Martian?' "

Of course not all collectors accumulate dolls of investment quality. Robin Schwartz, a photographer whose work is in the permanent collection of New York's Metropolitan Museum of Art and whose recent book, *Like Us*, was a collection of primate images, put me in touch with a collector of a wholly other stripe: Dot Paolo, proprietor of the Rabbet Gallery in New Brunswick,

New Jersey. If one anthropomorphizes Barbie, Paolo is the person who adopts the unadoptables—provides a foster home for the heartbreaking dolls that have been chewed or shorn or battered. Although she is a successful corporate art consultant, her "collecting" is more merciful than mercenary. "I don't have the dolls standing up with perfect clothes," she told me. "What I like is what the children have done to them, the way they cut their hair and drew on their faces."

Schwartz photographed Paolo's dolls—dozens of forlorn, damaged Barbies—with Paolo's dog, Starbuck, who is fifteen and deaf; Paolo's compassion does not extend only to plastic objects. It is not a comfortable photograph. Even though they are not human, there is something tragic about

STARBUCK AND BARBIES, COLLECTION OF DOT PAOLO   ROBIN SCHWARTZ

the flea-market Barbies; the sad, spent dolls cast away without so much as a glittering G-string. They will not be fought over at auction or cherished by grown men. But at least they are among their own kind, not condemned to the landfill, watching coffee grounds and banana peels disintegrate before their nonbiodegradable eyes.

CHAPTER FIFTEEN

BARBIE FACES
THE FUTURE

If Barbie were merely another global power brand like McDonald's or Coke, ending this book would be simple. One would focus on what Mattel has in mind for its billion-dollar damsel, as well as on the company's rapid growth. In 1993, it gobbled up Fisher-Price, a producer of preschool toys, and in 1994 it purchased Kransco, the maker of such classics as the Whamo Frisbee and the Hula Hoop. Today, it is as large as or larger than the industry's longtime Goliath, Hasbro.

But Barbie's story is, of course, far more than a tale of shareholders' meetings and annual reports. It is a saga of mothers and daughters, men and women, hope, despair, passion, and the striving after an impossible "American" ideal. Barbie is an emblem of "femininity," a concept quite different from biological femaleness. Barbie was invented by women for women, and the wrath brought to bear upon Barbie by some women is perhaps wrath deflected from themselves. For daughters are indoctrinated into "femininity" by mothers—not by a plastic object. "Even a generous mother," Simone de Beauvoir wrote, "who sincerely seeks her child's welfare, will as a rule think that it is wiser to make a 'true woman' of her, since

STITCHING OF BARBIE'S HAIR SYLVIA PLACHY

society will more readily accept her if this is done." Barbie permits such "generous" mothers to wash their hands of the taint of "femininity," to blast Barbie as a "bimbo," even as their conflicting messages and ambivalences etch their way onto their daughters' evolving minds.

Barbie is also a space-age fertility icon, a totem of an ancient matriarchal power. In the dark, primal part of our brains where we process primitive archetypes, she is Ur-woman. As an icon, she has come to represent not merely "American" women or consumer capitalist women, but a female principle that defies national, ethnic, and regional boundaries.

Nor is Midge to be overlooked as an archetype. If Barbie is Ur-woman, Midge is Ur-sidekick. The entire female sex can, for the most part, be divided into Barbies and Midges. From Gilgamesh and Enkidu to Achilles and Patroclus to the Lone Ranger and Tonto, epic pairings have historically involved men. But by the mid-twentieth century, the convention broadened to include women. For every Lucy, there began to be an Ethel.

Because of Barbie's archetypal resonance, to mutilate a Barbie doll is not to vandalize a toy; it is to attack a woman. As evidence, one need merely cite the police investigation of the "Sandusky Slasher," who within six months between 1992 and 1993 cut the breasts and mutilated the crotches of two dozen Barbie dolls at three stores in Sandusky, Ohio—where, incidentally, *Barbie Bazaar* is published. (Sandusky is also the hometown of Sugar Kowalsky, Marilyn Monroe's character in *Some Like It Hot*.) In February 1993, Perkins Township police received an FBI profile of the suspected slasher—a white male between the ages of sixteen and thirty. He is "an organized and controlled individual who is probably dominated in a relationship with a woman, possibly his mother," reported the *Chicago Tribune,* and is "considered harmless by friends." The FBI appears to have treated the crime as if the doll were an actual woman; it has constructed a psychological profile reminiscent of Hitchcock's Norman Bates. But my hunch is that the assault—like so much of the art that involves Barbie mutilation—may have been upon Barbie as a construct of femininity rather than Barbie as an archetypal woman. And if so, the perpetrator might well be female. (I find myself wondering if Andrea Dworkin can account for her time when the attacks took place.)

Nor has Barbie merely been a crime victim. In one of the more lurid kidnappings of 1993, she was an accessory. Accused Long Island child abductor John Esposito required a powerful magnet to lure seven-year-old Katie Beers away from a shopping mall and into a dungeon beneath his house. What was his bait? The Barbie exercise video.

Then there is the "Barbie strategy": a way of gaining attention for one's ideas by linking them to Barbie. Shortly before the 1992 presidential election, pop culture analyst Greil Marcus wrote an op-ed piece for *The New York Times* explaining Bill Clinton's "Elvis strategy"—how he grabbed press coverage by associating himself with the King. When President Bush accused him of promoting "Elvis Economics," Clinton raised a saxophone to his lips and belted out "Heartbreak Hotel" before the astonished eyes of Arsenio Hall and his television audience. "Slap Elvis on anything and you'll be noticed," Marcus wrote. "Elvis in a speech is a guaranteed soundbite on the evening news."

In 1992, the American Association of University Women demonstrated that Barbie was a guaranteed soundbite, too. When the group complained about a Barbie who said, "Math class is tough," the story made page one of *The Washington Post.* Like Clinton with Elvis, the AAUW used Barbie to direct attention to its own agenda—a 1991 study it had commissioned which showed that girls begin to lose their self-confidence at puberty. At age nine, the girls were assertive and academically self-assured; but by high school fewer than a third felt that way.

The upshot from the incident—a public discussion of how that age-old toxin "femininity" warps bright, androgynous minds—was, of course, a good thing. But I couldn't help feeling Barbie got a bum rap. After all, the doll didn't say, "Math class is tough *for girls,*" or "Math class is tough; let's study cosmetology." She simply said, "Math class is tough"—which struck me as a call to knuckle down and master the subject. Would a doll who said "Computers make homework fun" be likely to quake at the sight of an algebra problem? This underscores another pattern in Barbie's universe. People project fears and prejudices onto her; when a person talks at length about Barbie, one usually learns more about the speaker than about the doll.

Reinvention is a constant in Barbie's life, but at Mattel as in Ecclesiastes, there is nothing new under the sun. The 1993 Western Stampin' Barbie is a direct knockoff of the 1981 Western Barbie, except that the earlier model's eye winked. Similarly, Barbie has been pushing homeovestism—the masking of one's cross-gender strivings by decking oneself out like a parody of one's own gender—in slightly different guises for a decade. Modeled on the mid-eighties Day-to-Night Barbie, the current "We Girls Can Do Anything" Career Collection dolls are packaged with implicitly "masculine" daytime work outfits and absurd caricatures of "feminine" evening dresses. The contrast, for instance, between the 1993 Police Officer Barbie's work garb—a natty indigo uniform with trousers, a necktie, and a long phallic flashlight—and her "glittery" evening frock—a gilded bustier with a gold-flecked tutu—is particularly striking. No one but a drag queen—or a homeovestite—would be caught dead in it.

In response to tough new environmental laws in Europe, however, Barbie's chemical composition, while still plastic, has changed. It is no longer exclusively polyvinyl chloride (PVC), which, when incinerated, produces hydrochloric acid, linked to acid rain. The doll's arms are made from ethylene-vinyl acetate (EVA), its torso from acrylonitrile-butadiene-styrene (ABS), and its bend-leg armature from polypropylene. Only its outer legs remain PVC—but this, too, is a different formula from that of the early dolls. In the late eighties, the German government passed a law restricting the amount of plasticizer (a softening agent) permitted in PVC. German consumer watchdogs worried that if a child accidentally swallowed a toy made of PVC, his or her stomach acid would extract its plasticizer, leaving behind a hard, dangerous object.

"We tried to argue with them by conducting tests where we had plasticized PVC Barbie shoes tied on a tether fed to pigs," explained Maki Papavasiliou, Mattel's vice president of corporate environmental affairs. "For weeks on end they would fish them out and weigh them to demonstrate that there was no weight loss—no plasticizer loss." But the Germans remained unconvinced, so Mattel complied with the law, making Barbie's legs less flexible than they used to be.

Mattel has also adapted its packaging to comply with European regulations. The display windows in Barbie's European boxes are no longer made of PVC, and the company has made a commitment to use more recycled materials. The floor, in fact, in Barbie's three-story town house is made of postconsumer recycled ABS.

COLLECTOR'S ITEMS

Although Barbie wasn't sold in Europe until the early sixties, Germany and France are now among Mattel's most important markets. Likewise, Mattel has recently begun selling Barbies in Japan, instead of issuing Barbie-like teen fashion dolls through a Japanese franchise. Barbie kicked off her new internationalism in 1990 with the "Barbie Summit," a kiddie United Nations that took place at New York's Waldorf-Astoria. Its slogan, in English, was "One Child/One World," which was emblazoned in several languages on the official Summit doll's carton. But one had to question Mattel's phrasing. The translations were not always literal—the German version, for instance, was *"Eine Welt für alle Kinder"*—literally "One world for all the children." Yet the Italian translation needlessly preserved the English construction. Thus *"Un bimbo/un mondo"* was boldly displayed on the box.

Despite its economic problems, Eastern Europe is a new frontier for Barbie. Children in Moscow clamor for the doll, and often have to settle for stout Russian knock-offs with large feet, smudged makeup, and fright-wig hair. Families who can afford an authentic Barbie often cannot afford authentic clothes; they must sew outfits for the doll. To relieve the shortage, some American Barbie collectors organized a shipment of dolls to Russia, and even Cher, no fan of Barbie, brought dozens of them on her recent trip to Armenia, whence her family originated. "I always hated you, Barbie," Cher told *People* magazine, "I always thought you were a blond bimbo, but now I see that you have your uses."

Not all members of the former Soviet empire are welcoming Barbie with glee. In a full-page 1993 article in *Sobesednik,* a Russian pop cultural journal that had, until 1990, been a supplement to the Communist Youth Party newspaper, two waggish writers joked about Barbie's anatomical deficiencies and high cost—so steep, in fact, that in order to afford her, three families had to share her: "For a week the American girl will live with Masha; for a week with Dasha; for a week with Kolya." They describe Barbie as "the plaything of the century" and—racy pun intended—as "the most popular woman for sale in all the world."

One could end here, with Barbie's Eastern exodus, a path obliquely reminiscent of Hitler's annexation of the Sudetenland, Poland, and Czechoslovakia. But having opened this book with an emblematic spectacle, I had hoped to close with one—perhaps a snapshot of Teflon felon Ruth Handler restored to her rightful glory, autographing thirty-fifth-anniversary products for hundreds of fans in the Barbie boutique at Manhattan's FAO Schwarz. Yet the essence of Barbie—what makes her more than a global power brand—has to do with the way she colonizes the inner lives of children. Thus to describe an official corporate function would have been to slight Barbie's grass-roots identity.

I was about to abandon the anecdotal approach when I learned that the College Art Association's 1994 meeting was scheduled to take place at the New York Hilton the same week as the American International Toy Fair. A little over thirty blocks from the showrooms where Mattel would be hawking its latest Barbies, Erica Rand, a Bates College art historian, was slated to make a very different Barbie presentation. Rand wasn't interested in the doll per se, but in how it could be subverted for women's pleasure. Her work had been inspired, she told *Lingua Franca* magazine, by a 1989 photo spread in *On Our Backs*, a lesbian pornographic journal, that featured a Barbie-like doll used as a dildo. Presented as part of a panel cosponsored by the Gay and Lesbian Caucus, her paper was entitled "The Biggest Closet Ever Sold: Barbie's."

I soon found myself on the phone with artists, scholars, and other contributors to this book, urging them to hear Rand's talk with me. Many were interested; two academics, with whom I had talked through some applications of feminist and psychoanalytic theory, had planned to attend even before my call. A. M. Homes, author of "A Real Doll," agreed to come, as did my college pal Ella King Torrey, a grants officer for a foundation she prefers not to name, who had debriefed Charlotte Johnson and Jack Ryan. I had hoped that Donna Gibbs, the Mattel publicist I had grown to admire for her ability to translate deep distaste into remarkable courtesy, might leave Toy Fair and hear the talk, but she was needed on the display floor. Likewise, Maggie Robbins, the artist who makes "Barbie Fetishes" by hammering rusty nails into the doll, canceled at the last minute. Things were busy at *McCall's* and she couldn't get away.

As serendipity would have it, however, the admission pass I had obtained for Gibbs did not go to waste. Cindy Jackson, the woman who had been surgically remade into Barbie, was in town from London and called to say hello. Although it would cut into the time she had allotted to visit department stores, she agreed to show up, and materialized at the Hilton with an enormous shopping bag filled with L'eggs pantyhose. (She can't buy them on her side of the Atlantic.)

The panel—which also included papers titled "Warhol's Closet: Homosexuality, the Collection and the Articulation of Identity," "Is It Different Yet?," "Closet Ain't Nothin' but a Dark and Private Place," and "Heroic Swooners: The Androgyne and Homoerotic Impulse in Early French Romantic Painting"—was convened in an upstairs ballroom, that, fifteen minutes before the session began, was already packed. People stood two deep around the room's periphery and greedily eyed the seats I was saving. So large was the crowd that A. M. Homes and I missed each other; she wound up sitting across the room, invisible in an ocean of black leather and tweed.

The program did not start promptly. Jackson glanced at her watch; precious shopping time was ticking away. Rand's talk was scheduled first, but when the lights dimmed, slide after slide of provocatively sprawled youths flashed on screen—the heroic swooners. The friend seated beside me passed a note: "If Rand isn't next, I'm out of here."

As if in response, the androgyne apologist stepped down and Rand took the microphone. She was a reedy, dark-haired woman, and in her I thought I recognized a fellow Midge. But when she opened her mouth, the feelings of solidarity vanished. Rand's talk was an exercise in the "Barbie Strategy"—advancing one's political agenda by lashing it to Barbie. After what must have been the twentieth time she used the word "subversion," I began to be cross. Rand said Mattel had bought the patent to the Lilli doll, which it hadn't. She characterized the Random House Barbie novels, written by young female loose cannons at Mattel's advertising agency, as if they had been produced under tight corporate scrutiny. I don't often passionately identify myself as a journalist, someone who unearths facts and verifies them, but as Rand spoke, I embraced that tedious, literal-minded persona.

WHEN RAND FINISHED, I WALKED OUT OF THE HILTON with Ella King Torrey. (Stalked out might be more accurate.) An inveterate Barbie scholar, Ella, too, had caught factual errors, but they didn't seem to bother her. "Relax," she told me. "Rand's point didn't have anything to do with Barbie. It was about the politics of sexual identity. She could have just as easily been talking about toasters."

Ella is a tall woman with abundant blond hair who, in the muted February light, might have passed for an early-sixties executive Barbie—Busy Gal or Career Girl. She was not literally decked out in one of those outfits, but she wore the nineties equivalent—an expensive black silk pantsuit exquisitely offset with silver jewelry and a diaphanous scarf. Even in the seventies, when clothes were so ugly one could hardly bear to look at them, Ella had managed to accessorize. Her scarves always fell the way they were supposed to fall, and even when she wore whimsical jewelry, it looked drop-dead chic.

Ella, it is fair to say, brings out the Midge in me, as she has since we were undergraduates. So I was docile when she prescribed a shopping trip to ease my irritation, and steered us toward Takashimaya, the very grand Japanese department store one block east on Fifth Avenue. In the Random House novels, Midge never questioned Barbie; she trusted that Barbie knew best. And I liked the idea of visiting a store with ties to Tokyo. It harked back to those original Japanese Barbies with their hard mouths and seductive stares who had so beguiled us in our youth.

A doorman pulled open the portal to a vast, clean, perfect atrium that made us feel almost doll-like in scale. There was, I would like to say, a whiff of cherry blossoms, but, in fact, the smell was more like that of thirty-five-year-old vinyl. We stepped into the elevator and were transported.

The afternoon was young. We had credit cards. And somewhere deep in our intuitive intelligences, we accepted what we could not change: Barbie was us.

ACKNOWLEDGMENTS

LIKE THE DOLL ITSELF, *Forever Barbie* was not made by a lone extremist. Thanks to Paul Bresnick for coming up with the idea, and Janis Vallely for convincing him that I was the writer to implement it. To Sylvia Plachy, for those amazing photographs, as well as that weekend with Ella King Torrey in Niagara Falls. To Amy Bernstein, Corby Kummer, and Judith Shulevitz, for performing surgery without an anesthetic. To Anna Shapiro, the original Boho Barbie, for editorial and conceptual guidance. To Glenn Horowitz, for keeping me on track, and to the friends who kept my thinking on track: May Castleberry, Anne Freedgood, Ben Gerson, Marianne Goldberger, Caroline Niemczyk, Ellen Handler Spitz, and Abby Tallmer.

Because this book required extensive trips to Los Angeles and a monastic year of writing on Long Island, I must express thanks geographically: to the California contingent—Victoria Dailey, Barbara Ivey, Mike Lord, and Nancy Lord; the Sag Harbor contingent—Laurel Cutler, Dorothy Frankel, and Carol Phillips; and, in cyberspace, the Echo contingent—Marisa Bowe, Jonathan Hayes, Stacy Horn, and NancyKay Shapiro.

On the research front, thanks to Tom Fedorek, Caroline Howard, Jeremy Kroll, Donna Mendell, and Jessy Randall. And to Mary Lamont, my stalwart transcriber.

Nor could I have written this without certain spokespeople for the under-twelve set: Polly Bresnick, Honor McGee, Meredith Niemczyk, Gabriel Nussbaum, Lily Nussbaum, and Heather O'Brien.

Many people interviewed for this book provided background rather than extensive quotations. For a consumer-watchdog look at the toy industry and at children's television, thanks to Diana Huss Green and Peggy Charren. On the role of stylists in the fashion industry, thanks to Michele Pietre and Debra Liguori. On family dynamics and eating disorders, thanks to Laura Kogel and Lela Zaphiropoulos of the Women's Therapy Center Institute. On goddess iconography in visual art, thanks to Monte Farber and Amy Zerner. For an insider's perspective on collecting, thanks to Joe Blitman, Karen Caviale, Beauregard Houston Montgomery, and Marlene Mura. And to Gene Foote, for permitting Geoff Spear to photograph his "girls."

Then there were the friends who acquainted me with books, artwork, ideas, and people that I needed to know: Charles Altshul, Lauren Amazeen, Vicky Barker, Janet Borden, Russell Brown, Susan Brownmiller, Jill Ciment, Suzanne Curley, Deirdre Evans-Prichard, Eric Fischl, Henry Geldzahler, Arthur Greenwald, Vicki Goldberg, April Gornick, John G. Hanhardt, Lydia Hanhardt, Linda Healey, Phoebe Hoban, Margo Howard, Susan Howard, Deborah Karl, Delores Karl, Chip Kidd, Katie Kinsey, Jennifer Krauss, David Leavitt, Karen Marta, Yvedt Matory, Rebecca Mead, Louis Meisel, Susan Meisel, Anne Nelson, Dan Philips, Kit Reed, Bill Reese, Ken Siman, Barbara Toll, Frederic Tuten, Miriam Ungerer, Janet Ungless, and Katrina Vanden Heuvel. Also, Camille Paglia never missed—or failed to forward—a Barbie reference in *TV Guide*.

And finally, thanks to Glenn Bozarth and Donna Gibbs at Mattel, who deigned to give me access, and to all the present and former Mattel employees who told their stories. Without them, Barbie's synthetic tapestry would have been vastly less rich.

NOTES

All interviews for this book were tape-recorded.

CHAPTER ONE: WHO IS BARBIE, ANYWAY?

6 Impermanence of Warhol's icons: See Arthur C. Danto, "Warhol," *Encounters and Reflections* (New York: The Noonday Press, 1991), pp. 286–293.

7 The dark side of Dietrich: See Dietrich's cruelest biographer, Maria Riva, *Dietrich* (New York: Alfred A. Knopf, 1993).

7 Statistics on Mattel's sales furnished by the company.

8 "My life has been spent . . .": From *Boobs in Toyland*, a BBC TV production in association with Lionheart Television International, Inc., 1991. (Shown on the Discovery Channel in 1993 as *Dolls in Playland*.)

8 Nancy Rivera Brooks, "Barbie's Doting Sister," in the *Los Angeles Times*, December 10, 1990.

9 A "hooker or actress between performances": Interview with Jack Ryan by Ella King Torrey, Los Angeles, December 1979. (All Ryan quotations from this interview.)

10 F. Scott Fitzgerald's remarks on contradictory ideas: "The Crack-up," *Esquire*, February 1936, pp. 41, 164.

10 Quindlen and Goodman on Barbie: According to my informal scoring, Quindlen has chalked up the largest number of gratuitous assaults. For further thoughts on disparagement of Barbie as "simplistic, good-hearted feminism," see Mim Udovich, "Our Barbies, Ourselves," *The Village Voice*, June 15, 1993, p. 20. Udovich discusses the folly of an objective ideological corollary for the term *feminist*. "Anna Quindlen reviles Barbie ('I had never wanted American girls to have a role model whose feet were perpetually frozen in the high heel position,' she writes in her latest anthology, *Thinking Out Loud*)," Udovich

observes, (and) "this brand of simplistic, good-hearted feminism has seemingly come to be regarded as an objective ideological corollary."

10 "rough housework": Interview with Charlotte Johnson by Ella King Torrey, Hawthorne, California, December 1979. (All Johnson quotations from this interview.)

10 Vicarious leisure: See Thorstein Veblen, *The Theory of the Leisure Class* (New York: Penguin Books, 1979), p. 72.

11 "man shortage": See Susan Faludi, *Backlash: The Undeclared War Against Women* (New York: Crown Publishers, Inc., 1991).

12 "dynamic obsolesence": Harley Earl quoted by David Halberstam, *The Fifties* (New York: Villard Books, 1993), p. 127.

13 *"Gender is a kind of imitation . . .* impersonation and approximation": Judith Butler, "Imitation and Gender Insubordination," in Diana Fuss, ed., *Inside/Out: Lesbian Theories, Gay Theories* (New York: Routledge, 1991), p. 29.

13 "womanliness as a masquerade": Joan Rivière, "Womanliness as a Masquerade," in Victor Burgin, James Donald, and Cora Kaplan, eds., *Formations of Fantasy* (New York: Routledge, 1986), pp. 35–44.

14 Ru-Paul's Barbie mastectomies: See Ru-Paul's BBC documentary short on the introduction of the Shani doll, 1991.

14 The Barbi Twins diet: See Linda Stasi, Doug Vaughan, and Anthony Scaduto, "Inside New York," *New York Newsday*, January 11, 1993, p. 13.

15 "I believed in Barbie. . . . There's more Barbie dolls in this country than there are people": Michael Milken quoted on ABC News's *20/20*, June 4, 1993.

16 Baby dolls came into existence in 1820: See Antonia Fraser, *A History of Toys* (London: Weidenfeld & Nicolson, 1966), p. 160.

17 "Childhood was invented in the eighteenth century . . . the child became the savior of mankind, the symbol of free imagination and natural goodness": Louise J. Kaplan, *Female Perversions: The Temptations of Emma Bovary* (New York: Anchor Books, 1991), p. 411.

17 Americans lost their taste for German toys: See Fraser, op. cit., p. 206.

CHAPTER TWO: A TOY IS BORN

18 Marilyn Monroe's birth and childhood: See Norman Mailer, *Marilyn* (New York: Grosset and Dunlap, Inc., 1973).

18 Handler biographical information: Interviews with Ruth Handler, Los Angeles, July 7, 1992; Ruth and Elliot Handler, Los Angeles, April 26, 1993. (All Ruth Handler and Elliot Handler quotations, unless otherwise attributed in the text, are from these two interviews.)

21 Marx Toys' advertising budget: See Sydney Stern and Ted Schoenhaus, *Toyland: The High-Stakes Game of the Toy Industry* (Chicago: Contemporary Books, 1990,) pp. 35–37.

23 "When she walks . . . the earth shakes": Interview with Ken Handler, New York, January 22, 1993. (All Ken Handler quotations are from this interview.)

23 The Handlers' art collection described in Sotheby's catalogue, November 14, 1985.

24 Ryan "had a funny little body . . .": Interview with Gwen Davis, New York City, January 13, 1993.

24 Details of Ryan house: See Richard Warren Lewis, "Jack Ryan and Zsa Zsa: A Millionaire Inventor and His Hungarian Barbie Doll," *People*, July 14, 1975, pp. 60–63. Also, interview with Bill Smedley (one of the engineers who briefly lived in Jack's castle), San Bernadino County, California, May 2, 1993.

25 "He ruined a perfectly good . . .": Interview with Norma Greene, Bel-Air, California, October 30, 1992.

25 "torture chamber," "Jack's sex life would have made the average *Penthouse* reader blanch with shock": Zsa Zsa Gabor, *One Lifetime Is Not Enough* (New York: Delacorte Press, 1991), p. 235.

25 The birth of the *Bild* Lilli doll: See Billy Boy, *Barbie, Her Life and Times*

(New York: Crown Publishers, 1987), p. 19.

26 "We had a fight . . ." ("*Wir hatten Streit miteinander, und da hat er mir alle Geschenke wieder abgenommen.*"): Lilli, *Bild Zeitung,* June 26, 1952.

26 ". . . and in your opinion what should I take off?" ("*Und welchen Teil soll ich dann Ihrer Meinung nach ausziehen?*"): Lilli, *Bild Zeitung,* July 26, 1953.

26 "Can't you give me the name . . ." ("*Können Sie mir nicht Namen und Adresse dieses grossen, schönen, reichen Mannes sagen?*"): Lilli, *Bild Zeitung,* June 24, 1952.

26 Sculpted by Max Weissbrot: Billy Boy, op. cit., p. 19.

26 Images from Lilli promotional brochure, 1955.

27 "I saw it once in a guy's car . . . They were lifting up her skirts and pulling down her pants and stuff": Interview with Cy Schneider, New York City, June 26, 1992. (All Schneider quotations are from this interview.)

31 "The Lilli doll looked kind of mean . . . And Japanese people didn't like it at all.": Interview with Frank Nakamura, Santa Monica, California, September 19, 1992. (All Nakamura quotations are from this interview.)

34 "She was very resourceful . . .": Interview with Seymour Adler, Los Angeles, September 16, 1992; telephone interview, July 28, 1993. (All Adler quotations are from these interviews.)

34 The men "would go out to get bombed . . ." and other Japanese business practices: Telephone interview with Lawanna Adams, October 7, 1992.

35 "I think Japan was the perfect place . . .": Interview with Joe Cannizzaro, El Segundo, California, September 21, 1992. (All Cannizzaro quotations are from this interview.)

36 Ernest Dichter and motivational research: See Vance Packard, *The Hidden Persuaders* (New York: Pocket Books, 1981). (Dichter appears throughout the book; his research methods are discussed on page 29.)

36 "All you care about is having people come to the U.S. who have rich relatives": Ernest Dichter, *Getting*

Motivated (New York: Pergamon Press, 1979), p. 29.

37 "didn't dare" say . . . "naked girls" sold the magazine: Ibid., p. 34. (All references to Dichter's marketing strategy and psychoanalytic take on merchandise are from this book.)

37 Dichter's "depth interviews": Packard, op. cit., p. 29.

37 "He never asked a direct question": Interview with Hedy Dichter, Croton-on-Hudson, New York, August 10, 1993.

38 "Properly manipulated . . . American housewives can be given a sense of identity . . . by the buying of things": Betty Friedan, *The Feminine Mystique* (New York: Dell Publishing, 1984), p. 208. (Dichter referred to as "The manipulator," p. 211.)

38 Size of toy study control group: See Ernest Dichter, ed., *A Motivational Research Study in the Field of Toys for Mattel Toys, Inc.* Unpublished study prepared by the Institute for Motivational Research, Inc., Croton-on-Hudson, N.Y., June 1959, p. 5.

38 "The big long gun satisfies his need for power": Ibid., p. 122.

38 "Adults frown upon doll play on the part of little boys . . .": Ibid., p. 23.

39 Is Barbie "a nice kid . . . or a little too flashy?": Ibid., p. 7.

39 "should the wardrobe be sophisticated, even wicked?": Ibid., p. 6.

39 "the gift psychology of the adult . . . Are men afraid of their wives' taunts should they bring home a 'sexy' doll?": Ibid., p. 7.

39 "I know little girls want dolls with high heels . . . undue moral pressures": Ibid., p. 71.

39 (MRS. B. SEEMED VERY MUCH EMBARRASSED . . . "Maybe the bride doll is O.K., but not the one with the sweater": Ibid., p. 73.

39 "I'd call them 'daddy dolls' . . .": Ibid., p. 72.

40 "The face looks snobbish": Ibid., p. 50.

40 "I think they call these Barbies because they are so sharp": Ibid., p. 54.

40 "I would like her better if there was a little less eye makeup . . . But how else could she attract boy dolls?": Ibid., p. 50.

40 The tomboy who held her "at some distance": Ibid., p. 50.

40 Doll's neck "too long . . . legs too thin": Ibid., p. 48.

40 Ginny clothes "cheesily-made": Ibid., p. 59.

40 "I like Revlon dolls the best . . . They are . . . fatter.": Ibid., p. 54.

40 "She's so well groomed, Mommy.": Ibid., p. 70.

40 Convince Mom that Barbie will make a "poised little lady" out of her . . .: Ibid., p. 74.

41 "The type of arguments which can be used successfully to overcome parental objection are in the area of the doll's function in awakening in the child a concern with proper appearance": Ibid., p. 74.

41 "The child exerts a certain amount of pressure . . . The toy advertiser can help . . . by providing [the child] with arguments . . .": Ibid., p. 11.

41 The commercials should depict "a variety of teen-age social activities": Ibid., p. 47.

CHAPTER THREE: SEX AND THE SINGLE DOLL

44 "problem that has no name": Friedan, op. cit., p. 15.

44 "Ruth works a full day . . .": *Los Angeles Times,* September 29, 1959.

46 "If the growth Mattel has had . . .": Interview with Marvin Barab, Palos Verdes, California, May 1, 1993. (All subsequent Barab quotations are from this interview.)

47 "Ruth and Elliot ate in the cafeteria every day . . .": Interview with Beverly Cannady, Sherman Oaks, California, September 16, 1992. (All Cannady quotations are from this interview.)

47 Steve Lewis's remarks: Telephone interviews with Steve Lewis, April 2, 1993, April 16, 1993, September 1, 1993. (All Lewis's quotations are from these interviews.)

51 The Single Girl "supports herself": Helen Gurley Brown, *Sex and the Single Girl* (New York: Bernard Geis, 1962), p. 5.

51 "Sturdy, colorful . . .": *Mattel 1963 Toy Catalogue* (Hawthorne, Calif.: Mattel Toys, 1963), p. 34.

51 "If you are to be a glamorous . . .": Brown, Op. Cit., p. 119.

51 "When a man thinks of a single woman . . .": Ibid., p. 6.

51 "The first spokeswoman for the revolution . . .": Barbara Ehrenreich, Elizabeth Hess, and Gloria Jacobs, *Re-Making Love* (New York: Anchor Books, 1986), p. 56.

52 "Copycat a mentor . . .": Brown, op. cit., p. 193.

52 "time and often more money . . .": Ibid., p. 6.

52 "Men survey women before treating them . . .": John Berger, *Ways of Seeing* (New York: Penguin, 1977), p. 46.

52 "an object of vision": Ibid., p. 47.

53 "Nothing is as transient, useless, or completely desirable as a suntan . . .": Gloria Steinem, *The Beach Book* (New York: The Viking Press, 1963), p. 2.

53 "formative years were spent entirely in bathing suits": Ibid., dust jacket.

53 "I must . . . develop my bust": Ibid., p. 98.

53 "build" a bikini: Ibid., p. 101.

54 Steinem's failure to observe that Bunnies were exploited because of their gender: See Marcia Cohen, *The Sisterhood: The True Story of the Women Who Changed the World* (New York: Simon and Schuster, 1988), p. 114.

54 "It was interesting . . .": Ibid., p. 114.

54 "terrific good looks . . . If Gloria says it's otherwise . . .": Ibid., p. 114.

54 "There are many chic women in New York . . .": Cynthia Lawrence, *Barbie's New York Summer* (New York: Random House, 1962), p. 49.

54 Steinem's beach looks—"Ivy League," "Muscle Beach," "Pure Science": Steinem, op. cit., p. 111.

55 "One gets the sense talking to Gloria that she was born . . .": Leonard Levitt, "SHE: The Awesome Power of Gloria Steinem," *Esquire*, October 1971, p. 208.

55 "With every office clerk able to afford a vacation . . .": Steinem, op. cit., p. 83.

55 "Feminism didn't come into my life . . .": Telephone interview with Gloria Steinem, May 20, 1994.

55 Midge "is thrilled with Barbie's career . . .": Carson/Roberts, Midge's debut ad—videotape provided by Mattel.

56 "Basically, Tammy was a baby doll . . .": Interviews with Joe Blitman, Los Angeles, July 3 and July 6, 1992. (All Blitman quotations are from these interviews.)

57 The "togetherness" movement . . . in which a woman "exists only for . . . her husband and children": Friedan, op. cit., p. 47.

57 Marx alleged Mattel copied the "form, posture, facial expression . . ." of the *Bild Lilli* doll: *Louis Marx and Co., Inc., and Greiner & Hausser G.m.b.H. v. Mattel, Incorporated*, Civil Action No. 341-61-WB, filed March 24, 1961, in the U.S. District Court, Southern District of California Central Division. (RG 21 Records of the District Court of the U.S. for the Southern District of California, Central Division 1938–1961, Civil Case Files, Folder 341-61, Box #2276.) Quotation from reply to defendant's counterclaims in second amended answer; and plaintiffs' counterclaim against defendant, September 15, 1961, p. 10.

59 Mattel counters by alleging Marx has conspired with Germans to compete unfairly by "marketing an inferior doll in the United States of confusingly similar appearance to" Barbie: *Marx v. Mattel*, second amended answer to complaint and counterclaim and jury demand, September 11, 1961, p. 10.

59 Mattel introduced wooden dolls from the "collection of Miss Ruth Ellison . . .": *Marx v. Mattel*, Defendant's notice under title 35, section 282, p. 2. (News that the dolls were discovered by Jack Ryan's brother was provided in the Jack Ryan interview, op. cit.)

59 Judge Leon Yankwich dismissed claims "with prejudice as to all causes of action . . .": *Marx v. Mattel*, Decision filed March 4, 1963.

60 "I Am . . . Not a Toy . . .": Robin Morgan at the Miss America Pageant: See Cohen, op. cit., pp. 151–152.

61 "The typical George Wallace voter and the Bob Dylan fan lived in different worlds": Jim Miller, "The Best of the Summer of '68," *The New York Times*, July 25, 1993.

63 "a sort of ecstatic vision . . .": Arian and Michael Batterberry, *Mirror, Mirror* (New York: Holt, Rinehart, Winston, 1977), p. 388.

63 "a vision of sexuality freed from the shadow of gender distinctions . . . expand the possibilities.": Ehrenreich et al., op. cit., p. 35.

CHAPTER FOUR: THE WHITE GODDESS

66 Statistics on breast cancer: Susan Ferraro, "The Anguished Politics of Breast Cancer," *The New York Times Magazine*, August 15, 1993, p. 58.

67 "We were all raised on a . . . idea of what a sexually successful woman was supposed to look like . . . the official breast" was "Barbie's breast": Katie Davis, Report on Breast Implants, National Public Radio's *Morning Edition*, April 17, 1992. (Quotation checked against official transcript.)

67 "androgynous vacancy . . .": Susan Sontag, "Notes on Camp," *Against Interpretation* (New York: Farrar, Straus and Giroux, 1966), p. 279.

71 "If psycho-analytic theory . . .": Sigmund Freud, "The Uncanny," *The Standard Edition of the Complete Psychological Works of Sigmund Freud*, Vol. 17 (London: The Hogarth Press Limited, 1961), pp. 219–256.

71 Transitional objects: See D. W. Winnicott, "The Location of Cultural Experience," *The International Journal of Psychoanalysis*, Vol. 48 (1966), pp. 368–372; D. W. Winnicott, "Transitional Objects and Transitional Phenomena," *The International Journal of Psychoanalysis*, Vol. 34 (1953), pp. 89–97.

72 Transitional objects: Interview with Ellen Handler Spitz, New York City, August 7, 1992.

73 The masses' craving "to bring things 'closer' . . .": Walter Benjamin, "Art in the Age of Mechanical Reproduction," *Illuminations* (New York: Schocken Books, 1969), p. 223.

74 Plastic "is the very idea of its infinite transformation . . .": Roland Barthes, *Mythologies* (New York: Hill and Wang, 1982), p. 97.

74 a "magical substance which consents to be prosaic": Ibid., p. 98.

75 Venuses: See Lawrence Langer, *The Importance of Wearing Clothes* (Los Angeles: Elysium Growth Press, 1991), p. 99.

76 "crystalline Aphrodite": Kenneth Clark, *The Nude* (Princeton, N.J.: Princeton University Press, 1956), p. 71.

76 Cycladic idols: See H. W. Janson, *History of Art* (Englewood Cliffs, N.J.: Prentice-Hall, Inc., and New York: Harry N. Abrams, Inc., 1964), p. 68.

76 Egyptian *Ushabti*, Native American kachina dolls: See Fraser, op. cit., p. 34.

77 Genesis as "a male declaration of independence from the ancient mother-cults": Camille Paglia, *Sexual Personae* (New Haven: Yale University Press, 1990), p. 40.

77 Witches "raised storms . . . by unbinding their hair": Barbara Walker, *The Women's Encyclopedia of Myths and Secrets* (San Francisco: Harper & Row, 1983), pp. 367–368.

78 Saint Paul on women's hair: See 1 Corinthians 11:10.

78 American Association of University Women's survey on girls and self-esteem: See Suzanne Daley, "Little Girls Lose Their Self-Esteem on Way to Adolescence, Study Finds," *The New York Times*, September 1, 1991.

78 The White Goddess Maia, "ever-young Virgin . . .": Barbara Walker, *Women's Dictionary of Symbols and Sacred Objects* (San Francisco: Harper & Row, 1988), p. 465.

78 "The white goddess is anti-domestic . . .": Robert Graves, *The White Goddess* (New York: Farrar, Straus and Giroux, 1966), p. 449.

79 SunSpell, "fiery guardian of good," MoonMystic, "who wears the symbols of night": SunSpell, MoonMystic boxes, promotional flyer issued by Mattel in 1979.

79 Great Mother as "sexual dictator . . ." Paglia, op. cit., p. 43.

80 "Barbie is bigger than all those executives . . .": Interview with Robin Swicord, Santa Monica, California, September 18, 1992.

81 Piaget on play: See Jerome S. Singer, *The Child's World of Make-Believe* (New York: Academic Press, 1973), p. xi.

82 "When kids maneuver to form . . .": Barrie Thorne, *Gender Play* (New Brunswick, N.J.: Rutgers University Press, 1993), p. 4.

82 "I married a Ken . . .": Sarah Gilbert, *Summer Gloves* (New York: Warner Books, 1993), p. 9.

82 "A lot of them act out . . .": Telephone interview with Dorothy Singer, June 15, 1993. (All Singer quotations are from this interview.)

83 "The Geometry of Soap Bubbles": Rebecca Goldstein, *Strange Attractors* (New York: The Viking Press, 1993), pp. 163–178.

83 "Where's Barbie going?": Interview with Ann Lewis, Washington, D.C., January 31, 1992.

83 "There are a lot of mothers . . .": Singer interview, op. cit.

84 Mattel market research session: Interview with Alan Fine, El Segundo, California, October 29, 1992.

CHAPTER FIVE: THE BOOK OF RUTH

86 "man's relationships with *things* . . .": Alvin Toffler, *Future Shock* (New York: Bantam Books, 1988), p. 51.

89 Hobbling of women: See Langer, op. cit., p. 55.

89 Steinem as "a life-size counter-culture Barbie doll": Cohen, op. cit., p. 323.

90 Barbie encouraged girls "to see themselves only as mannequins . . .": "Feminists Protest 'Sexist' Toys in Fair," *The New York Times*, February 29, 1972.

90 Dawn as precursor of "disco consciousness . . ." Beauregard Houston Montgomery, "The Delirium That Was Dawn" in *Dolls*, Vol. 12, No. 3, May 1993.

90 "If you asked me to give you fifty words . . .": Interview with Rita Rao, El Segundo, California, September 14, 1992. (All Rao quotations are from this interview.)

91 "exploitative, parasitic, and . . . disgraceful . . .": U.S. District Court Judge Robert Takasugi quoted by Claudia Luther, "Mrs. Handler Gets Probation, Must Pay 'Reparations,' " *Los Angeles Times*, December 9, 1978.

91 Mattel's financial mess: See Stern and Schoenhaus, op. cit., pp. 64–76.

93 "There's a group of people . . .": Interview with Tom Kalinske, New York City, February 12, 1993.

95 Details of grand jury indictment: See Alexander Auerbach, "Indictment Names 4 Ex-Officials of Mattel," *Los Angeles Times*, February 17, 1978.

95 "I . . . will exert every ounce of strength . . .": Ibid.

95 Ruth Handler's sentence: See Luther, op. cit.

98 Ruth promotes Nearly Me: See "Barbie Doll Developer Ruth Handler Offers a New Look to Mastectomy Victims," *People*, April 11, 1977; Robert Lindsey, "A Million-Dollar Business from a Mastectomy," *The New York Times*, June 19, 1977.

100 "that dark involvement with birth and blood and death": Joan Didion, *The White Album* (New York: Simon and Schuster, 1979), p. 117.

100 "That thing was grotesque.": Interview with Aldo Favilli, El Segundo, Calif., July 13, 1992.

102 Barbie's SuperStar face: *Mattel 1977 Toy Catalogue* (Hawthorne, Calif.: Mattel Toys, 1977), pp. 2–3.

103 "In a world ordered by sexual imbalance . . .": Laura Mulvey, "Visual Pleasure and Narrative Cinema," *Screen*, Vol. 16, No. 3 (1975), pp. 6–18.

105 "Under Mr. Spear . . .": Pamela G.

Hollie, "Mattel's Diversified Comeback," *The New York Times,* June 21, 1979.

105 "His austere, no-nonsense style of management . . .": John Quirt, "Putting Barbie Back Together Again," *Fortune,* September 8, 1980.

105 "years of murky legal and financial battles . . .": "Mattel's Successful Retreat," *Business Week,* May 16, 1977.

CHAPTER SIX: SOME LIKE IT BARBIE

106 "She's got the billion-dollar look": *Mattel 1981 Toy Catalogue* (Hawthorne, Calif.: Mattel Toys, 1981) p. 2.

108 Hispanic Barbie: *Mattel 1980 Toy Catalogue* (Hawthorne, Calif., Mattel Toys, 1980), p. 6.

108 "Little Hispanic girls . . .": Ibid.

110 "The only way to keep ahead . . .": Barbara Ehrenreich, *Fear of Falling: The Inner Life of the Middle Class* (New York: Pantheon Books, 1989), p. 235.

110 "To achieve definition . . .": Ibid., p. 236.

111 Descriptions of Great Shape Barbies: See *Mattel 1984 Toy Catalogue* (Hawthorne, Calif.: Mattel Toys, 1984), p. 5.

112 Girls "didn't care if Barbie winked or not": Interview with Judy Shackelford, Bel-Air, California, April 28, 1993. (All Shackelford quotations are from this interview.)

113 Jill Barad biographical information: See Kim Masters, "It's How You Play the Game," *Working Woman,* May 1990, pp. 88–91.

115 "We Girls Can Do Anything": Launch commercial (Los Angeles: Ogilvy & Mather, 1984), tape provided by Mattel.

116 Tracy Ullman, the "ugly kid with the brown hair . . .": Ileane Rudolph, "The Many Faces of Tracy," *TV Guide,* October 9, 1993, p. 31.

116 "express where women were . . .": Interview with Barbara Lui, Santa Monica, California, April 28, 1993. (All Lui quotations are from this interview.)

117 "Womanliness therefore could be assumed and worn . . .": Joan Rivière, "Womanliness as a Masquerade," op. cit., p. 38.

117 "homeovestism": See Louise J. Kaplan, op. cit., pp. 250–262.

119 Homeovestism as a "perverse strategy": Ibid., p. 251.

119 "I thought Barbie would dress . . .": Interview with Carol Spencer, El Segundo, California, July 13, 1992.

119 "The fate of the world is in the hands of one beautiful girl"— She-Ra: *Mattel 1985 Toy Catalogue* (Hawthorne, Calif.: Mattel Toys, 1985), pp. 46–52.

120 She-Ra's sales estimated by Shackelford: Shackelford interview, op. cit.

120 "They looked like lady wrestlers": Interview with Beauregard Houston Montgomery, February 18, 1993. (Unless indicated otherwise in the text, all Mongomery quotations are from this interview.)

120 "It seemed time to offer little girls a role model . . .": Jill Barad quoted in Masters, op. cit., p. 90.

121 Atari's sales figures: See Stern and Shoenhaus, op. cit., p. 102.

121 Restructuring of Mattel's 1984 debt: See Scot J. Paltrow, "Mattel Plans to Give 45% Voting Stake to Group That Will Invest $231 Million," *The Wall Street Journal,* May 4, 1984; John D. Williams, "Mattel Investor Group Gets 45% Stake in Exchange for Rescue Financing Pact," *The Wall Street Journal,* July 16, 1984; Stephen J. Sansweet, "Mattel Quarterly Operating Profit Jumped by 81%," *The Wall Street Journal,* December 7, 1984.

123 Barad's ascendancy during Mattel's upheavals: See Masters, op. cit., pp. 89–90.

123 "The company was going to hell . . .": Ibid., p. 90.

123 Mattel's business misfortunes, 1984–1988: See Stern and Schoenhaus, op. cit., p. 300.

124 "The bee is an oddity of Nature": Barad's official Mattel biography, issued by Mattel public relations, 1992.

127 "The fact is, I really don't know what that means": Interview with Jill Barad, El Segundo, California, September 17, 1992. (Unless otherwise indicated in the text, all Barad quotations are from this interview.)

128 "Barbie truly is one of the dominant sexual personae of our time": Telephone interview with Camille Paglia, September 10, 1992.

128 "I've seen some very handsome men in business": Brooks, op. cit.

129 *Newsweek*'s 1988 report on the demise of the supermom, *Good Housekeeping*'s "New Traditionalist" ad campaign: See Faludi, op. cit., p. 90.

129 Lacroix quoted on bubble skirts ("for women who like to 'dress up like little girls' "): Ibid., p. 169.

130 "Bye-bye . . . little bow tie": *Mademoiselle,* quoted by Faludi, ibid., p. 177.

131 "When I as a futurist share our assumptions . . .": Telephone interview with Laurel Cutler, September 11, 1993.

CHAPTER SEVEN: PAPER DOLL

134 Circulation figures for Barbie novels: See Random House internal memos, 1962. (Random House archive, Columbia University Library.)

136 "The commodification of one's look became the basis of success": Winni Breines, *Young, White and Miserable: Growing Up Female in the Fifties* (Boston: Beacon Press, 1992), p. 105.

136 Being seen was "one of the main attractions of attending school": Ibid.

138 Paula Foxx slips into the Roberts "family circle as naturally . . . as any ordinary woman might have done": Bette Lou Maybee, *Barbie's Fashion Success* (New York, Random House, 1962), p. 21.

138 "what a pretty and talented daughter I have": Ibid., p. 27.

139 Barbie afflicted with "rare streaks of just being ornery": Ibid., p. 88.

140 "There are more important things to dream about than being rich": Ibid., p. 6.

140 Nancy Drew is "within reach. . . . She is pretty but not beautiful": Arthur Prager, *Rascals at Large, or the Clue in the Old Nostalgia* (Garden City, N.Y.: Doubleday and Company, Inc., 1971) p. 77.

141 Barbie afflicted by "emotions so strange that she could not understand them herself": Cynthia Lawrence, "The Size 10 Dress," *Here's Barbie* (New York: Random House, 1962), p. 94.

141 Barbie and Bertha hold hands in a "warm spotlight": Ibid., p. 100.

141 "A girl lives in some out-of-the-way town for nineteen years . . ." Sylvia Plath, *The Bell Jar* (New York: Bantam Books, 1972), p. 2.

142 "calm, steady" Ken Carson: Cynthia Lawrence, *Barbie's New York Summer* (New York: Random House, 1962), p. 21.

142 Genitals resembling "turkey neck and turkey gizzards": Plath, op. cit., p. 55.

142 Constantin's name as "full of S's and K's": Ibid., p. 41.

142 "Why did I attract these weird old women?": Ibid., p. 180.

142 Barbie wants "a whole New York wardrobe, free": Lawrence, *Barbie's New York Summer*, p. 5.

143 Esther Greenwood's mother "begging [her] with a sorrowful face . . .": Plath, op. cit., p. 166.

143 "I hate her": Ibid., p. 166.

143 "A girl . . . tries to resolve her ambivalent dependence . . .": Nancy Chodorow, *The Reproduction of Mothering: Psychoanalysis and the Sociology of Gender* (Berkeley, Calif.: University of California Press, 1979), p. 137.

144 "I felt like a piece of merchandise": Lawrence, *Barbie's New York Summer*, p. 62.

144 "A sudden gust of wind caught [Barbie's] full skirt . . .": Ibid., p. 107.

144 "It was probably Clara's British background . . .": Bette Lou Maybee,

Barbie's Hawaiian Holiday (New York: Random House, 1962), p. 39.

145 "I was born in the wrong part of the century . . .": Telephone interview with Bette Lou Maybee, May 21, 1993. (All Maybee quotations are from this interview.)

145 Rose Marie Reid: "a swimsuit wizardess . . .": Brown, op. cit., p. 94.

146 Bernard Gottlieb to Robert Bernstein: Letter dated August 31, 1965. (Random House archive, Columbia University.)

146 Sales of the later Barbie books recorded in internal Random House memos and royalty statements. (Random House archive, Columbia University.)

147 "With the donkey's noisesome voice . . .": Eleanor Woolvin, *Barbie and the Ghost Town Mystery* (New York: Random House, 1965), p. 50.

148 Thanks to former *Barbie* magazine editor Karen Tina Harrison for providing me with a copy of the unreleased *Barbie* magazine (*Barbie*, Christmas, 1984).

148 "Barbie Goes Milano," *House & Garden*, June 1986.

148 Sottsass intended the style as "an ironic gesture": Stephen Bailey, *Taste: The Secret Meaning of Things* (New York: Pantheon Books, 1991), p. 68.

149 "Barbie Goes to Brazil," in *Barbie*, Winter 1988.

149 "We couldn't show Barbie's family . . .": Interview with Karen Tina Harrison, New York City, February 23, 1993. (All Harrison quotations are from this interview.)

150 "I take my daughter to marches": Interview with Katy Dobbs, New York City, November 20, 1992. (All Dobbs quotations are from this interview.)

152 "the largest drug combination . . .": "When TV Kids Go Down the Tubes: Eight Stories You Won't See on Sitcoms," *People*, March 25, 1991, p. 38.

154 "I can remember sitting in meetings . . .": Interview with Barbara Charlebois, Los Angeles, May 2, 1993. (All Charlebois quotations are from this interview.)

155 "We Girls Can Do Anything," *Barbie Fashion*, June 1991.

155 "Aunt Rose Comes First," *Barbie Fashion*, June 1993.

155 "The Volunteers," *Barbie Fashion*, February 1993.

156 "I can have Ken being a feminist . . .": Interview with Barbara Slate, Sag Harbor, New York, July 1, 1993. (All Slate quotations are from this interview.)

CHAPTER EIGHT: BARBIE LIKE ME

158 They formed "a cluster of images . . .": Neal Gabler, *An Empire of Their Own: How the Jews Invented Hollywood* (New York: Anchor Books, 1989) p. 7.

161 "Our inner cities burned . . .": "It's a Wonderful Life: Thirty Years of Barbie and America," *Barbie Thirtieth Anniversary Magazine*, Winter 1990, p. 11.

162 "For six years, I had been preaching . . .": Interview with Yla Eason, New York City, January 22, 1993. (All Eason quotations are from this interview.)

163 "I'm not sure I'd go so far . . .": Interview with Ann duCille, New Haven, October 1, 1993. (All duCille quotations are from this interview.)

163 "Having been a little girl who grew up without the images . . .": Telephone interview with Lisa Jones, March 9, 1993. (See also Lisa Jones, "A Doll Is Born," *The Village Voice*, March 26, 1991 p. 36.)

164 Reclining Chinaman, Chicken Snatcher, other shameful historic toys: See Jo Ann Webb, Smithsonian News Service, "American Toy Makers Respond to the Call for Positive Ethnic Products," *Los Angeles Times*, August 16, 1992.

165 Details of Watts riots: See Paul Jacobs, *Prelude to Riot: A View of Urban America from the Bottom* (New York: Vintage Books, 1968), p. 30.

165 Jacobs "ought to be investigated" for having written it. Ibid., p. 16.

166 "To buy a house in the Valley . . .": Ibid., p. 102.

166 "I think what Lou and Robert . . .": Interview with Marva Smith, Los Angeles, February 1993. (All Marva Smith quotations are from this interview.)

167 "I know you don't agree . . .": Letter from Paul Jacobs to Ruth and Elliot Handler. (Paul Jacobs papers, Mugar Library, Boston University.)

168 "You'd sew it into the doll's head . . .": Telephone interview with James Edwards, January 15, 1994; interview, Los Angeles, February 22, 1994. (All Edwards quotations are from these interviews.)

168 All quotations from the 1977 Shindana Catalogue (Los Angeles: Shindana Toys, 1977).

168 "Black people were suspicious . . .": Cliff Jacobs memo. (Paul Jacobs papers, Mugar Library, Boston University.)

169 "Art was the kind of person . . .": Telephone interview with Robert Bobo, January 14, 1994. (All Bobo quotations are from this interview.)

170 "I can't even begin . . ." Telephone interview with Ralph Riggins, January 16, 1994.

170 Manipulation: The Mammoth Corporation Game, Shindana 1980 Catalogue (Los Angeles: Shindana Toys, 1980).

171 "Well, you know, they didn't have . . .": Interviews with Cliff Jacobs, Los Angeles, July 17, 1992, and April 27, 1993. (All Jacobs quotations are from these interviews.)

171 Shani story: Interview with Roger Wilkins, Washington, D.C., December 31, 1992.

172 "It was so disheartening": Interview with Darlene Powell Hopson, Middletown, Connecticut, April 22, 1993. (Unless otherwise indicated in the text, all Darlene Powell Hopson quotations are from this interview.)

172 "despair around the world": Derek Hopson and Darlene Powell Hopson, Different and Wonderful: Raising Black Children in a Race-Conscious Society (New York: Prentice-Hall Press, 1990), p. xx.

173 Skin color and social hierarchy within the African-American community: See Midge Wilson, Kathy Russell, and Ronald Hall, The Color Complex: The Politics of Skin Color Among African Americans (New York: Harcourt Brace Jovanovich, 1992), pp. 67–68.

174 There were "a lot of things that when I look at now . . .": Interview with Kitty Black Perkins, El Segundo, California, September 21, 1992. (All Black Perkins quotations are from this interview.)

176 "I'm an African American": Telephone interview with Jacob Miles, January 12, 1994. (All Miles quotations are from this interview.)

178 "You'd be surprised how many white people . . .": Interview with Susan Howard, New York City, November 16, 1992.

CHAPTER NINE:
MY FAIR
BARBIE

180 "I needed [the characters] . . .": Interview with Jill Ciment, New York City, September 30, 1992. (All Ciment quotations are from this interview.)

182 "nothing is as crass and vulgar . . .": Bayley, op. cit., p. 142.

183 "You'll notice prole women smile more . . .": Paul Fussell, Class (New York: Summit Books, 1983), p. 51.

184 "working class women . . . are less aware . . .": Pierre Bourdieu, Distinction: A Social Critique of the Judgment of Taste (Cambridge, Mass.: Harvard University Press, 1984), p. 206.

185 For an update on class-coding in dress and grooming: Joan Kron, "Secret Beauty Codes," Allure, August 1992, pp. 54–57.

186 "Nothing is too ugly . . .": Fussell, op. cit., p. x.

187 "proper tea ceremony": Pleasant Company Summer Catalogue, Summer 1992, p.4.

187 "Miss Crampton's Academy . . .": Ibid, p. 20.

187 Eleven million sold: American Girls' ad, Publishers Weekly, September 27, 1993.

188 "the poor and the relatively unschooled" favor brilliant colors: Packard, op. cit., p. 113.

188 "Scientific observation shows . . .": Bourdieu, op. cit., p. 10.

189 "We're fulfilling what we always said . . .": Interview with Meryl Friedman, El Segundo, California, July 15, 1992. (All Friedman quotations are from this interview.)

190 "Whatever the fashion, the California version . . .": Alison Lurie, The Language of Clothes (New York: Random House, 1981), p. 112.

190 "the opposition between the classical sports and the Californian sports . . .": Bourdieu, op. cit., p. 220.

191 "The prole bathroom . . .": Fussell, op. cit., p. 95.

192 "The first time I saw it happen . . .": Reyner Banham, Los Angeles: The Architecture of Four Ecologies (New York: Harper & Row, 1971), p. 213.

193 "the dream of a good life . . .": Ibid., p. 238.

193 "All the elegant accesories . . .": Mattel 1964 Toy Catalogue (Hawthorne, Calif.: Mattel Toys, 1964), p. 28.

194 "Well, there's a brick wall . . .": Interview with Aaron Betsky, Los Angeles, July 15, 1992. (All Betsky quotations are from this interview.)

194 Details of the Deluxe Reading Corporation's Dream Kitchen: See Mark Ouellette, "Dream Kitchen," Barbie Bazaar, May/June 1993, pp. 15–17.

195 "global power brand": Interview with Astrid Autolitano, El Segundo, California, April 27, 1993. (All Autolitano quotations are from this interview.)

CHAPTER TEN:
GUYS AND
DOLLS

200 "Woman with the Golden Hair": Robert Bly, Iron John (New York: Vintage Books, 1992), p. 141.

200 "Millions of American men . . .": Ibid., p. 136.

202 Readers of Leg Show . . . "tend to be white-collar, educated people . . .": Interview with Dian Hanson, New

York City, January 21, 1993. (All Hanson quotations are from this interview.)

204 Matrisexuality of children: See Chodorow, op. cit., p. 96.

207 "I rubbed . . .": Madonna quoted by Mark Bego in *Blond Ambition* (New York: Harmony Books, 1992), p. 15.

207 "If you look at any . . .": Sharon Stone quoted by Kevin Sessums in "Stone Goddess," *Vanity Fair*, April 1993, p. 207.

208 Vampiric female gaze: Telephone interview with Camille Paglia, October 28, 1992.

208 Men "create folk legends . . .": Chodorow, op. cit., p. 183.

208 A nude should arouse "some vestige of erotic feeling": Clark, op. cit., p. 8.

209 Erotization of medieval bellies in medieval times, other female body parts at other times: Anne Hollander, *Seeing Through Clothes* (New York: The Viking Press, 1975), p. 98.

209 Psychological meanings of milk: Packard, op. cit., p. 93.

209 "So long as only the upper parts . . .": Langer, op. cit., p. 44.

210 "stopped off to do a *Playboy* shoot on the way to cheerleading practice": Halberstam, op. cit., p. 575.

210 Eve's "golden tresses" and their meaning: John Milton, *Paradise Lost*, Book IV, vs. 305–306.

211 Erotization of female behind: See "The Bottom Line," *W*, December 7–14, 1992.

212 "The figure was almost like road kill . . ." and other facts about the new erotization of the female derriere, including the angles of primate bottoms in heat: Martha Barnette, "Perfect Endings," *Allure*, November 1993, pp. 160–163.

212 "taking the basic Ken and Barbie poses . . .": Walter Kirn, "Übersex: Has Hollywood Lost Sight of the Difference Between Erotic and Aerobic?," *Mirabella*, September 1992, p. 46.

212 Antics of Mattel engineers: Interview with Derek Gable, Palos Verdes, May 1, 1993. (All Gable quotations are from this interview.)

213 "Cults of beauty have been persistently homosexual . . .": Paglia, op. cit., p. 117.

214 "I loved the shiny hair . . .": Interview with the Lady Bunny, New York City, October 22, 1992. (All Lady Bunny quotations are from this interview.)

214 Drag queens on the runway: Patricia Jacobs, "He Is a She!," *New York Post*, December 21, 1992.

215 "Growing up in the inner-city . . .": Interview with Vaginal Davis, New York City, October 6, 1992.

215 Core gender identity: See Robert Stoller, "Primary Femininity," *Journal of the American Psychoanalytic Association*, Vol. 24, Supplement on Female Psychology, 1976, pp. 59–76.

216 "Drag constitutes the mundane way in which genders are appropriated . . .": Butler, op. cit., p. 21.

217 "the secret habits that seem normal enough to us . . .": A. M. Homes, "A Real Doll," in Richard Peabody and Lucinda Ebersole, eds., *Mondo Barbie* (New York: St. Martin's Press, 1993), p. 8.

217 "what it means to be a 'good girl' . . .": Interview with A. M. Homes, New York City, December 1, 1992. (All Homes quotations are from this interview.)

218 The Barbi twins as "truck drivers in drag": Stasi, Vaughan, and Scaduto, op. cit.

218 *Playboy* cover story on the Barbi Twins: "Seeing Double: The Barbi Twins Are a Couple of Dolls You'll Never Outgrow," *Playboy*, September 1991, pp. 137–145.

219 "Is this what you call erotic?": "Letters from Our Readers," *On Our Backs*, May/June 1989, p. 5. (The original "Gals and Dolls" pictorial, *On Our Backs*, March/April 1989, pp. 32–34. The credit reads: "Photos and Models: Evans, Brill, Smith.")

CHAPTER

ELEVEN: OUR

BARBIES, OUR

SELVES

222 "doll" as woman, "dolled up" as dressed up. Beauvoir, op. cit., p. 279.

224 "the whole Barbie phenomenon": Interview with "Jan," New York City, October 6, 1992.

226 Barbie at Sierra Tucson: See Alethea Savile, "Safe Haven Among the Sex Addicts," *Daily Mail*, October 8, 1992.

226 Barbie weight study at University Central Hospital in Helsinki, Finland: "Barbie's Missing Accessory: Food," *Tufts University Diet and Nutrition Letter*, Vol. 11, No. 11, January 1994, p. 1.

226 "The body of the Ceres . . .": Hollander, op. cit., p. 3.

227 Meredig's eating disorder statistics: See "She's No Barbie, Nor Does She Care to Be," *The New York Times* August 15, 1991.

227 "Wow! A doll with hips and a waist": *People* September 2, 1991.

227 "Stranglehold on distribution . . .": Meredig quoted by Lynn Smith in "Not Only Fun, but P.C. Too," *Los Angeles Times*, October 30, 1992.

227 Compromising material in Meredig's press kit, "Her Doll Is Built Like Real Women," Minneapolis St. Paul *Star Tribune*, August 19, 1991, p. 7E.

228 The *Venus de Milo* "legless by design": Hollander, op. cit., p. 214.

229 Plastic playthings lack "the pleasure, the sweetness, the humanity of touch": Barthes, op. cit., p. 54.

229 Parents' "prejudice" against plastic playthings: Brian Sutton-Smith, *Toys as Culture* (New York: Gardner Press, 1986), p. 11.

230 "Behind the anorexic's caricature . . .": Kaplan, op. cit., p. 457.

231 "While it may be hard to imagine the subtle transactions . . .": Susie Ohrbach, *Hunger Strike: The Anorectic's Struggle as a Metaphor for Our Age* (New York: W. W. Norton & Company, 1986), p. 81.

232 "The anxious mother was the agent of will . . .": Susan Brownmiller, *Femininity* (New York: Ballantine Books, 1985), p. 34.

232 "Women are traditionally the primary feeders": Interview with Laura Kogel, New York City, June 21, 1993.

(All Kogel quotations are from this interview.) See also Women's Therapy Center Institute, *Eating Problems: A Feminist Psychoanalytic Treatment Model* (New York: Basic Books, 1994).

234 *The Beauty Myth* as "the language of a science fiction writer describing the Blob": Elizabeth Kaye, "What Women Think of Other Women," *Esquire*, August 1992, p. 100.

235 Ann Landers's statistics on eating disorders: *New York Newsday*, April 29, 1992.

235 Columbia Pictures's shrinking logo: Jill Andresky Fraser, "What's in a Symbol? Not the Statue of Liberty," *The New York Times*, January 17, 1992.

235 "In *Superstar*, Haynes vindicates Karen . . .": Joel Siegel, "Barbies," *City Paper*, January 27–February 2, 1989.

236 "It is this small film's triumph . . .": Barbara Kruger, *Art Forum*, December 1987, p. 108.

237 "This work is part of a tradition of . . . antimainstream . . . filmmaking": Interview with John G. Hanhardt, New York City, February 14, 1993. (All Hanhardt quotations are from this interview.)

239 "When the film came out, we had many rentals to clinics . . .": Telephone interview with Christine Vachon, March 2, 1994.

239 "And they said no. . . . That really disappointed me": Haynes quoted by John Anderson in "The Final Cut," *New York Newsday*, April 4, 1991.

240 "When Karen Carpenter died of anorexia . . .": Christine Alt quoted by Marjorie Rosen in "Eating Disorders: A Hollywood History," *People*, February 17, 1992, pp. 96–99.

241 "When I first started modeling . . .": Telephone interview with Lauren Hutton, August 26, 1993. (All Hutton quotations are from this interview.)

241 "I thought it would be cool . . .": Interview with Glenn O'Brien, September 4, 1992.

241 "I ate nothing. I mean nothing": Beverly Johnson quoted by Rosen, op. cit.

CHAPTER TWELVE: THE WOMAN WHO WOULD BE BARBIE

244 "I'm registered with the British Internal Revenue Service . . .": Telephone interview with Cindy Jackson, April 13, 1993; in New York City, May 12, 1993. (All Jackson quotations are from these interviews.)

247 "ROSANNE'S HUBBY IN PLOT TO ROB BANK," etc. *National Enquirer* headlines, January 12, 1993, p. 1.

247 "Well, we're not in a perfect feminist world": Liz Logan, "Roseanne's Biggest Change," *The Ladies' Home Journal*, November 1993, p. 276.

249 "Although Cindy has always talked about this Barbie doll image . . .": Telephone interview with Dr. Edward Latimer-Sayer, April 19, 1993. (All Latimer-Sayer quotations are from this interview.)

251 Researchers at Dow Corning knew silicone harmed immune systems in mice: Sandra Blakeslee, "Dow Found Silicone Danger in 1975 Study, Lawyers Say," *The New York Times*, April 7, 1994, p. A18.

CHAPTER THIRTEEN: BARBIE OUT OF CONTROL

252 Telephone interview with the performance artist who masterminded the BLO, January 18, 1993. (All of this artist's quotations are from this interview.)

257 "I don't think the College of Cardinals used terms . . .": Telephone interview with Robert Sobieszek, February 25, 1994. (All Sobieszek quotations are from this interview.)

259 "If a company . . .": Interview with Deirdre Evans-Prichard, Los Angeles, May 18, 1994.

259 "the polyethelene essence . . .": Telephone interview with Barbara Bell, March 24, 1993.

259 "When I was a little girl . . .": Telephone interview with Grace Hartigan, April 28, 1994. (All Hartigan quotations are from this interview.)

261 "The portrait looks so bad . . .": Pat Hackett, ed., *The Andy Warhol Diaries* (New York: Warner Books, 1989), p. 713.

261 "I want to capture the soul of plastic": Telephone interview with Beauregard Houston Montgomery and Mel Odom, April 7, 1993. (All Odom quotations are from this interview.)

262 "The arid scimitar . . .": Virginia Woolf, *To the Lighthouse* (New York: Harcourt Brace Jovanovich, 1981) p. 38.

262 "It's about being angry about everybody wanting to look like a Barbie": Interview with Maggie Robbins, Brooklyn, New York, January 17, 1993. (All Robbins quotations are from this interview.)

263 "It was definitely cathartic for me . . .": Interview with Susan Evans Grove, New York City, June 23, 1992. (All Grove quotations are from this interview.)

264 "Do you have any female friends who look like me . . . ?": Interview with Julia Mandle, New York City, July 8, 1993. (All Mandle quotations are from this interview.)

265 "I wanted the doll to symbolize this kind of glamorous but secondary position": Interview with Ellen Brooks, New York City, November 6, 1992. (All Brooks quotations are from this interview.)

265 "the outstanding fashion doll . . .": A. Glenn Mandeville, *Fashion Doll Anthology and Price Guide* (Cumberland, Md.: Hobby House Press, 1987), p. 166.

266 "The early Barbie had an attitude . . .": Interview with Ken Botto, New York City, May 12, 1993.

266 "Barbie Noir": Alice Kahn, "A Onetime Bimbo Becomes a Muse," *The New York Times*, September 29, 1991.

266 "five hundred years of tourism in this country": Interview with Jaune Quick-to-See Smith, New York City, November 28, 1992. (All Smith quotations are from this interview.)

267 "glossy decapitated portrait of a hunky male": Interview with Roger Braimon, New York City, June 22, 1993.

268 "the greatest Romantic expositor . . .": Hollander, op. cit., p. 199.

268 "a man's big white handkerchief": Telephone interview with Dean Brown, February 24, 1993. (All Brown quotations are from this interview.)

270 "To me, Barbie dies when she puts on her wedding dress": Telephone interview with Felicia Rosshandler, April 25, 1994.

270 "In the era of AIDS, I'm overwhelmed . . .": Interview with Charles Bell, New York City, January 27, 1993.

270 Details of *The Barbie Project:* Interview with Lauren Versel, Sag Harbor, New York, August, 16, 1993.

270 Mattel's authorized Berlin show: *Barbie: Künstler und Designer Gestalten für und um Barbie* (Reinbek bei Hamburg, Germany: Rowohlt Verlag GmbH, 1994). (Elke Martensen, pp. 212–213; Holger Scheibe, pp. 154–155; Peter Engelhart, pp. 168–169; Frank Lindow, pp. 202–203.)

271 "I wanted people to look at these images . . .": Interview with David Levinthal, New York City, March, 24, 1994. (All Levinthal quotations are from this interview.)

CHAPTER

FOURTEEN:

SLAVES OF

BARBIE

276 "I stayed at the Beverly Hilton . . .": Interview with Fiona Auld, Niagara Falls, July 24, 1992.

280 "The bicycle is the most common transportation means . . .": Carol Spencer speech at the Barbie Collectors' Convention, Niagara Falls, New York, July 24, 1992.

281 "our Barbie Dean": Ruth Cronk, ed., *The Noname Newsletter,* June 1980, p. 8.

281 "got us started on the right foot . . .": *The Noname Newsletter,* September 1979, p. 2.

281 "in the process of struggling to hold her still . . .": *The Noname Newsletter,* January 1980, p. 2.

281 "The following day . . .": *The Noname Newsletter,* June 1980, p. 2.

281 "The thing that really rings . . ." *The Noname Newsletter,* February 1980, p. 3.

282 "in the objects that are always there . . .": Werner Muensterberger, *Collecting: An Unruly Passion* (Princeton, N.J.: Princeton University Press, 1994), p. 16.

283 "What else are collectibles . . .": Ibid., p. 31.

283 "It's an addiction": Interview with Jan Fennick, Rockville Center, New York, October 17, 1992. (All Fennick quotations are from this interview.)

283 "Ownership is the most intimate relationship that one can have to objects": Benjamin, op. cit., p. 67.

283 "People today are taking Barbie . . .": Interview with A. Glenn Mandeville, Rockville Center, New York, October 17, 1992. (Unless otherwise indicated, all Mandeville quotations are from this interview.)

285 "seems to swish off the page": R. L. Pela, "Malibu White House," *The Advocate,* January 26, 1993, p. 48.

285 "We're not totally object-oriented . . .": Interview with Karen Caviale and Marlene Mura, New York City, February 12, 1993. (All Mura and Caviale quotations are from this interview.)

287 "I belonged to . . .": Interview with Corazon Yellen, Los Angeles, October 30, 1992.

287 "Even though public collections . . .": Benjamin, op. cit., p. 67.

288 "She came out and said . . .": Interviews with Evelyn Burkhalter, Palo Alto, California, July 18, 1992 and April 30, 1993. (All Burkhalter quotations are from these interviews.)

289 "an insulting image of women": *Boobs in Toyland.*

289 "Billy Boy had a fight with the paparazzi . . .": Hackett, op. cit., p. 741.

289 "They meant everything to me": Offield quoted by Carol Masciola in "Goodby, Dollies as Collector's Treasure Is Lost," *Los Angeles Times,* October 14, 1992.

290 Details on Bruce Scott Sloggett: Associated Press wire story, October 25, 1992.

290 "It's literally . . .": Interview with Gene Foote, New York City, November 19, 1992.

292 "I don't have the dolls . . .": Telephone interview with Dot Paolo, April 6, 1994.

CHAPTER

FIFTEEN:

BARBIE FACES

THE FUTURE

294 "Even a generous mother . . .": Beauvoir, op. cit., p. 281.

296 He is "an organized and controlled individual . . .": Brenda Herrmann, "Tempo Update," *Chicago Tribune,* May 12, 1993.

297 Details of John Esposito's abduction of Katie Beers: Michael Salcedo and Gary Witherspoon, "Girl Missing," *Newsday,* December 30, 1992.

297 "Slap Elvis on anything . . .": Greil Marcus, "The Elvis Strategy," *The New York Times,* October 27, 1992.

297 For details of the "Math class is tough" flap, see Kevin Sullivan, "Foot-in-Mouth Barbie: Talking Doll's Patter Irks Math Teachers," *The Washington Post,* September 29, 1992. For details of the AAUW's report, "How Schools Shortchange Girls," which found that after sixth grade, boys tend to do better in math and take higher-level courses, see Laurie M. Gross, "Educators Give Barbie a Good Dressing-Down," *The Wall Street Journal,* September 25, 1992.

299 "We tried to argue with them . . .": Interview with Maki Papavasliou, El Segundo, California, October 29, 1992.

300 "I always hated you . . .": Susan Cheever, "In a Broken Land," *People,* May 17, 1993, p. 40.

300 "For a week the American Girl . . .": "The Plaything of the Century," *Sobesednik,* No. 26, June 1993.

301 Rand's work: See Polly Shulman, "Guises and Dolls," *Lingua Franca,* January/February 1994, p. 16.

BIBLIOGRAPHY

Ackroyd, Peter. *Dressing Up, Trans-vestism and Drag: The History of an Obsession.* London: Thames and Hudson, 1979.

Arnheim, Rudolph. *Art and Visual Perception: A Psychology of the Creative Eye.* Berkeley, Calif.: University of California Press, 1974.

Asakawa, Gil, and Leland Rucker. *The Toy Book.* New York: Alfred A. Knopf, 1992.

Baird, Robert M., and Stuart E. Rosenbaum. *Pornography: Private Right or Public Menace.* Buffalo, N.Y.: Prometheus Books, 1991.

Banham, Reyner. *Los Angeles: Archi-tecture of Four Ecologies.* New York: Harper & Row, 1971.

Banner, Lois. *American Beauty.* New York: Alfred A. Knopf, 1983.

Barthes, Roland. *The Fashion System.* New York: Hill and Wang, 1983.
———. *Mythologies.* New York: Hill and Wang, 1982.

Batterberry, Michael, and Ariane Bat-terberry. *Mirror, Mirror: A Social History of Fashion.* New York: Holt, Rinehart and Winston, 1977.

Bayley, Stephen. *Harley Earl and the Dream Machine.* New York: Alfred A. Knopf, 1983.
———. *Taste: The Secret Meaning of Things.* New York: Pantheon Books, 1991.

Beaton, Cecil. *The Glass of Fashion.* Garden City, N.Y.: Doubleday, 1954.

Beauvoir, Simone de. *The Second Sex.* New York: Vintage Books, 1989.

Bego, Mark. *Madonna: Blonde Ambi-tion.* New York: Harmony Books, 1992.

Bellah, Robert N., et al. *Habits of the Heart: Individualism and Com-mitment in American Life.* New York: Perennial Library, 1985.

Benjamin, Walter. *Illuminations.* New York: Schocken Books, 1969.

Bennett, Hal Zina. *Zuni Fetishes: Using Native American Objects for Meditation, Reflection and Insight.* San Francisco: Harper-SanFrancisco, 1993.

Berger, John. *Ways of Seeing.* New York: Penguin Books, 1977.

Bettelheim, Bruno. *The Uses of Enchantment: The Meaning and Importance of Fairy Tales.* New York: Alfred A. Knopf, 1975.

Blitman, Joe. *Vive la Francie.* Los Angeles: Joe Blitman, 1992.

Bly, Robert. *Iron John.* New York: Vintage Books, 1992.

Bourdieu, Pierre. *Distinction: A Social Critique of the Judgment of Taste.* Cambridge, Mass.: Harvard Uni-versity Press, 1984.

Boy, Billy. *Barbie, Her Life and Times.* New York: Crown Publish-ers, 1987.

Breines, Wini. *Young, White, and Miserable: Growing Up Female in the Fifties.* Boston: Beacon Press, 1992.

Brill, Dianne. *Boobs, Boys and High Heels, or How to Get Dressed in Just Under Six Hours.* New York: Penguin Books, 1992.

Brown, Helen Gurley. *Sex and the Single Girl.* New York: Bernard Geis Associates, 1962.

Brownmiller, Susan. *Femininity.* New York: Ballantine Books, 1985.

Butler, Judith. *Gender Trouble: Femi-nism and the Subversion of Iden-tity.* New York: Routledge, 1990.
———. "Imitation and Gender Insubordination," in Diana Fuss, ed., *Inside/Out: Lesbian Theories, Gay Theories.* New York: Rout-ledge, 1991, pp. 13–31.

Chernin, Kim. *The Hungry Self: Women, Eating & Identity.* New York: Perennial Library, 1986.
———. *The Obsession: Reflections on the Tyranny of Slenderness.* New York: Perennial Library, 1982.

Chodorow, Nancy J. *Feminism and Psychoanalytic Theory.* New Haven: Yale University Press, 1989.
———. *The Reproduction of Mother-ing: Psychoanalysis and the Soci-ology of Gender.* Berkeley, Calif.: University of California Press, 1979.

Ciment, Jill. *The Law of Falling Bod-ies.* New York: Poseidon Press, 1993.

Clark, Kenneth. *The Nude: A Study in Ideal Form.* Princeton, N.J.: Princeton University Press, 1956.

Cohen, Marcia. *The Sisterhood: The True Story of the Women Who Changed the World.* New York: Simon and Schuster, 1988.

Coleridge, Nicholas. *The Fashion Conspiracy.* New York: Harper & Row, 1988.

Coward, Rosalind. *Female Desires: How They Are Sought, Bought and Packaged.* New York: Grove Press, 1985.

Danto, Arthur C. *Encounters and Reflections: Art in the Historical Present.* New York: The Noonday Press, 1991.

DeWein, Sibyl, and Joan Ashabraner. *The Collector's Encyclopedia of Barbie Dolls and Collectibles.* Paducah, Ky.: Collector Books, 1988.

Dichter, Ernest. *Getting Motivated: The Secret Behind Individual Motivations by the Man Who Was Not Afraid to Ask "Why?"* New York: Pergamon Press, 1979.
———, ed. "A Motivation Research Study in the Field of Toys for Mattel Toys, Inc." Unpublished report prepared by the Institute for Motivational Research, Inc., Croton-on-Hudson, N.Y., June 1959.

Didion, Joan. *Slouching Towards Bethlehem.* New York: Farrar, Straus and Giroux, 1968.
———. *The White Album.* New York: Simon and Schuster, 1979.

Doane, Mary Ann. "The Economy of Desire: The Commodity Form in/of the Cinema." *Quarterly Review of Film and Video,* Vol. 22, pp. 23–33.

Duest, Marianne. *Barbie in Television.* New York: Random House, 1964.

Duhamel, Denise. *It's My Body.* Chicago: Egg in Hand Press, 1992.

Eames, Sarah Sink. *Barbie Fashion.* Paducah, Ky.: Collector Books, 1990.

Ehrenreich, Barbara. *Fear of Falling: The Inner Life of the Middle Class.* New York: Random House, 1989.
———. *The Worst Years of Our Lives: Irreverent Notes from a Decade of Greed.* New York: HarperPeren-nial, 1991.
———, Elizabeth Hess, and Gloria Jacobs. *Re-Making Love: The Feminization of Sex.* New York: Anchor Books, 1986.

Epstein, Cynthia Fuchs. *Deceptive Distinctions: Sex, Gender and the Social Order.* New Haven: Yale University Press, 1988.

Erikson, Erik H. *Childhood and Soci-ety.* New York: W. W. Norton and Company, 1963.
———. *Toys and Reasons.* New York: W. W. Norton and Com-pany, 1977.

Faludi, Susan. *Backlash: The Unde-clared War Against Women.* New

York: Crown Publishers, Inc., 1991.

Faulk, Gaby, ed. *Vargas.* Berlin: Benedikt Taschen Verlag Berlin GmbH, 1990.

Fausto-Sterling, Anne. *Myths of Gender.* New York: Basic Books, 1985.

Firestone, Shulamith. *The Dialectic of Sex: The Case for Feminist Revolution.* New York: William Morrow, 1993.

Formanek-Brunell, Miriam. *Made to Play House: Dolls and the Commercialization of American Girlhood, 1830–1930.* New Haven: Yale University Press, 1993.

Fraser, Antonia. *A History of Toys.* London: Weidenfeld & Nicolson, 1966.

Fraser, Kennedy. *The Fashionable Mind: Reflections on Fashion, 1970–1981.* New York: Alfred A. Knopf, 1981.

Freud, Sigmund. *The Sexual Enlightenment of Children.* Introduction by Philip Rieff. New York: Collier Books, 1963.

———. "The Uncanny" (1919) in *The Standard Edition of the Complete Psychological Works of Sigmund Freud,* Vol. 17. London: Hogarth Press Limited, 1961, pp. 219–256.

Friday, Nancy. *My Mother/My Self: The Daughter's Search for Identity.* New York: Delacorte Press, 1977.

Friedan, Betty. *The Feminine Mystique.* New York: Dell Publishing, 1984.

Fussell, Paul. *Class: A Guide Through the American Status System.* New York: Summit Books, 1983.

Gabler, Neil. *An Empire of Their Own: How the Jews Invented Hollywood.* New York: Anchor Books, 1989.

Gabor, Zsa Zsa. *How to Catch a Man, How to Keep a Man, How to Get Rid of a Man.* Garden City, N.Y.: Doubleday and Co., Inc., 1970.

———, with Wendy Leigh. *One Lifetime Is Not Enough.* New York: Delacorte Press, 1991.

Galasi, Peter. *Pleasures and Terrors of Domestic Comfort.* New York: The Museum of Modern Art, 1991.

Garber, Marjorie. *Vested Interests: Cross-Dressing and Cultural Anxiety.* New York: HarperPerennial, 1993.

Geldzahler, Henry. *Charles Bell: The Complete Works, 1970–1990.* New

York: Harry N. Abrams, Inc., 1991.

Gilbert, Sarah. *Summer Gloves.* New York: Warner Books, 1993.

Gilligan, Carol. *In a Different Voice: Psychological Theory and Women's Development.* Cambridge, Mass.: Harvard University Press, 1982.

Gitlin, Todd, ed. *Watching Television.* New York: Pantheon Books, 1986.

Glynn, Prudence. *In Fashion: Dress in the Twentieth Century.* New York: Oxford University Press, 1978.

Goldberg, RoseLee. *Performance Art: From Futurism to the Present.* New York: Harry N. Abrams, Inc., 1988.

Goldstein, Rebecca. *Strange Attractors.* New York: Viking, 1993.

Goodfellow, Caroline. *The Ultimate Doll Book.* New York: Dorling Kindersley, Inc., 1993.

Graves, Robert. *The White Goddess: A Historical Grammar of Poetic Myth.* New York: Farrar, Straus and Giroux, 1966.

Greer, Germaine. *The Female Eunuch.* New York: McGraw-Hill Book Company, 1971.

Hackett, Pat, ed. *The Andy Warhol Diaries.* New York: Warner Books, 1989.

Halberstam, David. *The Fifties.* New York: Villard Books, 1993.

Hirschmann, Jane R., and Lela Zaphiropoulos. *Preventing Childhood Eating Problems: A Practical, Positive Approach to Raising Children Free of Food and Weight Conflicts.* Carlsbad, Calif.: Gurze Books, 1993.

Hollander, Anne. *Seeing Through Clothes.* New York: The Viking Press, 1978.

Hopson, Darlene Powell, and Derek S. Hopson, *Different and Wonderful: Raising Black Children in a Race-Conscious Society.* New York: Prentice-Hall Press, 1990.

Horowitz, Jay. *Marx Western Playsets: The Authorized Guide.* Sykesville, Md.: Greenberg Publishing Company, Inc., 1992.

Howell, Barbara Thompson. *Tiara: An Insider's Guide to Choosing and Winning Pageants.* Whippany, N.J.: Tiara Publications, 1992.

Huizanga, J. *Homo Ludens: A Study of the Play-Element in Culture.* Boston: The Beacon Press, 1955.

Jacobs, Paul. *Prelude to Riot: A View of Urban America from the Bot-

tom.* New York: Vintage Books, 1968.

James, Cary. *The Imperial Hotel: Frank Lloyd Wright and the Architecture of Unity.* Rutland, Vt.: Charles E. Tuttle Company, 1968.

Janson, H. W. *History of Art: A Survey of the Major Visual Arts from the Dawn of History to the Present Day.* Englewood Cliffs, N.J.: Prentice-Hall, Inc., and New York: Harry N. Abrams, Inc., 1964.

Kaplan, Louise J. *Female Perversions: The Temptations of Emma Bovary.* New York: Anchor Books, 1992.

Kaye, Marvin. *A Toy Is Born.* New York: Stein and Day, 1973.

Kingsolver, Barbara. *Pigs in Heaven.* New York: HarperCollins, 1993.

Laake, Deborah. *Secret Ceremonies: A Mormon Woman's Intimate Diary of Marriage and Beyond.* New York: William Morrow, 1993.

Langer, Lawrence. *The Importance of Wearing Clothes.* Revised and updated with a new Introduction by Julian Robinson. Los Angeles: Elysium Growth Press, 1991.

Lasch, Christopher. *The Culture of Narcissism.* New York: W. W. Norton, 1978.

Lavitt, Wendy. *The Knopf Collectors' Guide to American Dolls.* New York: Alfred A. Knopf, 1983.

Lawrence, Cynthia. *Barbie's Easy-As-Pie Cookbook.* New York: Random House, 1964.

———. *Barbie's New York Summer.* New York: Random House, 1962.

———. *Barbie Solves a Mystery.* New York: Random House, 1963.

———, and Bette Lou Maybee. *Barbie and Ken.* New York: Random House, 1963.

———. *Barbie, Midge and Ken.* New York: Random House, 1964.

———. *Here's Barbie.* New York: Random House, 1962.

Lurie, Alison. *The Language of Clothes.* New York: Random House, 1981.

Mailer, Norman. *Marilyn.* New York: Gosset & Dunlap, Inc., 1973.

Mandeville, A. Glenn. *Doll Fashion Anthology and Price Guide.* Cumberland, Md.: Hobby House Press, 1987.

Manos, Paris, and Susan Manos. *The Wonder of Barbie: Dolls and Accessories, 1976–1986.* Paducah, Ky.: Collector Books, 1987.

————. *The World of Barbie Dolls.* Paducah, Ky.: Collector Books, 1988.

Martin, Richard. *Fashion and Surrealism.* New York: Rizzoli International Publications, Inc., 1987.

————, and Harold Koda. *Splash! A History of Swimwear.* New York: Rizzoli International Publications, Inc., 1990.

Mattison, Robert Saltonstall. *Grace Hartigan: A Painter's World.* New York: Hudson Hills Press, 1990.

Maybee, Bette Lou. *Barbie's Fashion Success.* New York: Random House, 1962.

————. *Barbie's Hawaiian Holiday.* New York: Random House, 1963.

Milton, John. *Paradise Lost.* New York: The Odyssey Press, 1962.

Montgomery, Beauregard Houston. "The Delirium That Was Dawn." *Dolls,* Vol. 12, No. 3, May 1993.

Moog, Carol. *Are They Selling Her Lips? Advertising and Identity.* New York: William Morrow and Company, Inc., 1990

Morris, Bernadine. *The Fashion Makers: An Inside Look at America's Leading Designers.* New York: Random House, 1978.

Muensterberger, Werner. *Collecting: An Unruly Passion.* Princeton, N.J.: Princeton University Press, 1994.

Mulvey, Laura. "Visual Pleasure and Narrative Cinema." *Screen,* Vol. 16, No. 3 (1975), pp. 6–18.

O'Brien, Richard. *The Story of American Toys.* New York: Artabras, 1990.

Orbach, Susie. *Fat Is a Feminist Issue.* New York: Berkley Books, 1981.

————. *Hunger Strike: The Anorectic's Struggle as a Metaphor for Our Age.* New York: W. W. Norton & Company, 1986.

Packard, Vance. *The Hidden Persuaders.* New York: Pocket Books, 1981.

————. *The Status Seekers.* New York: David McKay Company, Inc., 1959.

————. *The Waste Makers.* New York: David McKay Company, Inc., 1959.

Paglia, Camille. *Sexual Personae: Art and Decadence from Nefertiti to Emily Dickinson.* New Haven: Yale University Press, 1990.

Peabody, Richard, and Lucinda Ebersole, eds. *Mondo Barbie.* New York: St. Martin's Press, 1993.

Plath, Sylvia. *The Bell Jar.* New York: Bantam Books, 1972.

Poster, Mark, ed. *Jean Baudrillard: Selected Writings.* Stanford, Calif.: Stanford University Press, 1988.

Prager, Arthur. *Rascals at Large, or The Clue in the Old Nostalgia.* Garden City, N.Y.: Doubleday and Company, Inc., 1971.

Rhode, Deborah L. *Theoretical Perspectives on Sexual Difference.* New Haven: Yale University Press, 1990.

Riesman, David. *The Lonely Crowd.* New Haven: Yale University Press, 1961.

Rivière, Joan. "Womanliness as a Masquerade," in Burgin, Victor, James Donald, and Cora Kaplan, eds. *Formations of Fantasy.* New York: Routledge, 1986.

Robbins, Cynthia. *Barbie: Thirty Years of America's Doll.* Chicago: Contemporary Books, 1989.

Rousseau, Jean-Jacques. *Emile.* Rutland, Vt.: Charles E. Tuttle Co., Inc., 1992.

Rubin, Joan Shelley. *The Making of Middlebrow Culture.* Chapel Hill, N.C.: The University of North Carolina Press, 1992.

Russell, Kathy, Midge Wilson, and Ronald Hall. *The Color Complex: The Politics of Skin Color Among African Americans.* New York: Harcourt Brace Jovanovich, Publishers, 1992.

Schickel, Richard. *The Disney Version.* New York: Discus Books, 1971.

Schneider, Cy. *Children's Television.* Lincolnwood, Ill.: NTC Business Books, 1987.

Singer, Dorothy G. *Playing for Their Lives: Helping Troubled Children Through Play Therapy.* New York: The Free Press, 1993.

————, and Jerome L. Singer. *Make Believe: Games and Activities to Foster Imaginative Play in Young Children.* Glenview, Ill.: Scott, Foresman and Company, 1985.

Singer, Jerome L. *The Child's World of Make-Believe.* New York: Academic Press, 1973.

Singerman, Howard, ed. *Blueprints for Modern Living: History and Legacy of the Case Study Houses.* Published in conjunction with the exhibition presented at the Temporary Contemporary of the Museum of Contemporary Art, Los Angeles. Cambridge, Mass.: The MIT Press, 1989.

Sontag, Susan. *Against Interpretation.* New York: Farrar, Straus and Giroux, 1966.

Spitz, Ellen Handler. *Art and Psyche: A Study in Psychoanalysis and Aesthetics.* New Haven: Yale University Press, 1985.

————. *Image and Insight: Essays in Psychoanalysis and the Arts.* New York: Columbia University Press, 1991.

Spock, Dr. Benjamin. *Baby and Child Care.* New York: Pocket Books, 1971.

Squire, Geoffrey. *Dress and Society, 1560–1970.* New York: The Viking Press, 1974.

Steinem, Gloria. *The Beach Book.* New York: The Viking Press, 1963.

————. *Outrageous Acts and Everyday Rebellions.* New York: Signet, 1986.

Stern, Sydney Ladensohn, and Ted Schoenhaus. *Toyland: The High-Stakes Game of the Toy Industry.* Chicago: Contemporary Books, 1990.

Stewart, Doug. "In the Cutthroat World of Toy Sales, Child's Play Is Serious Business." *Smithsonian,* Vol. 20, No. 9, December 1989.

Suleiman, Susan Rubin, ed. *The Female Body in Western Culture: Contemporary Perspectives.* Cambridge, Mass.: Harvard University Press, 1986.

Sutton-Smith, Brian. *Toys As Culture.* New York: Gardner Press, Inc., 1986.

Talese, Gay. *Thy Neighbor's Wife.* New York: Ivy Books, 1993.

Tannen, Deborah. *You Just Don't Understand: Women and Men in Conversation.* New York: Ballantine Books, 1991.

Thorne, Barrie. *Gender Play: Girls and Boys in School.* New Brunswick, N.J.: Rutgers University Press, 1993.

Tocqueville, Alexis de. *Democracy in America.* New York: Anchor Books, 1969.

Toffler, Alvin. *Future Shock.* New York: Bantam Books, 1988.

Veblen, Thorstein. *The Theory of the Leisure Class.* New York: Penguin Books, 1979.

Vitruvius. *The Ten Books on Architecture.* New York: Dover Publications, Inc., 1960.

Walker, Barbara G. *The Woman's Dictionary of Symbols and Sacred*

Objects. San Francisco: Harper & Row, Publishers, Inc., 1988.

————. *The Woman's Encyclopedia of Myths and Secrets.* San Francisco: Harper & Row, Publishers, Inc., 1983.

Walsh, Mary Roth. *The Psychology of Women: Ongoing Debates.* New Haven: Yale University Press, 1987.

Whitton, Blair. *The Knopf Collectors' Guide to American Toys.* New York: Alfred A. Knopf, 1984.

Williams, Barry. *Growing Up Brady.* New York: HarperPaperbacks, 1993.

Winnicott, D. W. "The Location of Cultural Experience." *The International Journal of Psychoanalysis,* Vol. 48 (1966), pp. 368–372.

————. "Transitional Objects and Transitional Phenomena." *The International Journal of Psychoanalysis,* Vol. 34 (1953), pp. 89–97.

Wolf, Naomi. *The Beauty Myth: How Images of Beauty Are Used Against Women.* New York: William Morrow, 1991.

Woolvin, Eleanor K. *Barbie and the Ghost Town Mystery.* New York: Random House, 1965.

INDEX